# MASTERIN

# ENGLISH LITE

D0508712

# MACMILLAN MASTER SERIES

Banking
Basic English Law
Basic Management
Biology
British Politics
Business Communication
Chemistry
COBOL Programming
Commerce
Computer Programming
Computers
Data Processing
Economics
Electrical Engineering
Electronics
English Grammar
English Language
English Literature
French
French 2
German
Hairdressing
Italian
Keyboarding
Marketing
Mathematics
Modern British History
Modern World History
Nutrition
Office Practice
Pascal Programming
Physics
Principles of Accounts
Social Welfare
Sociology
Spanish
Statistics
Study Skills
Typewriting Skills
Word Processing

MACMILLAN MASTER GUIDES

Jane Austen: **Emma**
Robert Bolt: **A Man For All Seasons**
Emily Brontë: **Wuthering Heights**
Geoffrey Chaucer: **The Prologue To The Canterbury Tales**
Charles Dickens: **Great Expectations**
George Eliot: **Silas Marner**
George Orwell: **Animal Farm**
William Shakespeare: **Macbeth**
**A Midsummer Night's Dream**
**Romeo and Juliet**

# MASTERING ENGLISH LITERATURE

RICHARD GILL

M
MACMILLAN

© Richard Gill 1985

All rights reserved. No reproduction, copy or transmission of this publication may be made without written permission.

No paragraph of this publication may be reproduced, copied or transmitted save with written permission or in accordance with the provisions of the Copyright Act 1956 (as amended).

Any person who does any unauthorised act in relation to this publication may be liable to criminal prosecution and civil claims for damages.

First published 1985
Reprinted 1985

Published by
MACMILLAN EDUCATION LTD
Houndmills, Basingstoke, Hampshire RG21 2XS
and London
Companies and representatives
throughout the world

Printed in Hong Kong

British Library Cataloguing in Publication Data
Gill, Richard
Mastering English Literature.—(Macmillan
master series)
1. English literature—History and criticism
I. Title
820.9 PR83
ISBN 0–333–36107–5
ISBN 0–333–36108–3 (paperback)
ISBN 0–333–36109–1 (paperback export)

# CONTENTS

# CONTENTS

# CONTENTS

## CONTENTS

# CONTENTS

# PREFACE

I hope that this book will help you to enjoy English literature and be successful in public examinations. That is to say, I hope that reading it will help you think about the pleasures and values you find in English literature, and also that you will learn to write about poems, novels and plays in an appropriate way. Because all books are different from each other, studying English literature can never be a matter of learning a method which can be applied to every poem, novel or play. Each book, because it is different from any other, needs to be read, enjoyed, thought and written about in its own particular way. Nevertheless, an introductory book like this can help you in three ways: it can give you some questions to ask, it can provide you with examples, and it can offer hints about writing.

It is very difficult to study anything unless you know what you are looking for. By 'looking for' I mean finding what is important in the thing you are studying. The question is the best way of finding that. Therefore, in the chapters that follow, you will be provided with a number of questions that you can ask about English literature. The questions given are not the only ones that can be asked (this book is only an introduction) and, of course, some are not going to apply to the books you are studying. One of the things you learn during study is whether or not it is wise to ask a particular question. The fact remains, however, that the way into most books is through a question. My aim is to give you the basic ones. Your aim must be to master their use.

It is always much easier to understand a point about literature if you are given an example. In the following chapters you will find general discussion about how to read and think, but wherever possible I have provided examples. These examples are drawn from the books that are set at 'O' level, 'A' level, and other public examinations. Although some of them will be unknown to you, I hope that somewhere in the book you will find an example taken from one of the books you are studying. In addition to the examples I discuss, there are, where appropriate, exercises at the end of sections. These are to help you practise writing about books.

When you write about books, you will discover that you need to master a set of terms that describe certain literary effects. In addition, you will find that you need to master a wider vocabulary which deals with the thoughts, experiences and feelings with which literature is concerned. To help you do this I have included hints on how to write about poems, novels and plays. I have also explained some terms in the chapters and have provided a glossary which discusses the meanings of those terms. Some of the terms in the glossary are explained elsewhere in the book, whilst others are not. In some cases I have also tried to give some hints and warnings about how to use the terms. The glossary, therefore, is a guide as well as a source of explanation.

Once you have mastered the right questions, learned from the examples and exercises, and picked up some hints about how to write, you still have to face the examination. The last chapter aims to help you do this. It gives you advice about re-reading, interpretation, judging the effectiveness of literature, the kind of questions you face, and how to organise yourself in the examination room. I hope that the prospect of the examination will not dull the pleasure of the books you study. Quite often a book is enjoyed and valued more because you have looked at it in great detail. I hope this will be your experience, too.

RICHARD GILL

# ACKNOWLEDGEMENTS

The author and publishers wish to thank the following, who have kindly given permission for the use of copyright material: The Bodley Head Ltd, for an extract from *Tender is the Night* by Scott Fitzgerald; J.M. Dent, for extracts from *The Collected Poems* by Dylan Thomas; André Deutsch, for an extract from 'Not Waving but Drowning' by Stevie Smith and 'I Remember' by Stevie Smith; Gerald Duckworth, for an extract from *Complete Verse* by Hilaire Belloc; Faber and Faber, for extracts from *Collected Poems* by W.H. Auden, *Waiting for Godot* by Samuel Becket, *Collected Poems 1909–1962* by T.S. Eliot, *The Sense of Movement* by Thom Gunn, *Lupercal* by Ted Hughes, *The Hawk in the Rain* by Ted Hughes, *The Whitsun Weddings* by Philip Larkin, *The Collected Poems* by Louis MacNeice, *Collected Poems* by Edwin Muir, *Collected Poems 1908–56* by Siegfried Sassoon, *Rosencrantz and Guildenstern Are Dead* by Tom Stoppard; Granada Publishing Ltd, for extracts from *Poetry for Supper* by R.S. Thomas and *The Bread of Truth* by R.S. Thomas; for the extracts from *The Go-Between* by L.P. Hartley, © 1973 The Executors of the Estate of the late L.P. Hartley, published by Hamish Hamilton Ltd; Heinemann Educational Books, for an extract from *A Man for All Seasons* by Robert Bolt; William Heinemann Ltd, for an extract from *To Kill a Mockingbird* by Harper Lee; William Heinemann Ltd and The Bodley Head Ltd, for extracts from *Brighton Rock* by Graham Greene and *The Power and the Glory* by Graham Greene; The Hogarth Press, for an extract from *Cider with Rosie* by Laurie Lee; Provost and Fellows of Kings College, Cambridge, for an extract from *Aspects of the Novel* by E.M. Forster; London Management, for an extract from *The Royal Hunt of the Sun* by Peter Shaffer; for extracts from 'Church Going' by Philip Larkin, reprinted from *The Less Deceived* by permission of The Marvell Press, England; Methuen, London, for an extract from *The Homecoming* by Harold Pinter; for extracts from *The Crucible*, copyright © 1952, 1953 by Arthur Miller; John Murray (Publishers) Ltd, for extracts from *John Betjeman's Collected Poems* by John Betjeman; The Estate of the late Sonia Bronwell Orwell and Martin Secker and Warburg Ltd, for an extract from *1984* by George Orwell; The Society of Authors, for an extract from *Saint Joan* by G.B. Shaw; Dr Jan Van Loewen Ltd, for an extract from *The Winslow Boy* by Terence Rattigan; and Michael Yeats and Macmillan, London, for extracts from *Collected Poems of W.B. Yeats* by W.B. Yeats.

The author would like to acknowledge the help of the following: John Florance for innumerable discussions about literature and teaching; Pat Phillipps for reading and checking the manuscript, and Gillian Walters for typing it.

# PART I

# STUDYING POETRY

# CHAPTER 1

# READING, THINKING AND WRITING

## 1.1 WHERE YOU START: THE POEM ON THE PAGE

When you open a book of poetry, you may be struck by the thought that poems are odd things. Before you will be words organised into fixed lines. In some poems these lines will be further organised into regular units called stanzas. Moreover, some of the lines will be rhythmical, and words at the end of the lines might rhyme. People don't usually speak or write like that. Now, it is important to understand that this is not a silly reaction. Poetry is not like ordinary speech or writing, it is a specially made object in words. The word 'poetry', in fact, comes from a Greek verb which means to make.

When you take an examination in English Literature, you will probably study poetry. This means that you will have to learn to read, think, and write about it. Because poetry is not just like ordinary speech, you will have to learn to think and write about it in a special way. It would be wrong to write about it as if it were a letter to a friend, because you would be ignoring the special way in which it is made. On the other hand, poems are written by people for people, so you must not ignore the fact that it is a form of communication.

Each poem is different from every other poem. This point might seem too obvious to mention, but there is an important lesson to be learnt from it: because every poem is different, no two poems can be thought and written about in *exactly* the same way. Even if you are studying a number of poems by one author, each poem will make its own points in its own particular way. It would be wrong, therefore, to suggest that there can be a fixed method of studying a poem. What suits one poem will not suit another.

But this does not mean that no advice can be given. What this chapter sets out to do is introduce you to a way of reading and thinking about poetry that is broad enough to apply to every poem you read. It is not a fixed method but a general approach. Once you have mastered this approach, you will be able to look through the following sections and pick up advice on how to write in detail about the words, lines, rhythms, sounds, rhymes and shapes of poetry. Those, of course, are the aspects of poetry that make it different from ordinary speech and writing, the aspects that make it, at first glance, seem odd and unusual.

In the coming pages you will find a constant stress on the fact that poetry is both a specially made object and an important form of communication between people. You must remember that these are not two separate elements within any poem. Poetry communicates in and through those things that make it different from ordinary speech or writing. Therefore, this chapter will close on a very important idea that should control all your thinking and writing about poetry – the idea of enactment.

## 1.2 READING POETRY

How, then, should poetry be approached?

All study of poetry starts with reading. The first thing you should remember is that the voice is as much the medium of poetry as the page upon which it is written. Poetry, therefore, should be read aloud. This can be done in a number of ways. You can read to yourself. This is best done in your own room with a minimum of distracting noises. Another way of reading to yourself is to use a cassette recorder. It is a good idea to record yourself reading all the poems you have to study. You will probably find you can concentrate more when you are listening than when you are reading. Some students find it easier to listen to other people reading. There are recordings of poetry read either by actors, or, if the poetry is contemporary, by the poet, but these can be expensive, and there is no guarantee that the poems you are studying are on record or cassettes. You will probably, therefore, find it easier to ask a fellow student, friend or member of your family to read to you.

When you study a poem for the first time, you should read or listen to it, in part or whole depending on its length, four or five times. If a poem is introduced in class, it should be read once or twice either by the teacher or a student, and then everyone, including the teacher, should read it through two or three times to themselves. If you are studying at home, you can, of course, read or listen to it aloud any number of times. The rule is: the more the better. It is important to remember that reading or listening is not something you only do when you begin to study. When you re-read poems, study them afresh for an essay, or revise them for an examination, you should read or listen to them a number of times.

## 1.3 THINKING ABOUT WORDS

But what is it that you are reading? The simple but important answer is – *words.* A poem is made of words, and whatever is said in a poem is said in words. The words are organised in lines and stanzas. These are not just convenient ways of printing a poem but the very manner in which a poem exists. Any poem can be said to be: *these particular words organised in these particular lines.* It is these words, and the way they are organised, that you must attend to as you read. You should attend to them individually and as a whole group. You must try to see what they are saying and also be aware of the very way in which the words combine to say it. You should attend to the ideas, pictures and emotions of the poem, and you should be no less attentive to its sounds, rhythms and rhymes. The aim of reading should always be to come to grips with the poem in the fullest possible way.

Thinking and writing about a poem emerges from reading. It is reading that alerts you to the poem's ideas, its interesting words, its rhythms and shape and its human importance. Of course, once you start thinking you will discover more in the poem than you were at first aware of, but your starting point can only be your reading, for how else can a poem be known?

It is wise to have some idea of what emerges from reading. The starting point is your awareness of the words of the poem, and what it is the poet is making them do. A simple piece of advice will help: *when you are reading a poem, you should notice what you notice.* That is to say, you should be aware of what is going on. The words are saying something – be aware of what it is, and how they are saying it. The words are in lines – be aware of them. The words may be rhythmical, there may be rhymes, and there will certainly be sounds – be aware of them. The individual stanzas and the poem as a whole have shapes – be aware of them.

You will also be aware of something else – *your* reactions to the poem. Since you can only know a poem by reading it, you can only know it through your reactions to it. Therefore, you should notice how you are reacting to the poem. You can ask yourself: how am I reacting? What do I feel as I read these words? What thoughts and feelings do these words stir up in me? Am I enjoying this poem, and if so what kind of pleasure is it giving me? Am I being led to see things in a newer or deeper way by this poem?

If what emerges from reading a poem are thoughts about its words and an awareness of your own reactions to it, is there a particular way in which these thoughts can be organised? Because there are no fixed methods of studying a poem, there can be no fixed procedure for organising your thoughts about any poem you are studying. Nevertheless, an approach to any poem is bound to contain three elements. These are: assessing simply what the poem is about, questioning the words and your reactions to them, and seeing what the poem adds up to as a whole.

Most of this chapter, and the three chapters that follow, will be concerned with the second of these elements – questioning the words and your reactions to them. The last chapter of Part I – the poem as a whole – deals with the last of them. What, then, of the first?

## 1.4 WHAT THE POEM IS ABOUT

Before you start the detailed study of a poem, you should have a general idea of what it is about. Of any poem you can ask: what is this poem about? The answer you get will depend upon the kind of poem it is. If the poem is narrative, you should be satisfied that you understand the main events, and, if they are important, the motives of the characters. If the poem is a meditation or reflection upon life, you should make sure that you have a general idea about what is being said. If the poem is an argument about something, you should ensure that you can follow its main stages. It is not necessary that you understand every line or even every stanza, though it is worthwhile seeing if you can tease out the more difficult parts. What you should aim for is a state in which you could give a general summary of what the poem is about and be able to show the stages through which it goes. When you think about it in detail, you will no doubt become aware of many other things in it, and you will become clearer about what exactly is being said, but unless you have a general idea of what the poem is about, you will either be left with lots of ideas that don't add up to anything, or you will misinterpret the poem by fixing on one or two things in it whilst ignoring the others.

Once you have an idea of what the poem is about, you can question the words and your reactions to them. The best thinking gets under way when you have a question that you want to answer. Therefore, if you notice something when you are reading a poem, you should try to frame it in the form of a question. This is not always easy, so you should practise putting your reactions in the question form. For instance, if you notice a particular word you can ask: what is interesting about that word? Or, if you particularly enjoyed a line, you can ask: what was it about that line that I particularly enjoyed? If you find that difficult, there are two questions that can always be put: what do I feel about this poem? What is it about the poem that makes me feel this? You should remember that both these questions, and any others that you might ask, are, in one way or another, about the words of the poem.

It is helpful to realise where questions come from. Most come from three states – puzzlement, interest, and pleasure.

### 1.5 PUZZLEMENT, INTEREST AND PLEASURE

Puzzlement arises when you say: 'how strange!' or 'that's odd!' If you put your puzzlement in the form of questions, you can ask: Why does the poet say that? Why is that word used? Why does the poet move from that subject to this? Why write in this way about that subject? Let us look at an example.

Wordsworth's 'Resolution and Independence' (sometimes known as 'The Leech-gatherer') includes these lines upon the lives of poets:

> By our own spirits are we deified:
> We poets in our youth begin in gladness;
> But thereof come in the end despondency and madness.

Two words might puzzle you. Why does Wordsworth use such an elevated word as 'deified'? (It means made god-like.) What view of the poet, you might ask, emerges in the use of that extraordinary word? Even more puzzling is the plunge at the end from 'gladness' to 'madness'. A more obvious contrast would have been from 'gladness' to 'despondency', but Wordsworth descends into the frightening world of insanity, a descent which is made more disturbing by the fact that 'gladness' and 'madness' rhyme. It is very puzzling, and you may want to ask why he goes to this extreme.

Interest arises in a number of ways. You might say: 'that's intriguing' or 'how interesting'. There are a number of questions that can be framed out of expressions of interest. You can ask: am I interested because it reflects the way I feel? Am I interested because I've dimly felt like that but could never quite find the words? Am I interested because of the unusual way the poet thinks? Am I interested because this poem entices me to further thought?

Consider Tennyson's 'Ulysses'. The speaker, or protagonist, is the aged Ulysses, who is not content with ruling his island but yearns for more adventure. What is interesting is that his son, Telemachus, is content to stay and carry out the duties of a ruler. The younger man is said to be

> centred in the sphere
> Of common duties,

whereas the older wants

> To sail beyond the sunset, and the paths
> Of all the western stars, until I die.

Interest lies in the contrast, and the way in which it is different from what you might have expected. The young man is at the centre of a 'sphere / Of common duties' (words usually associated with older people), whilst the old man is full of adventure (something that characterises the young). You may be tempted to think further about why an old man speaks like a youth.

Pleasure occurs when you say' '*How* beautiful!' or '*How* wonderful for someone to say that!' When you frame such reactions as questions, you can ask: what is it about these words that I find beautiful? Is it their ease and naturalness? Is it that they are exciting and dramatic? Is it that the idea is very cleverly put?

Edward Thomas's 'Adlestrop' gives pleasure in a number of ways. Its ending is particularly haunting:

> And for that minute a blackbird sang
> Close by, and round him, mistier,
> Farther and farther, all the birds
> Of Oxfordshire and Gloucestershire.

What is so enjoyable about these lines? Is it something to do with the way that very precise phrase 'And for that minute' captures the stillness and wonder of an intense experience, or is it the contrast between the single blackbird 'close by' and, in the misty distance, 'all the birds / Of Oxfordshire and Gloucestershire'? In that contrast the poem, so to speak, opens up the landscape as it moves beyond Adlestrop to the remote countryside beyond. You may then want to ask why such a movement is so pleasurable.

## 1.6 WRITING: FINDING THE RIGHT WORDS

The reactions of puzzlement, interest and pleasure have all been given in words. More thought now needs to be given to the words in which these reactions have been expressed. Thought about the words you use is necessary when you come to writing about poetry. Every time you make a note, write an essay or take an examination you will have to find appropriate words. You will discover that you need two kinds of vocabulary. These two vocabularies correspond to what was said above about poetry being both a special way of using words and a form of communication.

As you think about your puzzlement, interest and pleasure, you will see that you need to write about *how* the words have stirred these reactions in you. You might want to write about how the words create meanings, about how they form lines, rhythms and stanzas, and about how they rhyme and make patterns of sounds. To do this you will have to master a specialised vocabulary of technical terms. The next three chapters help you to do this. Unless you can master these terms, your writing about poetry will become impressionistic and subjective. That is to say, you will be concerned with *your* feelings alone, with the result that you may ignore the words of the poem altogether.

But you need more than a vocabulary of technical terms. It is important to remember that poets often write because their thoughts and feelings have been stirred by important events. Owen, for example, wrote poetry because he was exposed to the horrors of the First World War, and Tennyson wrote *In Memoriam* in an attempt to understand his feelings of devastation and loss upon the death of his friend. Poets often deal with what most concerns them – their beliefs, loves, fears and hopes. The vocabulary you need to deal with such matters is one that covers human thoughts and feelings. You should master words that cover a great variety of emotions, moods and thoughts, and you must be sensitive and flexible about how they are used.

Of course, some of the thoughts and feelings you will need to discuss are yours. This means you should practise writing in the first as well as the third person. When you are discussing a stanza form, it is best to use the third person and say, for example: 'the simple four line stanza is very appropriate for telling a story.' When, however, you are writing about your reaction to a poem, you must use the first person. You could say: 'I find this poem very moving, because the poet is honest about his feelings.' A broad and flexibly used vocabulary of thoughts and feelings is necessary when writing about poetry, because without it your work will be cold and dry, conveying nothing of the poem's importance or impact.

An example will make these points clear. In his famous sonnet 'Upon Westminster Bridge Sept. 3 1820', Wordsworth writes:

> This City now doth, like a garment, wear
> The beauty of the morning . . .

In writing about this you should mention that Wordsworth uses a simile to evoke the beauty of the morning. (See p. 18 for simile.) But you should also bring out the way the simile expresses the awe and glad surprise of the poet. He does, after all, say 'This City *now*', as if he were held by the wonder that London, of all places, should wear 'The beauty of the morning' at that particular moment. 'Simile' is a technical word; 'awe' and 'glad surprise' are drawn from the more general vocabulary of human thought and feeling; *both* kinds are required when writing about how the words of the poem work.

## 1.7 TONE

When, in the next three chapters, technical words are introduced, they will be discussed in relation to words dealing with thought and feeling. There is, however, one term which is at the same time technical and more broadly human –tone. Tone is a technical word standing for the poise, mood, voice, manner, attitude and outlook of a poet, but because it is concerned with those things, it should be discussed in words from that broader human vocabulary. For instance, you may say that the tone of a poem is cold, cynical, bitter, troubled, uncertain, eager, bragging, gleeful, resigned or protesting. There are, of course, many others.

Tone is the most general of all the technical words because it can be applied to many aspects of poetry. For instance, you can ask about the tone of a simile, the tone of a particular rhythm, and, of course, the tone of a whole poem. That last point is very important – virtually *every* poem has a tone. The tone might be difficult to characterise, or you may be uncertain as to whether, for example, a poem is serious or amusing, but if it is a poem it almost certainly must take up an attitude or outlook, or have a mood, voice or manner. Therefore, it is wise to discuss tone before all the other terms, whether they come from the technical or broader human vocabulary.

In everyday conversation tone means the way in which people speak with a particular emotional colouring. A listener hears the tone of a speaker in the way the words are delivered. Tone is evident in the pace, the stress, and the length of the vowels; in fact, in the very way in which the mouth forms the sounds. But the listener does not hear tone simply as something physical. In the sounds, he or she hears, or senses, the mood of the speaker – the emotional pressure with which he or she speaks – and understands from these the attitude the speaker has taken up. Now in poetry you must decide what the tone is by attending to the words and trying to hear in them their tone. Once you feel you have picked up the tone, you can try reading the poem aloud to test out your judgement. You can't do this the other way round. To read a poem aloud is already to have decided what its tone is. To that extent, every reading is an interpretation. (It is important for you to remember this if you have recorded yourself on a cassette.) Needless to say, you will probably need to look at the poem a long time before you begin to pick up the tone. Even when you have begun to sense the emotional colouring of the words, you will still have to characterise it. This is often very difficult. You will probably have to use a number of adjectives and adverbs before you find a phrase that comes close to your experience of the tone. Let us look at a few examples.

The tone of Betjeman's 'A Subaltern's Love-song' is unmistakable. This is the second stanza about a tennis match:

> Love-thirty, love-forty, oh! weakness of joy,
> The speed of a swallow, the grace of a boy,
> With carefullest carelessness, gaily you won,
> I am weak from your loveliness, Joan Hunter-Dunn.

The tone there is ardent, admiring, boyish and breathless. The young man has been swept off his feet by Joan Hunter-Dunn and pours out his admiration with gleeful wonder at her 'speed', 'grace' and 'loveliness'.

More difficult to characterise, though very strong, is the tone of Dylan Thomas's 'Do not go Gentle into that Good Night', a villanelle which opens:

Do not go gentle into that good night,
Old age should burn and rave at close of day;
Rage, rage against the dying of the light.

Can that opening line be said to be both firm and fierce? The poet orders (in grammatical terms it is in the imperative mood) the one to whom he speaks not to go 'gentle'. The firmness is maintained in the power of 'burn' and 'rave' in the second line, and the return to the imperative in 'Rage, rage' is enough to justify saying that the conviction with which the poet speaks is fierce.

The tones of both the Betjeman and the Thomas poem are quite dramatic. This, however, is not true of Auden's poem about how painters have portrayed suffering, 'Musée des Beaux Arts'. Here are a few lines from the first part:

They never forgot
That even the dreadful martyrdom must run its course
Anyhow in a corner, some untidy spot
Where the dogs go on with their doggy life and the torturer's horse
Scratches its innocent behind on a tree.

The tone here is quiet, detached, even off-hand; the poet surveys the work of painters in a leisurely, almost nonchalant way. He is fascinated but not emotionally engaged or disturbed by the subject matter. Note how easily he uses a word such as 'even', and follows up 'dreadful martyrdom' with the everyday phrase 'must run its course / Anyhow', and then almost carelessly qualifies that with 'some untidy spot'.

Because every poem has a tone, you must think about it at some point when you study a poem. You can do this as soon as you are fairly clear what the poem is about. Sometimes you will feel you want to, because what has most interested you is the tone. On other occasions, other aspects of a poem will immediately puzzle, interest or give you pleasure, so you will want to think about them first. Still, you must not ignore tone, so it is wise to ask, at some time during your study of a poem, the following question: can I identify and characterise the tone of this poem?

## 1.8 ENACTMENT

There is one other aspect of poetry that, like tone, applies to every poem: enactment. When in the next three chapters a number of technical terms are introduced, you can think about them all in terms of how they enact the meaning of the poem.

Enactment depends upon an idea that is central to the study of literature. People often talk about what a book says – its subject-matter, meaning, or content – and the way it is written – its form, shape or structure. Sometimes the distinction is useful when you wish to isolate a particular aspect of a literary work. Yet it can be misleading. A poem is not made of two things – form and content, subject and structure, meaning and shape – it is made of words, and words are indivisible. You can't take from a word the aspects that create form, shape or structure – its sound, the rhythms it can help to establish, the rhymes it can effect, and the stanza shapes it can be used for – and leave the content. If you did remove those things, you would be left not with the content of the word but with nothing at all. So every aspect of a word contributes to the word's meaning. In everyday language we are not usually aware of this, but in poetry we are. Poetry uses every aspect, or resource, of language to enact meaning. The word 'enactment' is useful because it suggests that all the aspects of words, so to speak, join together and act out their meaning. An example will help to make this clear.

Arnold's 'Dover Beach' is about the thoughts and feelings the poet has when he hears the waves breaking on the shore. At one point he writes about the sounds and rhythms they make:

> Listen! you hear the grating roar
> Of pebbles which the waves draw back, and fling,
> At their return, up the high strand,
> Begin, and cease, and then again begin,
> With tremulous cadence slow, and bring
> The eternal note of sadness in.

The sounds and rhythms of those words enact two things – the ebbing and flowing of the tide, which begins, and ceases, and then again begins, and the overwhelming sadness those sounds stir in the poet. We can hear the tide lapping up the shore and then relapsing before its inevitable return, and then the poetry becomes more still as we listen to the delicacy of the 'tremulous cadence slow'. This stillness ceases as the tide brings in 'The eternal note of sadness'. The word 'eternal' is long, yearning and weighty; and it enacts the immensity of the poet's sadness. The point about these words is that they are not just decorating the idea of tides and sadness, but words which actually enact the movements of the tide and the poet's feelings.

How far have we got with our idea of a general approach to a poem? The reading of a poem has been discussed, as has the advice that before you start detailed study you should make sure you have a clear idea of what the poem is about. Once you have got that idea, you can then proceed with questioning yourself about what puzzles, interests and gives you pleasure. Whatever you say about these things, you must, at some point, think about the tone of the poem. You must also expect to find the words enacting their meanings.

You can't, of course, predict what aspect of a poem will puzzle, interest or please you, but you may be sure that it will be related to the topics discussed in the following chapters. There you will find a guide to terms, hints on what questions to ask, and suggestions about how to write about them.

## EXERCISES

**1** Read through the poems you are studying a number of times, trying to detect their tone. When you think you have grasped the tone, try to characterise what it is in writing.

**2** Read the following poem by Hardy and answer the questions below. Hardy is writing about a folk tradition that on Christmas Eve all the animals kneel in honour of the birth of Christ.

*The Oxen*

Christmas Eve, and twelve of the clock.
'Now they are all on their knees,'
An elder said as we sat in a flock
By the embers in hearthside ease.

We pictured the meek mild creatures where
They dwelt in their strawy pen,
Nor did it occur to one of us there
To doubt they were kneeling then.

So fair a fancy few would weave
In these years! Yet, I feel,
If someone said on Christmas Eve,
'Come; see the oxen kneel

'In the lonely barton by yonder coomb
Our childhood used to know,'
I should go with him in the gloom,
Hoping it might be so.

(a) It looks as if the elder believes the tradition. In what tone do you think the second line of the poem should be read?
(b) When Hardy says:

Nor did it occur to one of us there
To doubt they were kneeling then.

he is looking back upon the beliefs of his childhood from a position of doubt. What tone do these lines have?
(c) Try to characterise the tone of:

So fair a fancy few would weave
In these years!

You might think about why he calls the idea a 'fair fancy'.
(d) What is the tone of the last two lines of the poem? What words can you find to characterise the mood of a man who would willingly return to the beliefs of his childhood, although he knows they were only a 'fancy'?

# CHAPTER 2

# WORDS AND MEANING

## 2.1 LOOKING AT WORDS

When you ask what puzzles you, interests you or gives you pleasure in a poem, you will find that the answer is something to do with the way that the *words work.* The particular function of words that will be dealt with in this section is the way they establish meaning. You will be told about what to look for, be given useful questions to ask, and provided with a guide on how to think and write about the figures of speech that poets employ.

You could write about every word in a poem, but if you did, your writing would be mechanical and you would probably lose sight of the poem as a whole. It is much better to read through the poem a number of times, looking out for the *striking* word. You should read a poem with this question in mind: are there words here that are particularly puzzling, interesting or pleasurable?

Here are some lines of poetry. Read them through with that question in mind and see if any of the words strike you:

And stare into the tangled fire garden (R.S. Thomas, 'On the Farm')

And a tense, musty, unignorable silence (Philip Larkin, 'Church Going')

Now as I was young and easy under the apple boughs (Dylan Thomas, 'Fern Hill')

The blue jay scuffling in the bushes follows (Thom Gunn, 'On the Move')

Till with a sudden sharp hot stink of fox (Ted Hughes, 'The Thought-Fox)

In the first line the words 'tangled' and 'garden' might have struck you. 'Tangled' points to an interesting complication, and 'garden' is a surprise, coming as it does after 'fire'. In the second line, a number of words might have struck you, though perhaps the most interesting is 'unignorable'. The words itself is that! In the Dylan Thomas line, it is surely the word 'easy' which attracts attention. It is both unusual and comes with a delightful lilt after 'young'. 'Scuffling' in the fourth line attracts attention, largely because it is the word dealing with sound among others concerned with sight. In the last line, you might be struck by one or all of the four 'sudden sharp hot stink'; they are emphatic and deliberate. In all the above examples, words are used in a rich and intriguing way. You are being invited to think about them, and as you do, you see more and more in them. This is what poetry does with words – enriches and deepens their meanings.

When you are looking for the striking word, you should not ignore the 'little' ones such as 'the', 'a', 'too', 'yet', 'in', 'and'. Sometimes, a poet can enrich even the simplest and humblest of words. In MacNiece's 'Prayer before birth', each irregular stanza begins: 'I am not yet born.' That simple word 'yet' is very poignant as it shows the unborn child poised on the edge of life, innocent of any corruption but aware of the dangers of what is ahead. In Stevie Smith's 'Not Waving but Drowning', there is the line

Oh, no, no, no, it was too cold always

which is a plaintive line of someone who is beyond hope, and its plaintiveness is enacted in its simple words. The 'it' – such an insignificant word, normally – refers to the sea and to life itself. The contrast between the insignificant word and the large things 'it' stands for is quite moving. Likewise, the 'too' is simple and deep. The 'always' confirms that life was at every moment much too much for him. The art of Stevie Smith lies in her ability to convey so much sadness in so few, seemingly ordinary words.

## 2.2 HOW POETS USE WORDS

You may feel that the advice to look for the striking word is too general. If so, what other more specific advice can be given? Sometimes a change in tone can indicate that a word is worth thinking about. In Blake's 'The Poison Tree', the tone is that of someone who obsessively nurses his anger, till, in the words of the poem, 'it bore an apple bright', which tempts his hated enemy to theft:

And into my garden stole
When the night had veiled the pole;
In the morning glad I see
My foe outstretched beneath the tree.

When the enemy is dead, the tone changes from being dark and furtive to one of relief, and even rejoicing. This change is focused in the word 'glad'.

If you had to write about that poem, you would have to discuss the shock that comes when a word as blithe and innocent as 'glad' is used in relation to death.

You can also look out for repeated words. When a poet uses a word more than once it is often because it is vital in the building up of the poem's meaning. Here is another example from Blake – the opening of 'London':

I wander through each chartered street,
Near where the chartered Thames does flow,
And mark in every face I meet
Marks of weakness, marks of woe.

Why does Blake repeat 'chartered' and 'mark'? It looks as if he is angry at the way in which everywhere in London – even the river! – is given over to trade (a charter being a licence to sell). This, he feels, has marked the people, and also marked him, for although he uses the word as a verb when he speaks of himself, it sounds harsh, as if he, too, is aware of 'marks of woe' in him.

Another guide to important words is contrast. Yeats's poem 'The Circus Animal's Desertion' ends with a striking contrast between two ideas. He writes of:

. . . the foul rag-and-bone shop of the heart.

The power of these words comes from the contrast between the filth associated with a 'rag-and-bone shop' and the word 'heart' with its associations of high and noble feelings. Such a striking contrast invites you to write about how the words work.

Sometimes a word may strike you but you are at a loss as to what to say about it. If you are stuck like that, you can always ask these questions: why was *this* word rather than a similar one used? What meanings does this word have in everyday speech that might be exploited here? How does the context enrich the meaning of the word? Let us look at how these questions can help.

Consider the opening of Blake's 'The Sick Rose':

O Rose, thou art sick!

Why does Blake use 'sick' rather than a similar word such as 'ill'? The answer must be that 'sick' is more forceful. The physical associations of 'sick' are more powerful than 'ill' (which can mean just being off-colour), and its sharp, abrupt sound enacts more dramatically the rose's diseased state.

Now think about the words 'a white celestial thought' from Vaughan's poem 'The Retreat'. What meanings does the word 'white' have in everyday speech that are exploited here? 'White' means a colour but it is also associated with purity, spotlessness, cleanliness, the angelic and the good. Surely all these meanings are present in Vaughan's usage. The thoughts in his mind are pure, spotless, holy and heavenly.

For the last question, think about the opening of Clare's 'I am':

I am: yet what I am none cares or knows . . .

How does the context enrich the meaning of 'I am'? 'I am', in itself, is affirmative – the poet is stressing his existence – but it is only in the context of the rest of the line that we can see just how brave and noble the affirmation is. What makes anyone an 'I' is the caring and knowing of other people, and yet in spite of the fact that 'none cares or knows', he poignantly and heroically declares himself *to be.*

When you are asking questions about words, you must not imagine that some words are more worthy of study just because they sound more poetic. This is particularly important in modern poems where quite ordinary words are used. Eliot uses 'cheap hotels', 'window-panes', 'coffee spoons', 'shirt-sleeves' and 'white flannel trousers' in 'The Love-song of J. Alfred Prufrock'; and in his poem, 'Lake District', Betjeman (a master of the ordinary word) uses 'cruet', 'non-alcoholic wine', 'the H.P. sauce' and 'Heinz's ketchup'. No word is more poetic than another word. What matters is *how the poet uses them.*

When you write about words that puzzle, interest or give you pleasure, you will need to master some technical terms. The ones the examiners will expect you to know are: simile, metaphor, conceit, personification, symbol, image, paradox and ambiguity. These are called figures of speech. You must show tact in using these terms. It is never sufficient merely to identify and label. No examiner will reward you for pointing out that a word is a metaphor. Your aim should always be to show *how* a figure of speech contributes to the poem. In order to show that, you will need to master both the technical term and the broader vocabulary concerned with thought and feeling. Of course, one way of showing how a figure of speech contributes to the poem is by writing about how it enacts its meaning.

## 2.3 SIMILE AND METAPHOR

Similes and metaphors can be dealt with together, because they both speak of one thing in terms of another. In a simile the relation is made clear by the use of the words 'like' or 'as', whereas in a metaphor the two things are fused. For instance, 'the fog descended *like* a blanket' is a simile, and 'the blanket of fog descended' is a metaphor. In R.S. Thomas's 'On the Farm' a simile is used about a grin:

. . . a grin
Like the slash of a knife on his face

and a metaphor about a face:

Her pale face was the lantern
By which they read in life's dark book . . .

When you write about similes and metaphors, you should bring out their distinctive qualities. Similes are close to ordinary speech; consequently they are often successful when they have an ease which makes you say: 'Yes, I would make that comparison if I were in that situation.' Sassoon's poem 'Everyone Sang' moves effortlessly from singing to a simile that freshly, yet naturally, expresses a sense of release:

Everyone suddenly burst out singing;
And I was filled with such delight
As prisoned birds must find in freedom . . .

Sassoon trusts that the reader will know what a sudden outburst of joy feels like and will therefore understand the quite standard comparison with freed birds.

But similes can also be unusual, and when they are, they offer, so to speak, an invitation to you to journey in imagination from one thing to another. In 'The Rime of the Ancient Mariner', Coleridge says this of a becalmed ship:

Day after day, day after day,
We stuck, nor breath, nor motion;
As idle as a painted ship
Upon a painted ocean.

The simile invites you to journey from a real ship to one which is only 'painted'. Notice how the repetition of 'painted' makes the picture seem more unreal and thus very distant from the actual ship. The distance travelled by the wind makes the simile unusual. Although not necessarily unusual, the epic simile also requires you to make an imaginative journey from the thing being described to that in terms of which it is described.

Metaphors, by contrast, are economical and immediate. In 'Ode on the Intimations of Immortality in Early Childhood', Wordsworth compresses a metaphor into a single word when he says that the earth seemed 'Apparelled in celestial light'. Look how much meaning Wordsworth packs into one word. 'Apparelled' means clothed regally in garments that lend a special importance to the wearer. The metaphor presents a very clear picture of the earth gloriously clothed in resplendent light.

This economy makes for immediacy – two things are fused in a single verb. In 'Mariana', Tennyson writes 'When thickest dark did trance the sky'. The dramatic picture of the dark acting as a hypnotist to mesmerise the sky is established in a single word – 'trance'.

When you write about similes and metaphor, you should try to bring out their distinctive qualities. Never suggest, as some people do, that metaphors are better than similes. Concentrate rather on the natural and adventurous nature of similes, and on the economy and immediacy of metaphors.

## 2.4 CONCEIT

When a simile or metaphor is elaborate or far-fetched, and strikes you at first as being inappropriate, it is called a conceit. These were popular in the seventeenth century. When you meet one, you will probably be struck by its artificiality and ingenuity; your thinking about it may start with a feeling of strangeness but end with your seeing that, though it is unexpected, the comparison is intriguingly right. Crawshaw's short poem on the crucifixion is built on an astonishing conceit:

> They have left thee naked, Lord. O that they had;
> This garment too, I would they had denied.
> Thee with thyself they have too richly clad,
> Opening the purple wardrobe of thy side:
> O never could there be garment too good
> For thee to wear, but this of thine own blood.

It is strange, and even shocking, to see Christ's naked, blood-stained body as an opened wardrobe of purple clothes, and yet the horror of the conceit drives home the point that no clothes but Christ's own blood were too good for him to wear. If you have to write about conceits, you should try to bring out this surprising blend of weirdness and appropriateness.

## 2.5 PERSONIFICATION

Personification is giving non-human things human qualities. Tennyson's metaphor 'When thickest dark did trance the sky' personifies the dark by giving it the power to hypnotise. Personification also occurs when an abstract noun is spoken of as a person as in this line from Gray's 'Elegy':

> Can Honour's voice provoke the silent dust?

There are two important effects which are very close to personification – pathetic fallacy, and mental landscape. You are likely to come across both of these in nineteenth and twentieth century verse.

Pathetic fallacy occurs when human feelings are given to objects without them. In 'The Lotus Eaters' Tennyson writes:

> All round the coast the languid air did swoon,
> Breathing like one that hath a weary dream.

Both the metaphor 'swoon' and the simile 'breathing like' bestow feelings upon the air, an object which, by its very nature, can't have them.

A mental landscape is one in which the feelings of the one who looks at it become attached to the landscape itself. The landscape thus expresses the inner feelings of the one who views it. Tennyson's *Maud* portrays a man on the brink of mental collapse, who is bitter and resentful. The poem starts with these lines of barely controlled violence:

> I hate the dreadful hollow behind the little wood,
> Its lips in the field above are dabbled with blood-red heath,
> The red-ribbed ledges drip with a silent horror of blood,
> And Echo there, whatever is asked her, answers 'Death'.

This grotesque and nightmarish picture of the heath is as much a portrait of the speaker's mind. It is dreadful because he is full of dread, and full of horror because his mind is, and Echo tells him what he already thinks of – 'Death'.

Personification, pathetic fallacy and mental landscape frequently occur in poetry. What they have in common is the feeling that in the poet's mind the world is alive with feeling. It is this sense of life in otherwise lifeless things that you should try to bring out in your writing.

## 2.6 **SYMBOL**

A symbol is a word that stands for, or points to, a reality beyond itself. Sunrise, for instance, is often used as a symbol for a new beginning. That example helps you to see something else about symbols – they often share in the reality for which they stand. A sunrise not only stands for a new beginning, it *is* also the new beginning of a day. This is true of symbols that are not words: a handshake is not just a symbol of welcome, it *is* part of the act of welcoming. Thus, Blake's 'The Tyger' is a symbol of terrifying, creative energy, and in itself a terrifying, energetic creature.

When you are reading poetry, you may be troubled by this question: how do I know whether a word is or is not a symbol? Unlike simile, you can't look for a 'like' or an 'as'. The help that you can be given will depend upon whether or not the symbol is traditional. If it is, then you can learn that some words function symbolically. For instance, you have already seen that sunrise stands for a new beginning. Other popular ones are sunset, sleep and night standing for death; flowers standing for shortness of life; water for purity; the sea for eternity; the garden for perfect order; and the sky for heaven. In English poetry the seasons take on a symbolic force: spring is new life and energy; summer the time of joy and carefree living; autumn for maturity and fulfilment; and winter for old age and death. The more you read, the more acquainted you will become with traditional symbols.

If, however, a poet has created a new symbol, you can't depend upon such knowledge. Instead, you must read the poem with three questions in mind: does a word have a central place in the poem? Is it used in an elevated way? Does it transform other elements in the poem? Consider Muir's poem 'The Horses'. It begins:

> Barely a twelvemonth after
> The seven days war that put the world to sleep,
> Late in the evening the strange horses came.

The horses have a central place in that opening sentence because they come at its climax. The first two lines are grammatically subordinate to the third, which means that we are not given the main subject and main verb of the sentence till the last four words – 'the strange horses came'. Grammatical expectation thus makes them central. The horses are also treated in an elevated way. Not only are they called 'strange' but they appear amid traditional symbols. The 'seven days' is a symbol of creation, and 'put to sleep' is a symbol of death. The order of events is thus creation, death, and the coming of the horses, suggesting that the horses are a new beginning, or even a resurrection. If you look through the rest of the poem, you will see how the horses transform other elements. The poem ends:

> Our life is changed; their coming our beginning.

That is very clear – the horses have brought a new start and have changed life.

Muir's horses are clearly symbolic, yet it is not easy to say *exactly* what they symbolise. This is often the case with symbols (particularly newly created ones), and you should try to capture this in your writing. Symbols are often rich and complex, so you should be careful to suggest this when you discuss their function. We have used 'stands for' and 'points to'; you could also use 'represents', 'suggests', 'evokes' or 'expresses'. Your aim should always be to capture the way in which, so to speak, a symbol glows or echoes with meaning.

## 2.7 IMAGE AND IMAGERY

The most popular technical word is image, or, in its plural form, imagery. It is also the most comprehensive, in that it means any figure of speech or piece of descriptive writing. Although the name suggests it should only be used of words that appeal to the eye, it is regularly used of anything that can be detected by the five senses. It may sound odd, but people do talk about an image of taste or of smell. Sometimes it is helpful to ask yourself which sense is being appealed to, because this can influence the effect of a poem. For instance, if there are many images of taste or smell, the reader will feel very close to the objects in the poem, whereas images of hearing create distance.

At both 'O' and 'A' level you may be asked to discuss the imagery of a poem. In fact, imagery is often mentioned in a question to cover simile, metaphor, conceit, personification and symbol. This is what was meant by saying it is the most comprehensive term – an image in a poem could also be one of those figures of speech. The advice given about those figures already discussed also applies to writing about imagery: you must never merely label it but always write about its place in the poem.

But what is that place? You will find that imagery often has three functions: it creates atmosphere, it establishes a pattern within a poem, and it focuses the meaning of the poem as a whole. Let us look at some examples.

In Tennyson's *In Memoriam,* a sequence of poems on the death of his friend Arthur Hallam, there are many sections made memorable by the way the imagery creates the atmosphere of a place or a season. One is set in London:

> Dark house, by which once more I stand
>    Here in the long unlovely street,
>    Doors, where my heart was used to beat
> So quickly, waiting for a hand.
>
> A hand that can be grasped no more –
>    Behold me, for I cannot sleep,
>    And like a guilty thing I creep
> At earliest morning to the door.
>
> He is not here; but far away
>    The noise of life begins again,
>    And ghastly through the drizzling rain
> On the bald street breaks the blank day.

The images in this poem are urban – 'dark house', 'the long unlovely street', 'Doors', 'the noise of life' and 'the bald street'. Together they create the vivid atmosphere of an anonymous, ugly and unfeeling city. This atmosphere, it should be noted, is very impressive when its unfeeling blankness is contrasted with the pain of the poet as he stands outside the house where his dead friend lived. When you write about how imagery creates atmosphere, you should follow the practice used here. Look for the images that create the atmosphere, group them together in a sentence, sum up the impression they make, and then comment on the emotional effect they have upon the whole poem.

In some poems you find words and phrases that relate to each other because they grow out of a common image. Wherever these words and phrases interconnect, a pattern emerges in the poem, creating tightness, order and coherence. In other words, the imagery creates a pattern, which draws the poem together. Look at Shakespeare's Sonnet 30:

When to the sessions of sweet silent thought
I summon up remembrance of things past,
I sigh the lack of many a thing I sought,
And with old woes new wail my dear time's waste.
Then can I drown an eye, unused to flow,
For precious friends hid in death's dateless night,
And weep afresh love's long since cancelled woe
And moan the expense of many a vanished sight;
Then can I grieve at grievances foregone,
And heavily from woe to woe tell o'er
The sad account of fore-bemoaned moan,
Which I new pay as if not paid before.
But if the while I think on thee, dear friend,
All losses are restored and sorrows end.

What does the word 'sessions' mean? It could mean periods of time, but it is also the word used for the sittings of a court of law. Now if that latter usage is the one intended here, things begin to fall into place. 'Summon' is the word used for calling someone to court; 'cancelled' and 'expense' are legal terms; 'tell' refers to the giving of evidence; and 'new pay' is a fine exacted by the court. All those words grow out of the unstated image of the court. Taken together they make a coherent statement. Time, the poem says, is like a court; it is hard and seeks to punish those who appear before it. Often you will need to read a poem a number of times before you see a pattern in the imagery. When you do, you should list the words and show that they are connected by a common image. Finally, you should try to see what the pattern of imagery contributes to the meaning of the poem.

Imagery is effective when it is central to the poem's meaning. In Yeats's 'The Second Coming' a concrete image establishes very forcefully the idea that order is breaking down and communication becoming impossible:

Turning and turning in the widening gyre
The falcon cannot hear the falconer . . .
('gyre' means a spiralling movement)

The meaning of the poem is focused in that image. Just as the falcon spirals in ever-increasing sweeps away from the falconer, so civilisation breaks away from its centre. The image enacts the meaning of the poem because it is concrete: that is, it does not merely say something but presents an image in which this idea can be *seen* at work. When writing about the way an image focuses the meaning of a poem, you should show how the image makes concrete what the rest of the poem is saying. 'The Second Coming' is about disintegration; the image of the falcon makes this visible.

When writing about the three functions of imagery, you should remember that one does not exclude another. The imagery of a poem may do all three – create atmosphere, form a pattern and focus meaning. It is up to you to decide how the image works by examining the poem as a whole.

## 2.8 PARADOX AND AMBIGUITY

Paradox and ambiguity are sometimes called figures of speech and sometimes simply regarded as ways in which language functions. Either way, you should learn to master the terms.

A paradox is an apparent contradiction which says something strange yet true. For instance, in Keats's 'Ode on a Grecian Urn' there are these paradoxical lines on music:

Heard melodies are sweet, but those unheard
Are sweeter . . .

That is contradictory; a melody you can't hear can never be sweeter than one you can. Nevertheless, the lines point to the strange truth that that which we imagine is often more beautiful than that which actually exists. When you write about paradoxes, you should bring out the element of surprise. What starts off as an apparent contradiction often yields truths that are more interesting than everyday ones.

Ambiguity is a very useful term to master, when you want to write about the richness of meaning in poetry. Unlike its use in ordinary speech, it does not mean a confusing mistake but is used to indicate the many nuances of meaning that can be found in poetic language. Because language is ambiguous, a poem can do justice at the same time to quite different ideas. In Book I of *Paradise Lost* Milton writes of Satan's pride in seeing his host of fallen angels assembling before him:

And now his heart
Distends with pride, and hardening in his strength
Glories . . .

The word 'pride' is ambiguous because it has two meanings: a praiseworthy delight in one's own achievements, and the sin of placing oneself before others and God. Satan is rightly proud to see before him all the angels who remain his faithful followers, but this pride is also a sin in that Satan is setting himself up in opposition to God.

Ambiguity can also be created by the syntax of a poem: that is, by the order of words in a sentence. Consider these lines from the opening poem of Blake's *Songs of Innocence:*

And I made a rural pen,
And I stained the water clear.

What do these lines mean? They are about making ink to use in his pen, but do they mean that the pen stained the clear water, or is the meaning that the water was stained in order to make it clear? The syntax makes *both* meanings possible.

You may find that the longer you think about poems, the more ambiguous they become. If this is the case, you should not try to simplify them. The best thing you can do when writing about them is to make clear that poems might mean a number of things. Indeed, the meaning of poems may be all the possible meanings that arise through the ambiguities.

## 2.9 **ADVICE ABOUT TECHNICAL TERMS**

As with all technical terms, you will learn to master them by usage. Whenever you take notes or write an essay, you should try to use the appropriate technical terms. When you first begin to use them, it is a good idea, particularly in the case of imagery, to think them through in detail. You can do this by picturing the effects created by similes and metaphors and listing all the shades of meaning that emerge in symbols. Although this is somewhat artificial, it will help you to see just how rich are the meanings that words convey.

There is, however, one warning to give. Sometimes it is not possible to identify a word as a particular figure of speech. For instance, in Blake's 'The Sick Rose' it is not clear whether the rose is a real, a symbolic or a metaphoric one. There is, of course, no virtue simply in labelling, so when you cannot use an appropriate technical term, you should just concentrate on writing about the richness of the language.

## EXERCISES

**1** Read through all the poems you have to study to see if there are any words that particularly strike you. If there are, try to write about them, bringing out why you feel them to be effective.
**2** Read through all the poems you have to study for any of the figures of speech explained in this section. If you find some, try writing about how they help to establish the meaning of the poem.
**3** Read 'To Autumn' by Keats a number of times, and then attempt to answer the questions below.

Season of mists and mellow fruitfulness!
Close bosom-friend of the maturing sun;
Conspiring with him how to load and bless
With fruit the vines that round the thatch-eaves run;
To bend with apples the mossed cottage trees,
And fill all fruit with ripeness to the core;
To swell the gourd, and plump the hazel shells
With a sweet kernel; to set budding more,
And still more, later flowers for the bees,
Until they think warm days will never cease,
For Summer has o'er brimmed their clammy cells.

Who hath not seen thee oft amid thy store?
Sometimes whoever seeks abroad may find
Thee sitting careless on a granary floor,
Thy hair soft-lifted by the winnowing wind,
Or on a half-reaped furrow sound asleep,
Drowsed with the fume of poppies, while thy hook
Spares the next swath and all its twined flowers;
And sometimes like a gleaner thou dost keep
Steady thy laden head across a brook;
Or by a cider-press, with patient look,
Thou watchest the last oozings hours by hours.

Where are the songs of Spring? Ay, where are they?
Think not of them, thou hast thy music too, –
While barred clouds bloom the soft-dying day,
And touch the stubble plains with rosy hue;
Then in a wailful choir the small gnats mourn
Among the river sallows, borne aloft
Or sinking as the light wind lives or dies;

And full-grown lambs loud bleat from hilly bourn;
Hedge crickets sing; and now with treble soft
The redbreast whistles from a garden-croft;
And gathering swallows twitter in the skies.

(a) Think about the ambiguous character of: 'Conspiring with him how to load and bless' (line 3), 'To bend with apples' (line 5). What view of Autumn emerges from these ambiguities?

(b) In the second stanza Keats speaks directly to a personified figure of Autumn. How does Keats build up this figure, and what is its effect in the poem?

(c) Compare the lush imagery of the first stanza with the more restrained imagery of the third one.

(d) What distinctive atmosphere is created by the following images: 'the soft-dying day' (line 25), 'in a wailful choir the small gnats mourn' (line 27), 'borne aloft / Or sinking' (lines 28–9) and 'gathering swallows' (line 33)?

**4** Read 'Lights Out' by Edward Thomas a number of times and then answer the questions below.

I have come to the borders of sleep,
The unfathomable deep
Forest where all must lose
Their way, however straight,
Or winding, soon or late;
They cannot choose.

Many a road and track
That, since the dawn's first crack,
Up to the forest brink,
Deceived the travellers,
Suddenly now blurs,
And in they sink.

Here love ends,
Despair, ambition ends;
All pleasure and all trouble,
Although most sweet or bitter,
Here ends in sleep that is sweeter
Than tasks most noble.

There is not any book
Or face of dearest look
That I would not turn from now

To go into the unknown
I must enter, and leave, alone
I know not how.

The tall forest towers;
Its cloudy foliage lowers
Ahead, shelf above shelf;
Its silence I hear and obey
That I may lose my way
And myself.

(a) Think about how the word 'sleep' is used in the first line.

(b) Would it be helpful to describe the forest as a symbol; if so, of what is it symbolic?

(c) Throughout the poem there are images of travelling. Think about what they mean in the poem, and consider whether the image is a traditional or new one.

(d) Do all the images stem from one basic idea, and if so what is that idea?

# CHAPTER 3

# LINE AND RHYTHM

## 3.1 LINES: END-STOPPED AND RUN-ON

Because poems are written in set lines, something about the way a line of poetry is constructed is bound to attract your attention. There are three features that you are likely to notice because they have an important effect upon poems: the way the line ends, the breaks, or pauses that occur within lines, and the many different rhythms that the words in a line can create.

A line can end in two ways: it can be end-stopped or run-on. In an end-stopped line the meaning is complete by the close, so it finishes with a punctuation mark; in run-on lines the meaning is left unfinished, so there is no punctuation at the end. The first lines of Yeats's 'Byzantium' are end-stopped:

> The unpurged images of day recede;
> The Emperor's drunken soldiery are abed;

whereas his 'Leda and the Swan' begins with two run-on lines:

> A sudden blow: the great wings beating still
> Above the staggering girl, her thighs caressed
> By the dark webs . . .

There is, of course, no point in just identifying one line as end-stopped and another as run-on. You should only use these terms if you can go on to show that they contribute to the impact of the poem. The question, then, that should be asked is: what effects are created by end-stopped and run-on lines?

End-stopped lines usually sound firm and finished, because meanings are completed within them. Consider the first verse of Gray's 'Elegy':

> The curfew tolls the knell of parting day,
> The lowing herd winds slowly o'er the lea,
> The ploughman homeward plods his weary way,
> And leaves the world to darkness and to me.

In those lines there is the satisfaction of finding the lines completing their meanings as the subjects of those lines complete their tasks. The curfew bell rings to tell us that day is over, and as soon as we have learned that the line itself is over; likewise, the herd winds over the lea as the line that tells us that winds to a close. The termination of the end-stopped lines beautifully enacts the completion of the four things with which the first stanza deals.

By contrast, run-on lines create feelings of expectation. At the close of a line the meaning is not yet complete, so you might ask: what is going to happen next? What is the full meaning going to be? Where is the thought of the poem going? Hopkins's 'God's Grandeur', which is about the presence of the glory of God in the world, starts with two firm end-stopped lines, and then offers the reader an enticing run-on:

> The world is charged with the grandeur of God.
> It will flame out, like shining from shook foil;
> It gathers to a greatness, like the ooze of oil
> Crushed.

Because the line ends half way through a simile, a great deal of expectation is aroused. The expectation is dramatically gratified by the word 'Crushed' – easily the strongest word Hopkins has yet used in the poem. As a result of the expectation being suddenly fulfilled, the run-on line is far more emphatic than the two end-stopped ones.

Sometimes very telling effects are created by combining the two sorts of lines. Hopkins offered two end-stopped lines before moving to a run-on, but in Wordsworth's 'The Solitary Reaper' there are six restrained, end-stopped ones before the line runs on:

> Behold her, single in the field,
> Yon solitary Highland lass!
> Reaping and singing by herself;
> Stop here or gently pass!
> Alone she cuts and binds the grain,
> And sings a melancholy strain;
> O listen! for the vale profound
> Is overflowing with the sound.

As Wordsworth becomes ever more deeply enthralled by the girl's singing, the emotional pressure, so to speak, builds up. In the sentence that begins 'Alone she cuts' it is very strong, and after the powerful outburst to the reader 'O listen!', the line, like the song itself, overflows. Needless to say, it is also Wordsworth's emotions that have overflowed. The change, therefore, from end-stopped to run-on lines can be effective because it marks a change in the emotions of the poet.

## 3.2 CAESURA

A break within a line is called a caesura. It can only be located by attending to the pauses you are obliged to make when *reading* the line, though sometimes it occurs at a punctuation mark. If you wish to indicate the presence of a caesura, the customary sign is ||. Caesuras are worth noting because they can have marked effects upon a poem. You should look out for three effects: the way they shape the emotional life of a poem, the humour they can help to create, and the way they can dramatise a poem's close.

To say that caesuras shape the emotional life of a poem is to say that breaks in a line of verse help to create distinctive tones. Consider the following lines:

Sweet day, || so cool, || so calm, || so bright!

(George Herbert, 'Virtue')

All's over then: || does truth sound bitter?

(Robert Browning, 'The Lost Mistress')

I sit in the top of the tree, || my eyes closed.

(Ted Hughes, 'Hawk Roosting')

The tone of Herbert's line is that of a quiet, loving appreciation of the day's qualities. Speaking to the day, the caesuras mark the pauses in his thought. It is as if he stops to think before he speaks, so the caesuras enact the very process of deep thought and careful speech. The line from Browning forms part of a question which is asked in a resigned tone. The caesura is a heavy one (emphatic and long) which comes after the very final sounding 'then'. The sense of finality and the break create the tone of resigned acceptance. The tone of the Hughes is firm and determined. The hawk coldly lists its position in the tree and the fact that its eyes are closed. The caesura marks the determined way in which the bird notes those things.

Caesuras also mark a change in the emotions of a poem. If you attend closely to a poem's mood you may enjoy the pleasure of recognising and following changes in feeling. A very moving example occurs in 'Thyrsis', the poem in which Arnold mourns the death of his friend by thinking about how the landscape around Oxford, where they used to walk together, seems utterly changed. At one point he appeals to the hills to recognise him. Note how the caesuras mark the emotional pulse of his appeal:

> See, ‖ 'tis no foot of unfamiliar men
> To-night from Oxford ‖ up your pathway strays!
> Here came I often, ‖ often, ‖ in old days –
> Thyrsis and I; ‖ we still had Thyrsis then.

The first caesura marks his attempt to reassure the hills as to who he is; the second is light and indicates that his mind is travelling over the past pleasures he and Thyrsis shared as they strayed up the pathways. In the third line he hesitates regretfully over the word 'often', remembering, no doubt, that these walks were so much a part of his life 'in old days'. The greatest change in emotion comes in the last line, where a heavy caesura marks the deep change from the companionship of the past to the desolation of the present; a desolation made all the more poignant by the knowledge, enacted in the finality of 'then', that the pleasures of companionship are over.

The humour made possible by a caesura also marks a change in mood. Consider these lines from Pope's *The Rape of the Lock*:

> Meanwhile, ‖ declining from the noon of day
> The sun obliquely ‖ shoots his burning ray;
> The hungry judges ‖ soon the sentence sign
> And wretches hang ‖ that jurymen may dine . . .

The caesuras here are all light; indeed in the second and third lines they are hardly noticeable. The one in the fourth line is also light, but Pope cleverly uses it to mark the division between the wretches who are sped to the gallows and jurymen who retire to enjoy their dinner. The humour of the line is increased when we see so light a caesura marking a gross miscarriage of justice that leads to a grotesque contrast in fates – the rope for some, and, let us imagine, roast beef for the others!

At the end of a poem a caesura can dramatise the meaning. The pause before the final word or words allows the reader time to recognise what has happened in the poem before it is completed. The end, therefore, when it does come, is felt to be even more final. Consider Larkin's short yet very moving poem, 'Home':

> Home is so sad. It stays as it was left,
> Shaped to the comfort of the last to go
> As if to win them back. Instead, bereft
> Of anyone to please, it withers so,
> Having no heart to put aside the theft

And turn again to what it started as,
A joyous shot at how things ought to be,
Long fallen wide. You can see how it was:
Look at the pictures and the cutlery.
The music in the piano stool. That vase.

The pathos of the poem lies in the way that objects are made to stand for ordinary but deeply felt hopes and longings. When these hopes and longings have come to nothing, the objects still remain expressive of them at the same time as recording their failure. The heavy caesura in the last line allows the reader to see all that. We are told to look at the pictures, the cutlery and the music in the piano stool. The pause allows us to see just how sadly expressive these objects are before the final words – 'That vase' – confirms the poignancy of items that remain when the hopes that put them there have come to nothing.

## 3.3 THE METRES OF VERSE

When you think about a line of poetry as a whole, you may be struck by the fact that a sequence of stressed and unstressed syllables creates a regular, or nearly regular, rhythm. On the other hand, the lines of a poem may be rhythmical, and you can't recognise it. This is not unusual. To use a musical term, many readers are tone deaf where rhythm is concerned. If you know that your ear is not good at detecting rhythms, you should make a special effort to hear them. You can do this by reading aloud, listening to poetry being read, and learning poems by heart so that you can repeat them to yourself.

Once you begin to detect rhythms, you should master some basic technical terms. Regular patterns of stressed and unstressed syllables are called metres. Identifying metres is called scansion. When metres are identified, the syllables in a line are divided into groups of two or three, each of which is called a foot. When, in scansion, you wish to note that a syllable is stressed you use the / sign, and when unstressed the ∪ sign.

The most basic point in English metre is whether the stress falls on the first syllable of a foot. If it does, the metre is trochaic, and each foot is called a trochee; if, however, it falls on the second, the metre is iambic, and each foot is called an iamb. For example, the introductory poem of Blake's *Songs of Innocence* is trochaic:

/ ∪ / ∪ / ∪ /
Piping down the valleys wild,
/ ∪ / ∪ / ∪ /
Piping songs of pleasant glee,

and Collins's 'Ode written in 1746' is iambic:

How sleep the brave who sink to rest
By all their country's wishes blest!

Trochaic and iambic metres are based on a two-syllable foot. When a foot has three syllables, two other metres occur – the dactylic and the anapaestic. A dactyl is a variation of a trochee in that it has two unstressed syllables after the stress, and an anapaest varies an iamb by having two unstressed syllables before the stress. For example, Hood's 'Bridge of Sighs' is dactylic:

Touch her not scornfully;
Think of her mournfully,

and Swinburne's 'Off Shore' is anapaestic:

As the veil of the shrine
Of the temple of old . . .

There are also names for the number of feet in a line. A one foot line is called a monometer, two a dimeter, three a trimeter, four a tetrameter, five a pentameter, six a hexameter, seven a heptameter and eight an octameter.

You will find that much English verse is iambic and is written in tetrameters or pentameters. One of the most popular metres in English is the iambic pentameter, also called blank verse. Anapaestic metres are rare, but individual anapaests occur as a variation in basically iambic poems. Trochaic metres are less common than iambic ones, and dactylic metres are very rare indeed.

Now, there are very few things that annoy examiners more than candidates who identify a metre and say no more about it. Hence, what you should always do is write about how the rhythm contributes to the poem as a whole. To help you to do this, four issues will be discussed: the character of metres, the importance of variation within a metre, additional ways of writing about rhythm, and the question of why rhythm matters at all.

## 3.4 THE CHARACTERS OF METRES

Rhythms enact the thoughts and feelings of poems, so it is a good idea to ask: is it significant that these thoughts and feelings have been expressed in this particular rhythm? That question leads to another: are some rhythms more appropriate to certain thoughts and feelings than others? Both those questions are about the character of metres.

It is important to understand that there are no hard and fast rules governing the character of metres. You can't assume that because a poem is written in a particular metre then it must have a particular emotional character irrespective of what is being said. Rhythm cannot be separated from meaning.

Nevertheless, even if there are no rules, there are certain aspects of metres that make them suitable for some subjects. What follows are tentative suggestions about the appropriateness of rhythms to certain thoughts and feelings.

Trochaic metres, because they start with a stress, can sound assertive. Look at the opening of Blake's 'The Tyger':

> Tyger! Tyger! burning bright
> In the forests of the night . . .

The 'Tyger' bursts upon the reader in assertive trochees. Not all trochaic metres will be as powerful as that, but it is a good idea to see if you can find this rhythm hammering out the meaning of the lines.

By contrast, iambic metres can be thoughtful and recollective, since they move from the uncertainty of an unstressed syllable to the certainty of a stressed one. Wordsworth's 'Tintern Abbey', a thoughtful poem about recollected experiences, is written in gentle and not always regular iambic pentameters. In this passage he writes about how his mind works:

> With many recognitions dim and faint,
> And somewhat of a sad perplexity,
> The picture of the mind revives again . . .

The iambic rhythm of the last line beautifully enacts the revival of which it speaks; the stresses on 'The picture', 'mind', 'revives', and 'again' create the increasing certainty that comes with the mind's revival. This is particularly so in the di-syllabic 'revives' and 'again', where the poetry observes the natural iambic rhythms of speech, so that within one word there is movement from unstress to stress, from uncertainty to certainty.

Dactylic metres tend to be sad. The two unstressed syllables which follow the stress create a feeling of decline, of a falling away from certainty. It is not surprising, therefore, that a poem of regret – Browning's 'The Lost Leader' – should be written in sad, heavy dactyls:

> We that had loved him so, followed him, honoured him,
> Lived in his mild and magnificent eye . . .

The sad regret of 'loved him so' is created by the two unstressed syllables that follow 'loved'. It is as if we hear the sighs of the protagonist as hope fades away. The dactyl, in other words, enacts the way love for the lost leader dies.

Anapaestic metres, by contrast, build up emotional tension by hurrying the reader through unstressed syllables to the stressed one. A famous example is Byron's 'The Destruction of Sennacherib':

> The Assyrian came down like the wolf on the fold,
> And his cohorts were gleaming in purple and gold.

The unstressed syllables create an anticipatory tension, which is released in powerful monosyllables – 'down', 'wolf', and 'fold'.

## 3.5 VARIATION IN METRES

When you write about the effectiveness of rhythm, you will mention the impact of variation more than any other factor. Because only the dullest of poems keep strictly to a set metre, you are likely to find variation in many of the poems you study. It is sensible, therefore, to ask these three questions of any poem. Is there variation from the basic rhythm? What kind of variation is it? What impact does the variation have upon the meaning? If the answer to the first question is yes, you should consider the second two together.

Variations are usually of two types: a change from one metre to another, and words that are stressed much more heavily than others. A line of poetry can display both, and, needless to say, the presence of either affects the meaning of what is said.

When a metre changes, though only for a few words, the effect created is called counterpointing. In Book IV of *Paradise Lost* Milton counterpoints the basic iambic metre. Here is the passage from Book IV without scansion marks:

> Now came still evening on, and twilight grey
> Had in her silver livery all things clad . . .

The first line can be scanned:

> Now came still evening on, and twilight grey

but what of the second? By itself it would be possible to scan the line as a set of iambs:

> Had in her silver livery all things clad . . .

But that would be to ignore the effect of the run-on line. If we recognise that the sense is carried over, the second line should be scanned:

> Had in her silver livery all things clad . . .

That is, it can be read as a dactyl followed by trochees, or as a trochee followed by iambuses. However the rhythm is interpreted, the first word –

a verb, 'Had' – is stressed. This affects the meaning. By placing a stress upon the verb, the evening is seen as an active power at work in the world. You may also notice that of the other stresses, the heaviest are 'all' and 'clad'. They further enforce the evening's active power; *all* things are affected, *all* things are *clad.*

Let us further consider the effect of some words being more heavily stressed than others. Think about the opening of Shakespeare's Sonnet 73, in which the poet tells his beloved that he is passing from the autumn to the winter of his life:

> That time of year thou mayst in me behold
> When yellow leaves or none, or few, do hang
> Upon those boughs which shake against the cold,
> Bare ruined choirs, where late the sweet birds sang.

The metre is basically iambic, but some words are more stressed than others. In the first three lines they are: 'yéllow̆', 'nóne', 'féw' and 'sháke'. In the fourth line, the metre is more irregular, and more weight is placed on 'Báre rúinĕd chóirs' and 'láte'. Now, what have these words in common? They are all concerned with growing old. When old, you are 'yellow', near to nothing – 'none', 'few' – you 'shake', are 'bare' and 'ruined', and your youth is 'late', that is, dead. The point is that the words that are more heavily stressed are central to the poem's meaning. It is as if the poet is pushing the important words at you by stressing them more heavily. Therefore, in any poem you can ask: are there words here that are more heavily stressed, and do they have a central place in the meaning of the poem?

## 3.6 WRITING ABOUT RHYTHM

There are two reasons why you should master ways of writing about rhythm that are additional to the technical terms outlined above. The first is that examiners won't reward you just for putting a label on a metre, and the second that rhythm, because it affects the impact a poem has, should be spoken about in ways appropriate to that. Let us look at some examples.

Consider these lines from Blake's 'Spring':

> Sound the Flute!
> Now it's mute.
> Birds delight
> Day and Night . . .

The metre is trochaic, but what else can be said about it? The rhythm can be said to be light and carefree. If you want to say further what 'light' means, you might say that the rhythm is deft and tripping.

A very different effect is present in the first two lines of Herbert's 'Affliction':

> Lord, how I am all ague, when I seek
> What I have treasured in my memory!

The opening is basically iambic, but its effectiveness depends upon the jerky and uncertain quality of the rhythm. The first line is about disease (that is what 'ague' means), and you can feel the discomfort in the stumbling rhythm. The second line, by contrast, is much more smooth and flowing.

A third example can be found in Shakespeare's Sonnet 12:

> When I do count the clock that tells the time,
> And see the brave day sunk in hideous night . . .

The metre is a regular iambic one, but it is still necessary to describe its effect. Would it be right to say the regular, insistent rhythm makes the poem grave, serious and slow? The rhythm is that of somebody deliberately counting time and being fully aware that it is ebbing inevitably away.

A contrasting example can be found in Donne's 'The Canonization':

> For God's sake hold your tongue, and let me love,
> Or chide my palsy, or my gout . . .

The metre here is appropriately irregular. The poet is angrily turning upon the person who is interrupting him and gesturing him away defiantly.

As you will see, some of the words used to characterise rhythm are concerned with feeling. Rhythms were said to be 'carefree', 'uncertain', 'grave' and 'serious'. If you can characterise the emotional impact of rhythm, you should, of course, do so.

You may also have noticed that some of the words used to describe rhythm were drawn from the vocabulary of physical movement. The rhythms were said to be 'light', 'tripping'. 'deft', 'jerky', 'stumbling' and 'slow'. When you consider how to describe the impact of rhythm, it is a good idea to draw on such words. Rhythm could be awkward, ponderous, heavy, swaying or rolling. Here it should be said that sometimes the word 'movement' itself is more appropriate than rhythm. 'Rhythm' suggests regularity, whereas 'movement' is much more general, covering, as it does, pace as well as metre.

Very close to physical movement is physical gesture. It is sometimes appprropriate to use words dealing with gestures to describe the effect of rhythm. In the above examples, the Donne passage was described as a defiant gesture. Some lines of poetry, or even whole poems, might be described as expansive, dramatic, inviting or tense.

Because rhythm is an element in music, it is often useful to turn to the language of music when you are looking for words to characterise rhythms. In the above examples a line was described as 'smooth' and 'flowing' words often used to describe the effect of a piece of music. Other words that might be used are ones associated with tempo, such as lively, quick and brisk; and ones associated with the movement and volume of sound, such as crescendo, diminuendo and cadence. Cadence is a particularly useful word because it describes the way the voice rises or falls in pitch as it comes to a close at the end of a sentence, line or caesura. Of course, you should always try to characterise the effect of a cadence. Shakespeare's song from *Cymbeline* contains this cadence:

Golden girls and lads all must
As chimney sweepers, come to dust.

The thought that even 'golden girls and lads' must come, in the end, to nothing but 'dust' is enacted in a falling cadence of sad resignation.

You should remember that once you step beyond using technical terms to describe rhythm, you are writing in a more personal way. This is good, but it does bring the danger of vagueness. Therefore, you should try to blend both the technical and the non-technical vocabulary.

## 3.7 WHY RHYTHM MATTERS

The final point about rhythm can be put as a question: why does rhythm *matter*? The answer is that it conveys the emotional weight of what is being said. Think, for instance, about sadness. If you are sad, you experience sadness in two ways – you *know* you are sad, and you *feel* you are sad. Now, consider how you could convey this to somebody else. If you say 'I am sad', you will convey the knowledge of your sadness, but those words alone won't bring over the feeling. But the rhythms of poetry can. They can convey the fact of an emotion and the feeling of that emotion. Consider the rhythms of Hardy's poem 'The Voice':

Woman much missed, how you call to me, call to me,
Saying that now you were not as you were
When you had changed from the one who was all to me,
But as at first, when our day was fair.

In those lines you not only learn about the sadness of loss, you feel the emotional weight of it in the rhythms. The repeated word 'call' is mournful and plaintive, and, like 'woman' and 'missed', it bears a very heavy stress. In the second line, the word 'not' is very strongly stressed, emphasising the change. In the third line it is the simple word 'all' that bears the most emphasis, an emphasis that brings home how someone who was everything to him has utterly changed in his affections. In the last line the heavy caesura isolates the distant past 'when our day was fair'. The rhythms of the poem enact the sadness of which they speak. And that is why many people value poetry – it enables a reader to feel what it is like to undergo an experience.

## EXERCISES

**1** Read through the poems you are studying and consider the effects of end-stopped and run-on lines. You should also consider the impact of caesuras.
**2** Read through the poems you are studying and consider the rhythms of the poetry. You should also consider any variations and try to write about how central rhythms are to the poems.
**3** Read Sonnet 97 by Shakespeare a number of times, and when you feel you know it, answer the questions below.

> How like a winter hath my absence been
> From thee, the pleasure of the fleeting year!
> What freezings have I felt, what dark days seen!
> What old December's bareness everywhere!
> And yet this time removed was summer's time,
> The teeming autumn big with rich increase,
> Bearing the wanton burden of the prime,
> Like widowed wombs after their lord's decease:
> Yet this abundant issue seemed to me
> But hope of orphans and unfathered fruit
> For summer and its pleasures wait on thee,
> And, thou away, the very birds are mute.
> Or, if they sing, 'tis with so dull a cheer,
> That leaves look pale, dreading the winter's near.

(a) What is the emotional effect of the first line being run-on, and how is this increased by the heavy caesura after 'thee'? Think, too, about the effect of run-on and end-stopped lines in the sonnet.

(b) Think about the rhythms of the third line. What is effective about 'dark days seen'?

(c) What word is heavily stressed in the fourth line, and what effect does this have on the meaning and emotional quality of the poem?

(d) How would you characterise the effect of the cadence at the close of line 12? What is its emotional quality?

**4** Read Hardy's 'At Castle Boterel' a number of times, and when you feel you understand it, answer the questions below.

As I drive to the junction of lane and highway,
And the drizzle bedrenches the wagonette,
I look behind at the fading byway,
And see on its shape, now glistening wet,
Distinctly yet

Myself and a girlish form benighted
In dry March weather. We climb the road
Beside a chaise. We had just alighted
To ease the sturdy pony's load
When he sighed and slowed.

What we did as we climbed, and what we talked of
Matters not much, nor to what it led, –
Something that life will not be baulked of
Without rude reason till hope is dead,
And feeling fled.

It filled but a minute. But was there ever
A time of such quality, since or before,
In that hill's story? To one mind never,
Though it has been climbed, foot-swift, foot-sore,
By thousands more.

Primaeval rocks form the road's steep border,
And much they have faced there, first and last,
Of the transitory in earth's long order;
But what they record in colour and cast
Is – that we two passed.

And to me, though Time's unflinching rigour,
In mindless rote, has ruled from sight
The substance now, one phantom figure
Remains on the slope, as when that night
Saw us alight.

I look and see it there, shrinking, shrinking,
I look back at it amid the rain

For the very last time; for my sand is sinking
And I shall traverse old love's domain
Never again.

(a) Think about how the basic rhythm is varied throughout the poem and consider the emotional effect of this.

(b) Which words are heavily stressed in the third verse, and what contribution do they make to the meaning of the poem?

(c) Think about the movement of the words in the fifth verse. You might like to think about the place of 'first and last', 'transitory', 'long', and the effect of the run-on line.

(d) Try to describe the emotional effects of the end-stopped lines, the run-on lines, the heavily stressed words and the closing cadence of the final verse.

CHAPTER 4

# SOUND, RHYME AND FORM

## 4.1 LISTENING TO SOUNDS

Every word that is spoken has a sound as well as a meaning. In everyday speech people do not call attention to the sounds that words make, but in poetry – a special way of using words – sounds are made to play a part in the impact of a poem.

You may find that you are deaf to sounds. If you know that when you read or listen to poetry the fact that sounds are made has no effect upon you, then you should make a special effort to hear them. When you read or listen to any poem, bear this question in mind: what effects are being produced by the sounds of the words?

Listen, for instance, to these lines:

Thou mastering me
God! giver of breath and bread;
World's strand, sway of sea;
Lord of living and dead . . .

(G.M. Hopkins, 'The Wreck of the Deutschland')

Somewhere afield here something lies
In Earth's oblivious eyeless trust . . .

(Thomas Hardy, 'Shelley's Skylark')

Beautiful lofty things: O'Leary's noble head . . .

(W.B. Yeats, 'Beautiful lofty things')

It seemed that out of battle I escaped
Down some profound dull tunnel, long since scooped
Through granites which titanic wars had groined.

(Wilfred Owen, 'Strange Meeting')

Underwater eyes, an eel's
Oil of water body, neither fish nor beast is the otter . . .
(Ted Hughes, 'An Otter')

The passage from Hopkins sounds majestic and powerful; in the sounds of the words you can hear the authority of God. Listen, for instance, to the authority God has over the sea in the sounds of 'sway of sea'. The sound of the Hardy is more difficult to describe. Could it be said that the passage is soft and lyrical, suggesting a safe keeping in the oblivious earth? The sound of the passage from Yeats is also lyrical. It is also elevated without being grand or oppressive. The Owen passage, by contrast, is grave and sonorous. In the very sounds of the words you can hear the descent into the earth and feel something of the power that opened up a way into the earth's core. The Hughes passage is agile and fluid; in the sounds of the words you can hear the lithe twisting of the otter, particularly in 'an eel's / Oil of water body'.

You will have noticed that it was not possible to write about the effects of the sounds without also commenting on the meanings of the words. That is as it should be: when writing about the sounds of words you must not separate them from their meanings. The reason for this is that every word is *both* a sound and a meaning; you can't have one without the other. Used sensitively, sounds can enact meanings. As Pope said in *An Essay on Criticism*:

'Tis not enough no harshness gives offence,
The sound must seem an echo to the sense.

When you write about sounds in poetry, you will find that you need to master a body of technical terms and use a wider vocabulary to characterise the effect of the sounds. Let us consider the technical terms first. There are four: alliteration, consonance, assonance and onomatopoeia.

## 4.2 ALLITERATION

Alliteration is the repetition of a consonantal sound. For instance, the 'w', 'l' and 'sh' sounds are alliterated in this line from Hopkins's 'Spring':

When weeds, in wheels, shoot long and lovely and 'lush',

and in this line from Dylan Thomas's 'Over Sir John's Hill' the 's' is repeated:

Stare for the sake of the souls of the slain birds sailing.

Many students find it quite easy to recognise alliteration but are less sure about how to describe its effects. You can look out for two things:

the way it helps to create tones, and its regularity or irregularity.

Alliteration often helps to create a poem's distinctive tone. Of any alliteration you can ask: does the alliteration help to create the tone of the poem? Listen, for instance, to the vigorous opening of Shelley's 'Ode to the West Wind':

> O Wild West Wind, thou breath of Autumn's being

The alliterated words powerfully enact the awe the poet feels in the presence of such a mighty force. You can hear that awe in the expansive sounds of 'Wild West Wind' and feel the power of the wind in 'breath' and the cleverly delayed echo of the 'b' sound in 'being'.

When alliteration strikes you as being interesting, it is worth asking: are the alliterated sounds regularly or irregularly spaced? When they are regular, they can sound very emphatic. Consider the last line of the 'dark house' poem from *In Memoriam*:

> On the bald street breaks the blank day.

The feeling of a lonely poet oppressed by the return of morning is enacted in the regularly spaced words beginning with 'b'; they hammer home his desolation. The irregularity of Hughes's 'Pike' is also impressive:

> Pike, three inches long perfect
> Pike in all parts . . .

The 'p' sound stands out, but because it does so irregularly it sounds more threatening. It is not relentless like the alliterated 'b's of Tennyson but sharp, quick and disturbing.

## 4.3 CONSONANCE

You will not use consonance very much. It describes the effect of *like* consonant but *unlike* vowel sounds, as in 'heat' and 'hate'. When you do come across consonance, it is worth while asking whether there is a relation in meaning between the words. If so, you can write about the pleasure of finding a closeness of meaning in the similarity of sounds. For instance, in Marlowe's 'The Passionate Shepherd to his Love', there is a clear relation between 'live' and 'love':

> Come live with me and be my love . . .

To 'live' with someone is to share their life, and that sharing is close to what we mean by 'love'. The consonance gives the satisfaction of ear and mind working together.

## 4.4 ASSONANCE

Assonance is the repetition of a vowel sound. The points that were made about alliteration often apply to it, though you will have to become used to assonance working on a smaller scale. Nevertheless, it can be effective. Consider the following two examples:

Prayer, the Church's banquet, Angels age . . .

(George Herbert, 'Prayer')

Such weight and thick pink bulk
Set in death seemed not just dead.

(Ted Hughes, 'View of a Pig')

The 'a's in 'Angels age' sound elevated and spiritual, and the line consequently sounds as if it is lifted to a higher plane. The 'i's in the 'thick pink' and 'in' sound blunt and insistent. In the assonance, you can hear the poet pointing to these features. In both cases, however, the assonance is on a small scale.

## 4.5 ONOMATOPOEIA

Onomatopoeia is the name given to the effect of sounds of words imitating, or miming, the sounds of the object. For instance, 'buzz' is the name for the sound a bee makes, and the sound of the word itself imitates that sound. Poets often write in such a way that the sounds of the words they use remind you of the sounds made by the objects about which they are writing. Listen to the way in which Owen uses his words to imitate the harsh, mechanical sounds of guns and rifles:

Only the monstrous anger of the guns.
Only the stuttering rifles' rapid rattle
Can patter out their hasty orisons.

('Anthem for Doomed Youth')

'Monstrous anger' mimes the explosive power of big guns, and 'stuttering rifles' rapid rattle' is close to the repetitive sound of infantrymen's quick firing.

There is no point in writing about onomatopoeia unless you can show that it is effective. A good question to ask is: does the onomatopoeia help to establish the atmosphere of the poem? If the answer is yes, then you can write about its effectiveness. Consider the close of Tennyson's 'Morte D'Arthur':

long stood Sir Bedivere
Revolving many memories, till the hull
Looked one black dot against the verge of dawn
And on the mere the wailing died away.

'Wailing' is an onomatopoeic word which in combination with 'away' creates a falling cadence which is expressive of the isolation and silence of the mere. It helps to establish the atmosphere of a solitary figure left on the edge of a vast lake.

## 4.6 WRITING ABOUT SOUNDS

In writing about these four technical terms, it has not been possible to exclude other ways of characterising sound in poetry. Let us now concentrate on a wider vocabulary that will help you to write about the effects of sound.

You could turn to the words we use to describe how people speak. The sounds of words in a poem might be characterised according to manner of speech. Here are some possible words: gently, whisperingly, stridently, mellifluously, forthrightly, smoothly, incisively, piercingly and flatly. As you will see, most of these words are closely connected with tone.

There are also words that describe the nature of sounds. Echo and pitch are useful, as are resonant and sonorous. Other words are: deep, harsh, grating, light and shrill.

How might some of these words be used? Listen to these lines from Tennyson's 'The Lotus Eaters':

The lotus blooms below the barren peak:
The lotus blows by every winding creek:
All day the wind breathes low with mellower tone:
Through every hollow cave and alley lone
Round and round the spicy downs the yellow lotus-dust
is blown.

How can the effect of the alliteration, assonance and onomatopoeia be described? Could it be said that because of the sounds of the words the lines sound gentle, mellifluous and smooth?

Dryden's verse sounds very different. How can these lines from *Absalom and Achitophel* be characterised?

Of these the false Achitophel was the first,
A name to all succeeding ages curst:
For close designs and crooked counsels fit,
Sagacious, bold and turbulent of wit,

Restless, unfixed in principles and place,
In power unpleased, impatient of disgrace . . .

The alliteration of the 'f' sound is forthright, and that on the 'c' incisive and even piercing in its forcefulness. Likewise, the 'p' sounds could be described as forthright.

The sound of Milton's verse is very impressive. Listen to this passage from Book II of *Paradise Lost,* in which Satan, having left Hell, launches on his journey to Paradise:

At last his sail-broad vans
He spreads for flight, and in the surging smoke
Uplifted spurns the ground, thence many a league
As in a cloudy chair ascending rides
Audacious, but that seat soon failing, meets
A vast vacuity: all unawares
Fluttering his penons vain plumb down he drops
Ten thousand fathoms deep, and to this hour
Down had he been falling, had not by ill chance
The strong rebuff of some tumultuous cloud
Instinct with fire and nitre hurried him
As many miles aloft . . .

In the very sound of the words you can hear that Milton regards Satan as small and insignificant in the vastness of the universe. The words associated with his flight are light and mellifluous – 'flight', 'uplifted' and 'failing', but when he falls into the 'vast vacuity', the words that alliterate with these – 'fluttering' and 'falling' – stand in marked contrast to the deeply sonorous ones which enact his descent – 'plumb', 'down', 'drops', 'fathom' and 'deep'. The contrast between light and sonorous words enacts the slightness of Satan when compared to the fathomless tracts of space.

## 4.7 THE EFFECTS OF RHYME

The most common sound in poetry is that of rhyme. Most people's idea of poetry is of rhyming lines, and sometimes they are puzzled when they read poetry that doesn't rhyme. Their reaction is understandable. It is only in poetry that rhyme becomes an important feature. In everyday speech, for instance, it is treated as an embarrassment.

Whilst nearly everybody can recognise rhyme, few people can talk about its effectiveness. It is clearly not good enough to point out that lines rhyme. To help you think about it, five points will be made in guidance: the technical terms, the harmony rhyme creates, its role in giving emphasis to the words of a poem, its ability to focus the meaning of a poem, and its capacity to produce comic effects.

There are two technical terms associated with rhyme: masculine and feminine. Masculine rhyme occurs when the words are monosyllabic, and feminine when they are polysyllabic. 'Bold' and 'old' are masculine, and 'leaving' and 'weaving' feminine. You will notice that in the case of 'leaving' and 'weaving' the first syllable is stressed, whilst the second is not. This is called a feminine ending. The terms are of little use as most rhyme in English is masculine. Nevertheless, it is worth noting that masculine rhyme often sounds settled and determined, whereas feminine rhyme is fluid and musical. For instance, in Blake's 'Infant Sorrow' from *The Songs of Experience* the masculine rhymes create a hard and fixed effect:

My mother groaned! my father wept.
Into the dangerous world I leapt:
Helpless, naked, piping loud:
Like a fiend hid in a cloud.

The arrival of the child has a dramatic effect; the settled, determined rhymes give the impression that he is tough. By contrast, listen to the effect of these lines from Betjeman's 'Indoor Games near Newbury':

Rich the makes of motor chirring,
Past the pine-plantation purring
  Come up, Hupmobile, Delage!
Short the way your chauffeurs travel,
Crunching over private gravel
  Each from out his warm garage.

The feminine rhymes help to enact the sense of speed. Each flows musically after the other to create a feeling of quick yet smooth movement.

When we hear one word rhyme with another, we usually experience pleasure in finding harmony between the two. Harmony creates a feeling of completeness, the sense that something has been resolved or finished. This is particularly true when we expect a rhyme; our ears wait for the rhyming word, and, when it comes, we enjoy feeling that something – a meaning, a line, a stanza – has been completed. Listen to the neat first stanza of Eliot's 'Burbank with a Baedeker: Bleistein with a cigar':

Burbank crossed a little bridge
Descending at a small hotel;
Princess Volupine arrived,
They were together, and he fell.

That stanza is a little story in itself: Burbank, who is associated with small hotels, meets the exotic Princess Volupine and falls for her. The rhymes 'hotel' and 'fell' enact the sense of finality: Burbank, we feel, has fallen hopelessly in love, and nothing can be done about it. The rhyme, to put it simply, says: 'that's it'.

Eliot's rhymes give a sense of completeness. In Stevie Smith's strangely moving little poem 'I remember', the rhymes, at the end, create a touching feeling of harmony:

It was my bridal night I remember,
An old man of seventy-three
I lay with my young bride in my arms,
A girl with t.b.
It was wartime, and overhead
The Germans were making a particularly heavy raid
on Hampstead.
What rendered the confusion worse, perversely
Our bombers had chosen that moment to set out for
Germany.
Harry, do they ever collide?
I do not think it has ever happened,
Oh my bride, my bride.

The poem is full of interesting effects created by rhymes (look, for instance, at the deliberately clumsy yet amusing rhyme of 'overhead' and 'Hampstead'), but at the end the swell of emotion in the last line ('Oh') is completed by the rhyming word 'bride'. That creates harmony: in all the confusion, two people, one old and one young, can share in love.

When two words rhyme, you notice them. Poets can exploit this by using rhyme to emphasise important words. There are two particular ways in which this can be done: the frequent use of rhyme and internal rhyme.

In Betjeman's delightful 'Pot Pourri from a Surrey Garden', three lines of the last six-lined stanza rhyme. The poet is anticipating his marriage to Pam:

Over the redolent pinewoods, in at the bathroom casement,
One fine Saturday, Windlesham bells shall call:
Up the Butterfield aisle rich with Gothic enlacement,
Licensed now for embracement,
Pam and I, as the organ
Thunders over you all.

Rhyme brings together 'casement', 'enlacement' and 'embracement'. As well as admiring these polished, feminine rhymes, you might note that these prominent words are important to the poem's meaning. The 'casement' is open to admit the sounds that dominate the last stanza; 'enlacement' is a clever way of describing architectural detailing and it also suggests the loving ties that are made in marriage, an idea also present in 'embracement'.

Internal rhyme, which occurs when a word within a line rhymes with the one at the end, surprises the reader, who is compelled to listen to what the words say. It also tends to quicken the pace of a line. In the last stanza of 'The Garden of Love', Blake sees with increasing horror how black gowned priests energetically destroy his beloved garden:

> And I saw it was filled with graves,
> And tombstones where flowers should be,
> And priests in black gowns were walking their rounds
> And binding with briars my joys and desires.

Internal rhyme emphasises that 'briars' are binding 'desires' and increases the pace of the line so that the dark, purposeful priests seem unstoppable. By emphasising 'briars' and 'desires', internal rhyme enacts the conflict in the poem: the priests want to discipline and inflict pain upon someone who wants to express his feelings.

Rhyme's ability to focus the meaning of a poem is an extension of the way it emphasises certain words. In the Blake poem the theme is the conflict between 'briars' and 'desires'. Poets use rhyme to focus the reader's attention upon words that are central to the poem's meaning. There is a chilling moment in Chaucer's *The Pardoner's Tale* when this happens. Three reckless young men are in a town one morning:

> These riotoures three, of which I telle,
> Long erst er prime rang of any belle,
> Were set hem in a taverne for to drinke;
> And as they sat, they herde a belle clinke
> Biforn a cors, was carried to his grave.

It is a grim picture: early in the morning the wild young men are drinking but as they do so they hear the sound of a bell rung as a body is taken for burial. The central conflict of the poem between worldly, self-seeking pleasure and the inescapable presence of death is focused in the rhyme 'drinke' and 'clinke'. Their first pleasure in the morning is 'drinke', but this is interrupted by the sinister 'clinke' of a bell; not one for the first service of the day, but the one that precedes a body to burial. (Note how the run-run-on line dramatically leads to the grim word 'cors' – corpse.) When they learn the body is that of a friend of theirs, they rush out to find Death, a search which is successful in a grotesquely unexpected way, for they all die. Of course, it will not be evident that 'drinke' and 'clinke' are the central words of the poem till you have finished it. Therefore, you will need to know a poem well before you will be able to see that rhymes focus words that are central to the meaning.

Rhyme can be comic, particularly when it comes in short lines. Belloc is a master of the short line; in 'Lord Lucky' he tells of how a Mr Meyer accidentally kills a lord while out shooting:

As he was scrambling through a brake
Discharged his weapon by mistake
And plugged about an ounce of lead
Piff-bang into his grace's head –
Who naturally fell down dead.

The humour comes from the way the deft rhymes make a ghastly accident sound very clean and neat. The harmony of rhyme lends an inappropriate, and hence funny, smoothness to an unhappy event. Indeed, the sharp contrast between events that are ghastly or absurd and the neat harmony of rhyme may be the reason why comic poetry usually requires rhyme to be funny.

## 4.8 HALF-RHYME

There is one poetic feature that is related to rhyme but which, strictly speaking, is not rhyme at all. This is half-rhyme, or para-rhyme. It is not rhyme because words either do or do not rhyme; nevertheless, it depends upon rhyme for its effectiveness, because the ear wants the full harmony of rhyme but instead experiences discord. Owen uses the incompleteness of half-rhyme to enact the destruction of order and harmony that occurs in war. In the first stanza of 'Insensibility' he writes of those who have become insensible to the horrors surrounding them:

Happy are the men who yet before they are killed
Can let their veins run cold.
Whom no companion fleers
Or makes their feet
Sore on the alleys cobbled with their brothers.
The front line withers,
But they are troops who fade, not flowers,
For poet's tearful fooling:
Men gaps for filling:
Losses, who might have fought
Longer; but no one bothers.

The half-rhymes 'killed' / 'cold, 'fleers' / 'flowers', 'feet' / 'fought', 'brothers' / 'bothers', and 'fooling' / 'filling' enact the disharmony of war by hinting at a rhyme which we do not get. There is discord in ideas as well as sound: 'brothers' are those for whom we should be concerned (that is what 'brother' means), but in war 'no one bothers' about them. When you write about half-rhyme, you should look for discord in meaning and sound.

## 4.9 RHYME SCHEMES

When rhymes are regularly spaced, stanzas are formed. Stanzas can be formed other than by rhyme schemes, and, occasionally, rhyme schemes stretch across from one stanza to another; nevertheless, it remains true that stanzas are usually shaped by rhymes.

There is a simple way of classifying rhyme schemes. The word at the end of the first line, and any later one in that position that rhymes with it, is called A; the word at the end of the next line that does not rhyme with the previous one is called B; the one after that C, and so on. Even if words do not rhyme, they should still be given a letter. When a rhyme scheme is regular, you need only classify the first stanza. Thus, you would classify Larkin's 'An Arundel Tomb' as ABBCAC:

> Side by side, their faces blurred,
> The earl and countess lie in stone,
> Their proper habits vaguely shown
> As jointed armour, stiffened pleat,
> And that faint hint of the absurd –
> The little dogs under their feet.

The examiner, of course, is not interested in whether you can classify rhyme schemes. What interests him or her is whether you can write about how the form of a poem, created by the rhyme scheme, helps to enact its meaning. You should, therefore, be able to recognise standard verse forms and be aware of the particular effects they make possible.

## 4.10 STANZA FORMS

The simplest form is the rhyming couplet. Sometimes a couplet is the only structural unit in a poem, and sometimes it is part of a larger rhyme scheme. A very common couplet is rhymed iambic pentameters; these are called heroic couplets. The special effect this form creates is of self-affirmation; what is said in the first line is developed in the second, and then completed by the rhyme to make a strong, self-contained statement. In other words, the couplet is self-affirming because the second line and the rhyme develop and complete what the first line began. Because the experience of reading couplets is of moving from one statement to another, it is a form that is particularly suited to argument. Dryden translated the Roman poet, Lucretius, who wrote about death. Here are two couplets:

From sense of grief and pain we shall be free,
We shall not feel, because we shall not be.
Though earth in seas, and seas in Heaven were lost,
We should not move, we only should be tossed.

You can see how appropriate the couplet is for argument by looking at the first one. The bold, monosyllabic words of the first line assert strongly that in death we shall be free from pain, while in the second a general statement – 'We shall not feel' – is followed by the reason, which, in rhyming, completes both argument and the couplet. This self-affirming quality of the couplet is often used by poets to conclude poems. By placing a couplet at the end, a firmness and strength is added to the whole poem.

Stanzas of three lines are rare in English, though occasionally a tercet – three rhymed lines – is introduced to give variety or emphasis in a poem of couplets. Two three-lined stanzas which you might come across are terza rima and the villanelle. They are challenging forms, and, perhaps for that reason, rarely adopted.

The most common stanza is the quatrain. This four line stanza is used in ballads and lyrical verse. It can be structured in a number of ways: ABCB, ABBA, ABAB, AABB, ABCA. There are also non-rhyming quatrains. Quatrains can be neat and economical; there is pleasure in finding an argument or story, or a stage in either, neatly framed in four lines and held harmoniously together by rhyme. Consider the opening of Herrick's 'To the virgins, to make much of Time':

Gather ye Rose-buds while ye may,
   Old Time is still a flying:
And this same flower that smiles today
   Tomorrow will be dying.

The order of the argument is neat, and it is pleasing to find its four stages given a line each. Pleasing, too, is the contrast between the masculine rhymes which deal with what might be done and the flowing feminine rhymes that express the quick passing of time. Like all successful quatrains, this one creates the feeling that it needs just four lines to say all that needs to be said.

There are stanza forms of five, six, seven, eight and nine lines in length. Stanzas of seven lines that rhyme ABABBCC are called rime royal; they were used by Chaucer in some of his long, narrative poems. Eight line stanzas that rhyme ABABABCC are examples of ottava rima. Spenser used a nine line stanza for his long poem *The Faerie Queene*; it rhymes ABABBCBCC. Stanzas can be longer, but that is unusual.

## 4.11 SONNETS

You may not come across long stanza forms on 'O' and 'A' level syllabuses, but you are likely to meet sonnets. A sonnet is a fourteen line poem. It is usually formed in one of two ways: either it consists of an eight line section (octave) followed by a six line one (sestet), or of three quatrains and a concluding couplet. The first is called a Petrarchan, and the second a Shakespearian sonnet.

It is important to understand that the way a poet structures a sonnet, or for that matter any verse form, shapes what the sonnet says. In the Petrarchan sonnet the two-fold structure of octave and sestet makes possible an argument in two stages; in the first half the poet can explore a situation or an idea and then in the second come to a conclusion. If you look at sonnets written in the Petrarchan form you will often find the sestet beginning with words such as 'and', 'if', 'thus', 'so', 'but', 'for', and 'then'. In Sidney's sonnet 'Loving in truth, and fain in verse my love to show', the persona is that of a poet who longs to find the right words to express the anguish of his love:

> Loving in truth, and fain in verse my love to show,
> That she, dear she, might take some pleasure of my pain,
> Pleasure might cause her read, reading might make her know,
> Knowledge might pity win, and pity grace obtain,
> I sought fit words to paint the blackest face of woe;
> Studying inventions fine, her wits to entertain,
> Oft turning others' leaves to see if thence would flow
> Some fresh and fruitful showers upon my sun-burned brain.
> But words came halting forth, wanting invention's stay;
> Invention, nature's child, fled step-dame Study's blows,
> And others' feet still seemed but strangers in my way.
> Thus, great with child to speak, and helpless in my throes,
> Biting my truant pen, beating myself for spite,
> Fool, said my muse to me, look in thy heart and write.

Sidney structures the poem in an octave, rhyming ABABABAB, and a sestet, rhyming CDCDEE. This division shapes the experience the poem deals with. In the octave he yearns and desires (you can feel the yearning in 'That she, dear she') to write in such a way that his beloved will realise his pain. To that end he studies and reads ('others' leaves' means pages of their books) in the hope for relief and inspiration. The sestet, however, begins on a note of disappointment:

> But words came halting forth, wanting invention's stay . . .

Yet that 'But' does not mark the mood of the entire sestet; the poet, in an agony, which through a striking metaphor he compares to childbirth, gains inspiration (that is what 'muse' means here) to write, not from other poets' ideas but from his own feelings:

> Fool, said my muse to me, look in thy heart and write.

The sestet thus expresses both the disappointment of failure and the triumph of inspiration, and in so doing brings the sonnet to a satisfying close.

It is obvious that the English, or Shakespearian, sonnet, structured as it is in three quatrains and a couplet, will present a different set of opportunities to the poet. It is a more flexible form. The poet can develop an argument in two or three stages and then conclude it with a couplet, or produce one idea and two variations upon it before moving to the conclusion. Another option is that of using the entire twelve lines to build up a picture, recount an experience, or develop a single argument, and then using the couplet to affirm, deny or modify what has been said. You will see from this that the Shakespearian sonnet lays more importance on the concluding couplet. This, in itself, is a challenge, particularly when the couplet has to deny or overturn what the first twelve lines have been saying.

Some of these points can be seen in Shakespeare's 'Sonnet 130'. It is a deliberately amusing poem which mocks the conventional language adopted by many poets when they imagine that their beloveds are more beautiful than they really are. Against the conventional ideal – sparkling eyes, red lips, white skin, golden hair, etc. – we are offered a 'mistress' who has none of these qualities:

> My mistress' eyes are nothing like the sun;
> Coral is far more red than her lips' red;
> If snow be white, why then her breasts are dun;
> If hairs be wires, black wires grow on her head.
> I have seen roses damasked, red and white,
> But no such roses see I in her cheeks,
> And in some perfumes is there more delight
> Than in the breath that from my mistress reeks.
> I love to hear her speak, yet well I know
> That music hath a far more pleasing sound.
> I grant I never saw a goddess go;
> My mistress when she walks treads on the ground.
> And yet, by heaven, I think my love as rare
> As any she belied with false compare.

The three quatrains, rhyming ABABCDCDEFEF, do not develop an argument or produce variations on a basic idea; rather, Shakespeare builds up a picture (by no means a conventionally flattering one) of his mistress by comparing her features with those ideals honoured by other poets. By the end of the quatrains our picture of the mistress is fuller and more vivid, but it would be wrong to say that it has developed through a number of clearly defined stages. The couplet is problematic. The persona tries to do two things: insist that his mistress is wonderful to him, and make clear that what other poets write is 'false compare', that is, untrue. The latter works better than the former. By the end of the quatrains, it is clear that the poet's mistress is a real woman; after all, don't most girls walk on the ground! But does the couplet sufficiently overturn the impression that his mistress is horrible: dull eyes, indifferent lips, wild hair, pale cheeks and, worst of all, breath that 'reeks'? (Are there stronger words concerned with smell than 'reeks'?) Shakespeare tries to overcome this problem by saying 'And yet', following this with a colloquial phrase, the rhythm of which is very close to ordinary speech – 'by heaven' – and closing the line with the simple praise of one of his favourite words – 'rare'. But is it enough? If you feel it is not, then the reason for this is that Shakespeare, in structuring the sonnet this way, has given himself too much to do in the concluding couplet. The success of the poem, then, is related to the way it is constructed.

The Petrarchan and the Shakespearian sonnets offer different opportunities to the poet, but they do have this in common. They allow a poet to handle difficult and varied ideas in a concentrated way. That is why readers value sonnets for their economy and complexity.

## 4.12 WHY STANZA FORMS MATTER

The question that should govern all your thinking about stanza forms is: how does the form of the poem shape the meaning? Unless you can show that the form the poet has chosen is appropriate to the meaning and mood of the poem, it is pointless identifying and classifying stanzas. Look, for instance, at the stanza Tennyson adopted for *In Memoriam.* Here is a quatrain in which he is writing about his puzzlement in the face of the cruelty of nature and his doubts about the presence of God:

> I stretch lame hands of faith, and grope,
> And gather dust and chafe, and call
> To what I feel is Lord of all,
> And faintly trust the larger hope.

The rhyme scheme is ABBA, a couplet enclosed by another couplet. This is appropriate in a poem which is inward looking; the stanza contains

Tennyson's thoughts in the way in which those very thoughts are contained within his mind. But the enclosing rhyme also creates another effect. Because the enclosing rhyme (the A rhyme) is separated by the couplet it seems, by contrast, less strong. In the above example 'all' directly answers 'call', but 'hope' is distant from 'grope', thus ending the stanza on an unresolved note of hesitancy and doubt. This is, of course, deeply appropriate to a poem that deals with doubts and uncertainties.

## EXERCISES

**1** Read the poems you are studying, paying particular attention to how the poets use sound. Write about how the sounds contribute to the meaning of the poems.

**2** Read the poems you are studying, paying particular attention to the effects of rhymes and the appropriateness of stanza forms. Write about any rhymes you think are particularly successful, and about how the form of a stanza is appropriate to the meaning of a poem.

**3** This is the first verse of the 'Song of the Lotus Eaters' by Tennyson. Read it through a number of times and answer the set questions below.

> There is sweet music here that softer falls
> Than petals from blown roses on the grass,
> Or night-dews on still waters between walls
> Of shadowy granite, in a gleaming pass;
> Music that gentlier on the spirit lies,
> Than tired eyelids upon tired eyes;
> Music that brings sweet sleep down from the blissful skies.
> Here are cool mosses deep,
> And through the moss the ivies creep,
> And in the stream the long-leaved flowers weep,
> And from the craggy ledge the poppy hangs in sleep.

(a) What is the effect of the rhyme scheme upon the mood of the poem?

(b) Tennyson has clearly made use of alliteration. What are the different patterns of alliteration, and what is their effect?

(c) What is the effect of the assonance in the poem?

(d) Would you describe the sound effects as onomatopoeic? If so, what is the effect created?

**4** This is one verse from Shelley's *Adonais,* a poem written about the death of Keats. Read it a number of times and answer the questions below.

> Peace, peace! he is not dead, he doth not sleep –
> He hath awakened from the dream of life –
> 'Tis we, who lost in stormy visions, keep

With phantoms an unprofitable strife,
And in mad trance, strike with our spirit's knife
Invulnerable nothings. – *We* decay
Like corpses in a charnel; fear and grief
Convulse us and consume us day by day,
And cold hopes swarm like worms within our living clay.

(a) Describe the rhyme scheme and suggest what contribution it makes to the meaning of the poem.

(b) What is the effect of rhyming 'life' with 'strife' and 'knife'? Do these words focus the meaning of the verse?

(c) Think about the change in the sounds from the opening two lines to 'And in mad trance, strike with our spirit's knife'.

(d) Are there any cases of alliteration in the verse, and do they contribute anything to the impact of what is being said?

# CHAPTER 5

# THE POEM AS A WHOLE

## 5.1 A POEM IS NOT LOTS OF BITS

Let us summarise what the last four chapters have said on how to write about poetry.

Each poem you study should be read a number of times, preferably aloud. Before you start detailed thinking, you must be sure that you have a general idea of what it is about. Detailed thinking starts when you try to make sense of what puzzles, interests or gives you pleasure. You do this by asking questions. All the questions that you ask should be about the words of the poem. When you question yourself about your reactions to a poem you should ask what it is about the words that has made you feel the way you do. When you come to examine the words of a poem, there are a number of aspects that might strike you. You may be attracted to the wide variety of ways in which words create meanings. In that case, you may discuss the effects created by figures of speech. The way in which a poem is arranged in lines may also interest you. If so, you may investigate how the words create rhythms, and how these rhythms contribute to the poem's impact. The sounds, rhymes and stanza-forms that words create may strike you as important. You would then consider what effects they have on the meaning and mood of the poem. Whatever aspect of words you choose to write about, you should always try to show that words are indivisible, and that, therefore, all their aspects work together to enact what is being said in the poem.

But you must not stop there. A poem is not lots of bits. All the words of a poem add up to something – the poem as a whole. When, therefore, you study a poem, you should always do so with this aim: I must try to write about the poem as a whole. There are two ways in which you can be helped to do this. First, you can identify what *kind* of a poem it is. Once you have done this, you will have an idea of how to look at it as a whole. The second thing you can do is look out for the ways in which poets construct poems. When you see how the poem is made, you will be more able to see it as a whole.

To know what kind of a poem you are studying helps you to write about it as a whole, because you will have some idea of what its shape is. There are, of course, many different kinds of poem, but some are so popular that you are likely to meet them at 'O' and 'A' level. The very popular ones are those based on a story, those built on an argument, those that develop from an observation or an incident, those that trace the growth or change of emotions, and those that engage in a kind of game between poet and reader. (Of course, a poem can do more than one of these things at the same time.) Let us look at some examples of each of these kinds and see how knowing what sort of a poem is before us helps us to see it as a whole.

## 5.2 POEMS THAT TELL A STORY

When a poem tells a story, it is easy to see its shape as a whole, and to appreciate how each event contributes to the general design. There is no point in simply telling the examiner what the story is. Instead, you should repeat the story over to yourself, concentrating on how the events relate to each other. If you can see *why* one event follows another, you will have understood how the poem is designed. That is what you should write about. If you can convey to the examiner how and why the poem is built up, you will be writing about it as a whole.

Betjeman's 'A Subaltern's Love-song' tells a story. The created voice, or persona, is a breathless and ardent young man who, from the very start, is wildly in love with 'Miss Joan Hunter-Dunn'. The first three stanzas are concerned with the tennis match, in which she beats him. In the fourth stanza we should picture them walking around her father's spacious garden, and in the fifth and the sixth they prepare for the Golf Club dance. In stanzas seven and eight they drive through the Surrey countryside, which is atmospherically full of the sounds and smells of high summer. The order of events has led us to expect a scene at the dance, but here Betjeman springs his surprise – the last three stanzas record that the couple spent the whole evening ('until twenty to one') in the car park, with the result that the young man can proudly say 'And now I'm engaged to Miss Joan Hunter-Dunn'. The story thus depends upon a surprise. Looked upon as a whole, you can also see that the story has a delightful shape. Its design is a happy reversal. At the beginning of the poem the young man is beaten by the lovely Joan – 'love-thirty, love-forty, oh! weakness of joy' – and at the end there is another love game which, you may gather from his pleasure, he thinks he has won.

It is worthwhile thinking about the three ways in which Betjeman engages the reader's interest in the story. He leads you to expect something, he surprises you, and he produces a reversal. These three elements – expectation, surprise and reversal – are common to many poems that relate stories.

Look at how Keats arouses expectation at the beginning of 'La Belle Dame sans Merci':

O what can ail thee, knight-at-arms,
Alone and palely loitering?
The sedge has withered from the lake,
And no birds sing.

The poem starts with a question: what is the knight doing in this bleak and eerily silent place? Something is wrong, and the possibility that the scene might be a mental landscape reflecting his inner desolation raises the expectation that the knight has a strange story to tell. The rest of the poem fulfils that expectation.

Sometimes, particularly in ballads, the fulfilment of what we expect has a grim power. The ballad 'Sir Patrick Spens' is given shape by the expectation of disaster. Sir Patrick knows that the sea journey he has to undertake is dangerous, and when he and the whole ship's crew drown, there is a sombre feeling of fulfilment. Likewise, in the dialogue poem 'Lord Randal' we know that he is very ill and probably dying, and we wait in expectation for him to realise that he has been poisoned by the one he thought was his true love. In both poems expectation helps us to see the design as a whole.

Surprise accompanies the reversal of expectation. Take, for instance, Scott's 'Proud Maisie'. The opening is fresh and beautiful:

Proud Maisie is in the wood
  Walking so early;
Sweet robin sits on the bush
  Singing so rarely.

The words suggest the coming of new life; Maisie is 'walking so early' in the woods, and the robin sings 'so rarely' – both symbols of new beginnings. Yet an uneasy tension creeps in when Maisie questions the robin; his answer is surprising:

'When six braw gentlemen
  Kirkward shall carry ye' . . .

The rest of the poem spells out this unnerving reply: what lies in wait for Maisie is death.

## 5.3 POEMS BASED ON ARGUMENTS

Many poems are in the form of arguments. What you should attend to is the structure of what is being said. If you can see the stages through which the argument passes, you will be aware of the design of the whole poem. It is a good idea to make clear to yourself the poem's starting point. You could ask yourself the following questions about how the poem begins. Does it start from a widely held idea? Does it start with a question? Is there an event that presents a problem or a challenge to thought? Is there a situation out of which the argument arises? Then it is important to be aware of the stages through which the argument moves. A good question to ask is: why does the argument move from that stage to this? Finally, you should look at the conclusion of the argument. You can ask: is the end logical? Is the end effective? Has the argument achieved what it set out to do? Am I convinced by what has been argued?

Marvell's 'To his Coy Mistress' is a poem with a distinctive design. It is an invitation to a lady to enjoy the pleasures of love while there is still time. The theme is popular in poetry (Herrick's 'To the Virgins, to make much of Time' is another example), but Marvell makes it distinctive by his almost philosophical approach. The poem opens in this way:

> Had we but world enough and time,
> This coyness, lady, were no crime . . .

That is the first stage in the argument; the poet starts with the condition that if they had a great deal of time, it would not be wrong for the lady to be coy, that is, reluctant to love. Marvell then launches into a delightful fantasy of what he would do if he had that much time, but the tone changes for the second stage. It begins:

> But at my back I always hear
> Time's winged chariot hurrying near . . .

His point is a simple one – time is short. He presses this point home by inviting her to think about the certainty of death. The argument of the poem has been: if we had much time, I would spend it courting you, and it would not be wrong for you to refuse me, but the fact is that we haven't. This leads to the third and final part of the argument:

> Now, therefore, while the youthful hue
> Sits on thy skin like morning dew . . .

The conclusion is logical: since we have only a little time, we had better love *now*.

The structure of the poem is the structure of the argument. It arises out of a situation in which a man would love, and a woman would not. It moves from an impossible condition to a present reality, and then, in the eyes of the poet at least, to a logical conclusion. If you can grasp the order of the argument, you can understand the poem as a whole.

## 5.4 POEMS BASED ON OBSERVATIONS

In poems that develop from an observation you can see the poet at work. The poet is struck by something seen or heard, which starts a train of thought about its meaning or significance. In order, then, to see the poem as a whole, you have to follow those thoughts and reflections. One of the interesting features of this kind of poetry is the way the poet moves from observation to thought.

Philip Larkin's 'Church Going' is a reflection upon the fact that the poet stops and looks at churches. The first two stanzas recall familiar features – the way the heavy door closes, the flowers, the organ, the unique silence of the place and the lectern with its great Bible open. As he leaves, he says that the place 'was not worth stopping for'. And then the questioning begins:

> Yet stop I did: in fact I often do,
> And always end much at a loss like this,
> Wondering what to look for; wondering, too,
> When churches fall completely out of use
> What we shall turn them into . . .

The transition from detailed observation to thought comes with those questions. It is the last one that he concentrates on: will we keep cathedrals as tourist attractions, or will we treat churches as places of magic? He then asks who will be the last person to visit the church 'for what it was'. Will he be a historian, someone who loves antiquity, a Christmas church-goer or someone like the poet? That leads to the poem's conclusion. It is an answer to the question of why he stopped:

> A serious house on serious earth it is,

and since it is a place where people can be serious about their lives, he concludes that someone will always be 'gravitating' towards 'this ground' because he has discovered 'A hunger in himself to be more serious'.

## 5.5 POEMS BASED ON CHANGES IN EMOTION

Poems that develop from an observation are often similar to poems built upon an argument. The fourth kind of poem – that which traces the growth and development of an emotion – has also links with argument and observation poems. Indeed, in a poem that follows an argument, or one that reflects upon an observation, you can trace the change in emotion. For instance, the Marvell poem starts in a tone of cheerful playfulness, becomes serious and ends on a note of urgent passion. In the Larkin poem the emotions move from puzzlement to a quiet certainty about the significance of churches. In some poems, however, the feelings of the poet, and the changes they undergo, are central. In order to grasp such poems as a whole, you will need to follow the changes in mood. That is, you will have to understand what has generated the emotion, be attentive to the changes through which it passes, and, most important of all, appreciate why the poem ends when it does. It may be that a poem ends because the poet has found the words to express his emotion, or that the act of expressing emotion has brought relief.

Take, for example, a poem that is often studied at both 'O' and 'A' level: Owen's 'Anthem for Doomed Youth'. It is a poem of very powerful emotions which starts on a note of outrage:

> What passing bells for those who die as cattle?
> Only the monstrous anger of the guns.
> Only the stuttering rifles' rapid rattle
> Can patter out their hasty orisons.

Amid the mechanical noises of war, the poet angrily demands to know how the deaths of the soldiers are marked. It is not clear whether or not he wants bells tolled, because in the next line he calls the customary rituals of death 'mockeries':

> No mockeries for them from prayers or bells . . .

But it does not matter whether the poet is against funeral rituals or not, because the poetry should be read not as an argument but as a powerful discharge of emotion, as powerful, in fact, as the terrible guns. Yet that tone is not maintained. The second part (the sestet of the sonnet) begins more quietly:

> What candles may be held to speed them all?

and from then on the feelings of outrage give way to a sad contemplation of the very genuine ways in which the soldier's death will be marked: tears in the eyes, the pale faces of grieving girls, the tender thoughts of the mind and, quietest of all, the image of a slowly darkening English evening, which is compared to the drawing of a blind:

> And each slow dusk a drawing-down of blinds.

The feeling at the end of the poem is of emotion that has been expressed, leaving a calm, resigned acceptance. If you are to understand that poem as a whole, you must trace the emotions as they move from outrage to sad acceptance.

## 5.6 POEMS AS GAMES

Occasionally a poem is designed as a kind of game between poet and reader. Often the poet leads the reader to think the poem is going in a particular direction and then springs a surprise. A delightful example of this is Donne's 'Woman's Constancy'. The poet begins by mocking a woman for her unfaithfulness:

> Now thou hast lov'd me one whole day,
> Tomorrow when thou leav'st, what wilt thou say?

The tone is one of bitter amusement: she has loved 'one whole day' (so long!) and naturally will desert him tomorrow. Donne, again mockingly, furnishes reasons why she might go: she said she would, they are now different people from the ones who swore faithfulness, anyone may change a vow made in love, and so on. It appears that he is angry, and the reader may well pity his distress, until, that is, the poem ends:

> Vain lunatic, against these 'scapes I could
> Dispute and conquer, if I would,
> Which I abstain to do,
> For by tomorrow, I may think so too.

The reader, and the woman, have been caught out. The surprise of the ending reveals that the poem is not a bitter reaction to rejection but a cunning game he has been playing with an unsuspecting woman *and reader*. It looks as if the woman, after all, was the faithful one, and it was he who wanted to leave.

There are, of course, other kinds of poems, but the above examples are sufficient to make this point: if you want to talk about the poem as a whole, you should find out what kind of a poem it is, for that controls its shape and structure. When you see what the poet is wanting to achieve, you will be able to follow through his intention and so see the poem as a whole.

The second way of looking at a poem as a whole is that of examining how it is constructed. If you are aware of the ways in which a poet could make a poem, you might be able to see a poem not as lots of bits but as an organised whole. To help you to do this, here are five ways in which a poet can form a poem: use a persona, repeat central words, employ contrasts, link beginning and end, and use consistent imagery. Some of these have been mentioned before. The reason for referring to them again is to drive home the point that they help to make a poem a complete, organised object.

## 5.7 PERSONA

A persona is a specially made voice or self who speaks in a poem. Whenever there is an 'I' – that is, whenever the poem is written in the first person singular – that 'I' is a persona. Even when the self does not speak as an 'I', it is sometimes appropriate to call it a persona. For instance, in Keats's 'Ode on a Grecian Urn' the voice is not in the first person singular, but since the whole poem is an expression of a particular mind – an intent, sensitive, probing one – it is proper to call it a persona when writing about the poem. A persona gives a poem unity, because all that is said in it comes from one voice. This means that, whenever you write about a persona, you should also discuss tone, the changes, if any, in attitude, the build-up of emotional pressure, and the character of the voice.

Let us look at an example. Tennyson's 'Ulysses' is given both unity and interest through the creation of a very distinctive persona. The Ulysses who speaks is not the vigorous hero of the battles around Troy or of the adventures he met on his way home, but an old man, tired and yet discontented, who can only look back on his glorious past. Listen to the despairing tones and sluggish movement of the opening:

> It little profits that an idle king,
> By this still hearth, among these barren crags,
> Matched with an aged wife, I mete and dole
> Unequal laws unto a savage race,
> That hoard, and sleep, and feed, and know not me.

The cadence at the end of the sentence is so dark and flat that a reader may wonder whether such an exhausted and dispirited man could ever change. Yet in the next line, the attitude of the persona does change:

> I cannot rest from travel: I will drink
> Life to the lees . . .

The movement is still sluggish and the cadences fall heavily, yet the attitude is different: Ulysses is trying to stir himself; the caesura after 'travel' marks the end of one and the beginning of another deliberate effort to force himself into action. And with the change in attitude there comes a rise in the emotional pressure of the poem. This reaches its height when the old man summons his companions from the past to accompany him on one final journey:

> Come, my friends
> 'Tis not too late to seek a newer world.
> Push off, and sitting well in order smite
> The sounding furrows; for my purpose holds
> To sail beyond the sunset, and the baths
> Of all the western stars, until I die.

That is both invigorating – listen to the forceful imperatives, 'Come', 'Push off' and 'smite' – and, surprisingly enough, weary. The second sentence falls away with a wistful cadence in which the persona contemplates not success but his own death. But that is the character of the persona Tennyson has created – a tired old man who still longs for action, even though death is close.

Persona is not an easy idea to understand, so you should remember two things about it: the persona need not be that of the poet, and a poet is free to adopt a number of different personas.

It is a mistake to assume that the 'I' which gives a poem unity is the 'I' of the poet. In other words, the voice *within* the poem need not be identified with the voice of the poet *outside* the poem. Many students find this difficult, but there is no reason why they should. In novels it is quite usual to have the story told in the first person by a character whom no reader identifies with the novelist. It is the same with poetry: an 'I' can be a fictional one which has been specially created in the words of that particular poem. In Browning's dramatic monologues the personas range from a famous painter, 'Fra Lippo Lippi', to a young man who strangles his girl friend with her own long (and beautiful) hair, 'Porphyria's Lover'. Nobody should try to identify Robert Browning with them! It is, however, worth asking why the poet was interested in the personas he or she has created. For instance, Craig Raine's 'A Martian sends a post-card home' reveals an interest in taking an unengaged, alien view of human life, and Sylvia Plath's 'Lady Lazarus', a poem in which the persona looks to be very close to that of the poet herself, discloses a strange preoccupation with suicide.

The second point is an extension of the first: poets can create as many different personas as they like. Some of them can be close to their own selves, others can be entirely fictional, though in both cases the creation of a persona can show that the poet is interested in a particular experience. At the beginning of his poetic career T.S. Eliot wrote two poems in which two distinct and different personas bestow a unity upon varied, though very interesting, poetic material. In 'The Love-Song of J. Alfred Prufrock' the persona is a timid man who yet has wildly romantic fantasies about himself. The presence of this split personality gives cohesion to a dream-like succession of memories and imagined scenes. In 'Portrait of a Lady' the persona is a young man who is caught up in a barren friendship with a rather gushing older lady. The lady speaks for much of the poem, but the rather bored young man's thoughts – wandering, trivial, frustrated – give the poem unity.

## 5.8 THE REPETITION OF WORDS

When a poet uses a word more than once, you should concentrate on it because it could reveal something of importance about the poem as a whole. It was said above that Blake's repetition of 'mark' in 'London' was important. It shows that life in London marks people like a disease; and that is what the poem is about – the outer and inner corruption that London generates in people.

Now, read R.S. Thomas's 'Evans':

> Evans? Yes, many a time
> I came down his bare flight
> Of stairs into the gaunt kitchen
> With its wood fire, where crickets sang
> Accompaniment to the black kettle's
> Whine and so into the cold
> Dark to smother in the thick tide
> Of night that drifted about the walls
> Of his stark farm on the hill ridge.
>
> It was not the dark filling my eyes
> And mouth appalled me, not even the drip
> Of rain like blood from the one tree
> Weather-tortured. It was the dark
> Silting the veins of that sick man
> I left stranded upon the vast
> And lonely shore of his bleak bed.

You will notice that the word 'dark' occurs three times: the poet goes into 'the cold / Dark', the 'dark' that is 'filling' his eyes and mouth does not appal him, but 'the dark / Silting the veins of that sick man' does. 'Dark' is central to the atmosphere of the poem; together with words such as 'bare', 'gaunt', 'stark' and 'bleak', it creates the feeling of life reduced to a minimum, shorn of luxuries and pleasures. Yet the word does more. If you follow the way the word's meaning is enriched, you will see it is central to the poem's meaning. 'Dark' at first is nothing more than the night. The next time it is used it is associated with the poet's feeling of being appalled, and its last use suggests it is something that has physically invaded Evans and left him lonely and stranded, beyond help. Dark, then, expresses Evans's condition: he is lost, isolated, and in the shadows of human life.

## 5.9 THE USE OF CONTRAST

When a poet employs contrasting words, the meaning of the whole poem emerges in and through the tensions created by the contrasts. Look at Owen's 'Futility', a poem about a dead soldier:

> Move him into the sun –
> Gently its touch awoke him once,
> At home, whispering of fields unsown.
> Always it woke him, even in France,
> Until this morning and this snow.
> If anything might rouse him now
> The kind old sun will know.
>
> Think how it wakes the seeds, –
> Woke, once, the clays of a cold star.
> Are limbs, so dear-achieved, are sides,
> Full-nerved – still warm – too hard to stir?
> Was it for this the clay grew tall?
> – O what made fatuous sunbeams toil
> To break earth's sleep at all?

The poem is built on a set of contrasts. There is the contrast between the sun and the earth. The poet says 'Move him into the sun', and then follows this with references to the whispering fields and the snow. In the second stanza the sun is said to wake the seeds in the earth, just as it once woke the earth itself to life; but when it is evident that it can't wake the limbs of the dead man, the poet scornfully asks why it began *the whole* process of life at all. That contrast is linked to another: life and death. The sun wakes the seeds but it can't wake one who is dead. The contrast between life and death is close to the one between warmth and cold. The warm sun used to wake the soldier and it even woke the clays of a cold star, but though the man's sides are 'still warm', he can't be woken. Throughout the poem there is the contrast of sleep and waking. The sun always woke the soldier, but now he is in that sleep from which he can't be woken. The contrasts shape the whole poem and give it meaning. The poet is appalled by the fact that life and death seem so close yet are so far apart that no one can travel back from death to life.

## 5.10 BEGINNINGS AND ENDS

Owen's poem begins and ends with the sun warming the earth. At first the sun is welcome, but at the end the poet turns against it. That is one way in which the end of a poem can relate to its beginning. There are others. The end of a poem can return the reader to the beginning and invite a sad or happy comparison, or it can prove, or disprove, what was at first stated. Because poems are specially made objects in words, their beginnings and ends are important. Unlike everyday experience, a poem has a clear start and a clear end. Thus they give a poem a formal shape. It is therefore always worth your while comparing them.

Read Hardy's 'A Church Romance':

> She turned in the high pew, until her sight
> Swept the west gallery, and caught its row
> Of Music-men with viol, book, and bow
> Against the sinking sad tower-window light.
>
> She turned again; and in her pride's despite
> One strenuous viol's inspirer seemed to throw
> A message from his string to her below,
> Which said: 'I claim thee as my own forthright!'
>
> Thus their hearts' bond began, in due time signed.
> And long years thence, when Age had scared Romance,
> At some old attitude of his or glance
> That gallery-scene would break upon her mind,
> With him as minstrel, ardent, young, and trim,
> Bowing 'New Sabbath' or Mount Ephraim'.

The delightful thing about this poem is the way it moves in a circle. This circle is the poem's shape, and meaning, for the poem, like so many of Hardy's, is about the importance of the past in people's lives. The poem starts in the past. The girl is in church, and as her eyes sweep the west gallery, one of the members of the church band communicates his love to her. The poem then moves to a much later period, which finds them both too scared to express love, but even so, a glance of his can carry her back to the moment in the past when she sat in the congregation and he played in the gallery. Hence, at the end of the poem, there is the enjoyable feeling of returning to the past and finding it wonderfully unchanged.

## 5.11 CENTRAL IMAGES

The point about a poem being based upon a central, organising image has already been made. All that must be added is that you should be prepared to find the central image unusual. Hughes's short poem 'Snowdrop' is strangely impressive because its imagery is unexpected:

> Now is the globe shrunk tight
> Round the mouse's dulled wintering heart.
> Weasel and crow, as if moulded in brass,
> Move through an outer darkness
> Not in their right minds,
> With the other deaths. She, too, pursues her ends,
> Brutal as the stars of this month,
> Her pale head heavy as metal.

Hughes is writing about the flower that most people regard as both dainty and beautiful, but, as with many subjects, Hughes transforms the snowdrop into something hard, heavy and impressive. He does this by employing imagery associated with metal. The weasel and crow could be 'moulded in brass', an image that prepares us for the 'brutal' snowdrop with 'Her pale head heavy as metal'. The image transforms the everyday idea of a snowdrop and in doing so is central to the poem as a whole.

### EXERCISES

**1** Read through the poems you have to study, trying to identify what kind of poems they are. See how this helps you to write about the meaning of the poem as a whole.
**2** Read through the poems you have to study to see if they are formed upon recurring words, contrasts, a relation between their beginnings and ends, or their imagery. Write about how these features help you see each poem as a whole.
**3** Read Wordsworth's 'She dwelt among the untrodden ways' a number of times and then answer the questions below.

> She dwelt among the untrodden ways
> Beside the springs of Dove,
> A maid whom there were none to praise
> And very few to love:
>
> A violet by a mossy stone
> Half hidden from the eye!

Fair as a star, when only one
  Is shining in the sky.

She lived unknown, and few could know
  When Lucy ceased to be;
But she is in her grave, and, oh,
  The difference to me!

(a) How does each verse further the progress of the poem?

(b) What is the effect of the contrasts between the 'none' and 'very few' in the first verse, and the 'few' and 'me' in the third?

(c) Try to describe the importance of the imagery of the poem.

(d) What do you think of the end of the poem? Is there anything in the poem that has prepared you for it, or does it come as a surprise?

**4** Read Yeats's 'An Irish Airman foresees his Death' a number of times, and then answer the questions below.

I know that I shall meet my fate
Somewhere among the clouds above;
Those that I fight I do not hate,
Those that I guard I do not love;
My country is Kiltarten Cross,
My countrymen Kiltarten's poor,
No likely end could bring them loss
Or leave them happier than before.
Nor law, nor duty bade me fight,
Nor public men, nor cheering crowds,
A lonely impulse of delight
Drove to this tumult in the clouds;
I balanced all, brought all to mind,
The years to come seemed waste of breath,
A waste of breath the years behind
In balance with this life, this death.

(a) The word 'balance' occurs a number of times in the poem. What is its significance, and what does it contribute to the whole meaning?

(b) What is the effect of the contrasts in the poem?

(c) Does the mood of the poem change at any point? If so, what is the contribution of these changes to the poem as a whole?

(d) The poem is about coming to a decision: trace the various stages of this decision by examining the changes in mood and argument.

# PART II

# STUDYING NOVELS

# CHAPTER 6



# AUTHORS

## 6.1 NOVELS ARE SPECIALLY MADE WORLDS IN WORDS

When people talk about books they say such things as: 'Have you read Orwell?' or 'You should read Dickens'. Why, you may ask, do they single out the author of the book? In a trivial sense they do so because without an author there could be no book at all, but there is also a much more important reason: *a novel is a world specially made in words by an author.* A novel exists in the way it does because an author has chosen to put it together in that particular way.

This means that novels are not real life. Like all works of art – poems, plays, pots or pieces of music – they have been constructed or crafted. You might think that this is obvious, yet it is surprising how many 'O' and 'A' level candidates write about novels as if they were word for word records of events in everyday life. Novels, however, are fictional; that is to say, they have been made up. A character in a novel can't be compared to a real person from whom he or she has been copied, because, for example, there is no Jane Eyre in real life. She, or any other character in a novel, only exists on the page. If an author tells you that a character is five foot five with blue eyes, you can't say: 'No, I think the character is nearly six foot with brown eyes'.

When you write about novels, it is very important to make clear that they are not direct records of real events. Imagine two candidates, one bad and one good, writing about Orwell's *1984*; this is what they might say:

> In *1984* society is ruled by Big Brother. There are posters of him everywhere, and pictures of him are frequently shown on the telescreen. Big Brother is a dictator who wants to control everything, even the thoughts inside people's heads. One man, Winston Smith, tries to rebel against this society.

> In *1984* Orwell creates a society which is ruled by Big Brother. In order to show the control Big Brother has, Orwell writes that posters of him are everywhere, and that he frequently appears on the telescreen. Orwell wants to make his readers disapprove of Big Brother so he shows that Big Brother's aim is to control everything, even the thoughts inside people's heads. Orwell voices the reader's outrage at this society in the character of Winston Smith, who tries to rebel.

What is wrong with the first piece? The answer is that apart from the title nothing suggests that it is a *book* that is being written about. Big Brother and Winston Smith could be real people living in a real society. By contrast, the good candidate's piece recognises that Orwell has created this society. Moreover, the good candidate gives a reason why Orwell says that posters of Big Brother are everywhere, and, in the third sentence, suggests that Orwell wants the reader to take up a particular attitude to the events. In the final sentence, the good candidate writes about Orwell's purpose in creating Winston Smith.

What would an examiner make of these two pieces? He or she would not reward the bad candidate highly, because there is no evidence that it is a *novel* that is being written about. The good candidate, however, would be rewarded, because in the writing there is a recognition that a novel is something specially made by an author so that a reader will respond to it in a particular way.

The good candidate has recognised three things about a novel: the events of the novel, the author who has created them, and the reader for whom the novel is written. In any good writing about a novel these three things should be mentioned. They are, however, not separable. For instance, the events of a novel are only there because the author has put them there, and they are only recognised as events when read by a reader.

The author, of course, is the most important element; the events of the novel and the reactions of the reader depend upon what he or she chooses to do. This chapter, therefore, will concentrate on what an author does. Three major points will be discussed: the way an author arranges events, the way an author tells a story, and the attitudes an author can take towards characters and readers. Finally, some advice will be given on how to write about what an author does.

## 6.2 HOW AUTHORS ARRANGE EVENTS

The basic question you should ask about any novel is: how does the author arrange the events of the book? The most important way in which any author arranges events is by *controlling the viewpoint of the reader.* If you fail to attend to the particular way in whcih a novelist invites you to see events, you will misunderstand the novel. Therefore, you should ask of any novel: how is the author inviting me to view the events?

An example will help. In Charlotte Brontë's *Jane Eyre* the story is told by the central character. Jane is sent to Lowood School, where life is hard, discipline strict and the buildings cold and damp. She makes friends with a sickly girl, called Helen Burns. When Helen is dying (a fact of which Jane is unaware), Jane creeps into her bed. The passage ends in this way:

> She kissed me, and I her, and we both soon slumbered. When I awoke it was day: an unusual movement roused me; I looked up; I was in somebody's arms; the nurse held me; she was carrying me through the passage back to the dormitory. I was not reprimanded for leaving my bed; people had something else to think about; no explanation was afforded then to my many questions; but a day or two afterwards I learned that Miss Temple, on returning to her own room at dawn, had found me laid in a little crib; my face against Helen Burn's shoulder, my arms round her neck. I was asleep, and Helen was – dead.

How does the author invite us to view these events? She shows us Helen and Jane kissing each other before they sleep. What she then gives us is a series of disconnected statements about what happened to Jane. Because the statements are disconnected, Jane does not know what they mean. When Jane is told what has happened to her, we hear the events from Miss Temple's viewpoint. Miss Temple returned to her room, found Jane in bed with her face against Helen's shoulder, and her arms around her. And then both Jane and the reader are told the truth – Jane was asleep and Helen was dead. It is only at that point that Jane and the reader can make sense of the other events.

Why does Charlotte Brontë do this? She could have written: 'We went to sleep, and when I awoke, Helen was dead.' But if she had, we would not have *felt* the events very keenly. What Charlotte Brontë has done is invite us to view the events through the puzzled confusions of her story-teller, so that the reader can feel very close to Jane.

That is just one way in which an author can arrange the events of a novel. There are many others: an author can use letters, can rely on the conversation of characters, can write about characters' thoughts, can concentrate on the expressions on characters' faces, can employ a number of characters who tell the story from their points of view, and can invite the reader to have doubts about the reliability of the one who is telling the story. You should concentrate on two things: how the author is arranging the events, and the effect of this particular arrangement.

Though less important than viewpoint, you can ask another question about how an author arranges events: what events does the author choose to write about? Because there are many things an author could write about, and because these could be written about in great or little detail, you can learn a great deal about an author by looking at what he or she chooses to say. One author might concentrate on creating characters in a very detailed way, while another might devote a great deal of space to actions and hardly create character at all. It is often interesting to see what an author does not mention. Goerge Eliot, for instance, is interested in work, whereas Dickens is not. In *Middlemarch* George Eliot devotes much space to the young Dr Lydgate's attempt to introduce new medical practices, but in *Hard Times* Dickens never mentions what work people do, even though the novel is set in the industrial north. You should not assume that this makes George Eliot a good and Dickens a bad novelist. The point is that George Eliot has *chosen* to show people working and Dickens has not.

## 6.3 HOW AUTHORS TELL STORIES: FIRST-PERSON NARRATION

Telling a story is a complex business because the relation between the events, the author and the reader can vary a great deal. There are, in other words, a number of ways in which an author can tell a reader a story.

When you study a novel you should ask this question: in what person is this novel written? 'Person' is a grammatical term; verbs can be used in three persons. Take, for instance, the verb to write:

| | |
|---|---|
| first person: | I write |
| second person: | you write |
| third person: | he, she, it writes. |

When a novel is written, the relation between the novelist and events is conveyed in two of these three persons – the first and the third. (The second is not used because the novelist could only address one person.) It is important to ask which, because the first and third persons provide different opportunities for the author. Let us think about these.

When a novel is written in the first person, it is as if the novelist *is* the character telling the story, because the verbs will be in the form of: 'I saw . . . I thought . . . I did . . .' In fact, the character telling the story is not the novelist but a persona whom the novelist has created to tell the story from his or her point of view. Because the character telling the story – the narrator – is not the novelist, certain effects are possible. One of the most important is that the novelist can invite the reader to judge the narrating character. The novelist can do this either by making the narrator say things which he or she expects the reader will or will not approve of, or by making the narrator someone who is aware of his or her faults. Two examples will make this clear.

Charlotte Brontë expects the reader to approve of Jane Eyre's decision not to live with Mr Rochester when she knows he is married to someone else. This is what Charlotte Brontë makes Jane say:

One clear word comprised my intolerable duty – 'Depart!'

The reader should agree; 'duty' might be 'intolerable' but it remains duty – that which must be done. In *Great Expectations* Dickens asks us to judge many of Pip's actions severely by inviting us to agree with Pip's own judgements against himself. After Pip has received his 'expectations' – his fortune – he becomes ashamed of Joe, the good blacksmith who has helped to bring him up. At one point Dickens shows us how Pip, now living in London, reacts to the news that Joe is to visit him:

> Let me confess exactly, with what feelings I looked forward to Joe's coming.
>
> Not with pleasure, though I was bound to him by so many ties; no; with considerable disturbance, some mortification, and a keen sense of incongruity. If I could have kept him away by paying money, I would certainly have done so.

That is Pip's own judgement on his conduct. He says he is confessing; that is, owning up to what he has done wrong. The worst thing he confesses is the thought that, if it would have worked, he would have used bribery to prevent Joe from visiting him. Dickens intends that admission to lower Pip in our eyes.

You should learn from these examples to ask this question: what attitude does the novelist take towards the first person narrator? It could be approval, disapproval or, more likely, a balance between the two. What you must not assume is that you know what the attitude will be before you read the novel.

What other opportunities does first person narration provide? One has already been suggested: *we feel very close to the narrator.* First person novels are closer than any other to how we experience life. We know our own thoughts and feelings but can only observe and guess what other people do and think. Consequently, we feel close to Jane and Pip and are puzzled by what puzzles them. When we first read *Jane Eyre,* we wonder, as Jane does, what Mr Rochester feels for her, and a first reading of *Great Expectations* makes us wonder with Pip why Miss Havisham takes an interest in him. You should remember that it is the aim of the author to make you ask these questions. Part of the pleasure of reading these novels is living with the puzzlements that face the central character.

If you share the feelings of the central character, you will be appreciating another of the opportunities offered by first person narration – access to the mind of the narrator. First person narration allows the novelist to show you how the narrator thinks, feels and reacts. In some novels many very different states of mind are covered. In *Great Expectation* Dickens explores fear, guilt, ambition, snobbery, pretence, love, embarrassment, disappointment, shock, regret and gratitude. He also explores extreme mental states such as nightmarish dreams and fevers.

Although as a reader you are close to the experience of the narrator, you must remember that the novelist is not presenting your experience. One of the pleasures of first person novels is that you experience what, in ordinary life, you never can: how the world looks to somebody else. To follow Jane's or Pip's life is to be given another view of the world. Only first person novels can give you this, so it is worth asking yourself whether you learn from them how other people think and feel.

One of the most important opportunities offered by first person narrations is that of seeing how a narrator grows. Pip is a good example. *Great Expectations* is about what makes a true gentleman. Pip believes that wealth, London society, education and refined manners can make him a gentleman. But they don't; Pip merely becomes snobbish, resentful and unhappy. Dickens shows Pip's growing awareness of his own shallow beliefs until, in the end, he realises that the true gentleman is faithful, kind, generous and loving Joe, who has by nature all those qualities that Pip hoped to gain through money. The reader can appreciate Pip's painful growth towards true understanding, because the first person narration has made possible an inside view of the narrator.

## 6.4 HOW AUTHORS TELL STORIES: THIRD-PERSON NARRATION

Third person novels are more common. Third person narrators do not, so to speak, take part in the novel. In the eighteenth century the narrator often announced that he or she was the story-teller, but since then the practice has been for the narrator to be 'invisible'; that is, narrators have not called attention to themselves. Third person narrators are very powerful (they have been comapred to God) because they order events as they please. In addition, they can choose to know what they like about their characters' minds. It is always useful to ask: what does the narrator choose to know about the minds of his or her characters? That question comes down to whether or not the novelist chooses to have access to the characters' minds, and if so, which ones. Most novelists do one of two things: they either choose to have access to one character or to all.

Having access to only one character is a way of combining third person narration with one of the opportunities offered by writing in the first –

the reader sees all that is going on but is privileged to know the thoughts of only one character, usually the central one. Golding's *The Spire* is written in this way. Though the novel is written in the third person, all the events are seen from the point of view of Jocelin, the Dean of the Cathedral. As a result of that, it is easy to feel sympathy for him. Yet it is difficult not to be annoyed by his smug assumption that he, and only he, knows best. In the end, it is not easy to make a judgement, because Golding has written the book so that the reader is pulled two ways – access to his mind inclines us towards sympathy, but what we find in his mind leads us to judge him harshly.

When novelists choose to know everything about all the characters, they are called omniscient. George Eliot is a famous example. We come away from one of her novels with the feeling that we know the characters intimately, because Eliot writes about the thoughts, feelings and reactions of each in great detail in the hope that we will understand them. In *The Mill on the Floss* she presents the brother and sister, Tom and Maggie Tulliver, eating jam puffs. It is an ordinary incident, but Eliot intimately explores their feelings. Tom has given Maggie the best piece, and she has gently protested that she doesn't want it:

> Maggie, thinking it was no use to contend further, began, too, and ate up her half puff with considerable relish as well as rapidity. But Tom had finished first and had to look on while Maggie ate her last morsel or two, feeling in himself a capacity for more. Maggie didn't know Tom was looking at her; she was see-sawing on the elder bough, lost to almost everything but a vague sense of jam and idleness.
>
> 'Oh, you greedy thing!' said Tom when she had swallowed the last morsel. He was conscious of having acted very fairly and thought she ought to have considered this and made up to him for it.

We can see into *both* of their minds. We know that Tom would like some more food – 'feeling in himself a capacity for more' – but we also know that Maggie is unaware of this. Hence, when Tom feels angry, we understand why. Yet we also know why Maggie might be surprised by this reaction. By showing us what is going on in both their minds, Eliot enables us to understand both their points of view.

You must not expect every novel to be written in the above ways. Indeed, you should be prepared to find interesting variations on first and third person narratives. For instance, Jane Austen's *Emma* is written in the third person, yet whole paragraphs of it are written in the style and from the point of view of Emma herself. In Emily Brontë's *Wuthering Heights* there are two narrators, Nelly and Lockwood. It is, therefore, worthwhile asking yourself: is there anything unusual about the way the story is told? If there is, you must try to describe the effects of this.

## 6.5 AUTHOR'S ATTITUDES, AND IRONY

You can't discuss how a story is written in isolation from the novelist's attitude. The attitudes of a novelist – the interests taken in characters, and the interpretations of and judgements upon them – will be evident in the way the novel is written. Of every novel you can ask: what attitude is the novelist inviting me to take towards the events of the novel? The question has two parts: what are the attitudes, and how does the novelist put them over?

Consider the passage from *The Mill on the Floss.* What is Eliot's attitude to Tom and Maggie? It is a kind and understanding one. She does not take sides but shows that neither sees what the other wants. She, herself, is understanding and wants us to be the same. She does this by creating a detailed picture of their feelings: we are invited to share Maggie's 'vague sense of jam and idleness' and to be aware that Tom feels he has 'acted very fairly', though without reward.

Of course, a novelist can invite readers to take up many different attitudes. It would be foolish to try and describe them all here, yet there is one that deserves particular attention, because examiners will expect you to recognise it. This is irony. You must learn to recognise it, and be able to write about the ironic attitude that some novelists invite you to take towards their characters.

Irony occurs when a reader sees that an author is showing that there is a gap between what a character thinks is true and what is really true. Whenever this occurs, you can say that the attitude of the author is ironic. Irony can occur in a number of ways. A character may say something that you see is mistaken. The gap in that case is between words and truth. Or a character can say something, the real meaning or implication of which is very different from what that character supposed. The gap, or discrepancy, then, is between words and meaning. Again, a character can confidently expect certain events to happen or can set out to achieve something, but you will see that things won't work out as expected. The gap is then between intention and result. Finally, a character can interpret the world one way, but you will see that the author is leading you to see that that is wrong. This is the gap between appearance and reality.

When you write about irony, you will have to master words that describe the gaps between author, character and reader. Discrepancy has been mentioned; you could also use difference or incongruity. Hence, you might say there is an incongruity between what a character says and what his or her words actually mean. You will also have to be careful when you write about what authors are doing when they take up, or invite, ironical attitudes. Authors very rarely state ironies; rather they create ironies by hinting or implying differences. This is what most readers prefer; enjoying ironies is sharing an understanding with the author. If ironies are too obvious, or heavy, you will feel you are being treated as a child rather than an equal.

In novels (irony can, of course, be present in poetry and plays) ironies usually occur in one of two ways: either the reader sees an irony present in a situation, or the reader, recalling an earlier incident, sees an ironic discrepancy between two events. This is often called dramatic irony. Discrepancies between words and truth, words and meaning, and appearance and reality are usually seen as present in a situation, whereas the discrepancy between intention and result only happens when a past event is recalled.

Let us look at an example of irony in a novel. In *Emma*, Jane Austen employs most subtle and entertaining ironies. The plot centres on the efforts of Emma Woodhouse to find marriage partners for her friends. She persuades Harriet Smith, a pleasant but rather dull girl, that the new vicar, Mr Elton, is in love with her. Harriet, rightly as it turns out, can hardly believe that this is true, but Emma has no doubts: 'I cannot make a question, or listen to a question about that. It is a certainty.' The reader can see an ironic gap between Emma's smugly confident words and the truth. It is by no means certain that Mr Elton is in love with Harriet. For a start, it looks as if he is actually courting Emma, a fact of which she is quite unaware. Because of this, she says things of Harriet which the reader sees really apply to herself.

For example, Mr Elton gives Harriet a charade (a riddle in verse) for her collection. He intends it for Emma's eyes, but when Emma sees it she says: 'I never read one more to the purpose . . .' She's right. There is a purpose behind it, but *not* the one that she supposes. She thinks it means one thing; the reader can see it means another. The gap is between words and meaning.

Emma is so blind to Mr Elton's intentions that when her brother-in-law points out that he may have designs upon her, she dismisses the idea as ridiculous. The irony is intense; she is told the truth but cannot see it. She thanks her brother-in-law for his concern but assures him that he is 'quite mistaken':

> 'Mr Elton and I are very good friends, and nothing more'; and she walked on, amusing herself in the consideration of the blunders which often arise from a partial knowledge of circumstance, or the mistakes which people of high pretensions to judgement are for ever falling into; and not very well pleased with her brother for imagining her blind and ignorant, and in want of counsel.

The ironies here show just how wrong Emma's view of the world is; she confuses what she takes to be appearance with what is real. She considers those who commit blunders because of 'partial knowledge', but fails to see that that is what she is doing. She also is amused by people of 'high pretensions' who fall into error, without realising that that is a just remark about herself. And she is not very pleased with her brother-in-law imagining that she is 'blind and ignorant'; Jane Austen invites us to see that she is, and that her blindness is due to her imagining.

*Emma* abounds in dramatic irony. When Emma discovers that Mr Elton is actually in love with her, and when he discovers that what he took for encouragement was her attempts to marry him off to Harriet, both are shocked, and the reader sees the irony of the gap between their intentions and the result.

Even more enjoyable are those moments when the reader was not expecting the outcome. Readers learn to ignore Mr Woodhouse, because he is a fussy man who measures everything by how it might affect people's health – particularly his own. When Frank Churchill pays a visit, nearly everybody is delighted, one of the exceptions being Mr Woodhouse, who makes a characteristic complaint about Frank leaving doors open: 'He does not think of the draught. I do not mean to set you against him, but indeed he is not quite the thing!' His remark is ignored by both the characters and the reader. But, as it turns out, he is right: Frank Churchill is deceitful. He is, indeed, 'not quite the thing!'

Detecting irony is difficult. The best thing you can do is read with certain questions in mind. When characters speak, or when you are told their thoughts, you can ask: is that true? When the novelist makes a comment, you can ask: does he or she really mean that? In the case of dramatic irony, you can ask: have there been situations like this one before, and if so, do they cast an ironic light on this event?

It is not sufficient just to say that an author takes up an ironic attitude. You should always try to write about the *point* of the irony. There is no way of predicting the effects of irony, but you might look to see if it has a moral purpose. That is to say, the irony could be a way of showing up a character's moral defects. Emma, for instance, is too confident, gives way to her powerful imagination and enjoys controlling other people. These are moral defects. Irony might also show that a character is too proud, too self-centred or too idealistic. It is also worth noting that whatever the point of irony, it is often brought over by laughter. The reader is amused by the irony and sees in it a moral point about the characters.

## 6.6 WRITING ABOUT AUTHORS

The way authors arrange events, tell stories and take up attitudes to their characters are all examples of the basic theme of this section: novels are worlds specially created by authors. It is very important that you recognise this in your writing by being very careful about the words you use. Too many students write about how an author 'describes' a scene or a character, but if you think about it, this is an inappropriate way of thinking. You can only describe what is already there, but in the case of characters, there is nobody in the real world of which they are a copy. Characters, therefore, are not described but created. If you don't want to use the word 'created' all the time, you can turn to others. Here are some: arrange, shape, present, show, mould, make and imagine. Of course, there are occasions when you want to say that an author portrayed a feature of ordinary life. Let us imagine that you have been impressed by the way in which an author has understood the pains of growing up. How should you write about this insight into everyday life? The answer is to make clear that you see the difference between life and the novel. You could say: 'the author has closely observed the pains of growing up and has created characters in whom these feelings are expressed.'

**EXERCISES**

**1** Look at the novels you are studying from the point of view of how the author arranges the events and the person he or she adopts for the narration. What effects do these have?
**2** Ask yourself whether any of the novels you are studying invite you to look upon the characters ironically. If they do, write about how the irony works and the points which it makes.
**3** Read the following extract from Orwell's *1984* and answer the questions below.

The members of the department in which Winston Smith works are gathering for a daily ritual – the two minutes hate.

> The other person was a man named O'Brien, a member of the Inner Party and holder of some post so important and remote that Winston had only a dim idea of its nature. A momentary hush passed over the group of people round the chairs as they saw the black overalls of an Inner Party member approaching. O'Brien was a large, burly man with a thick neck and a coarse, humorous, brutal face. In spite of his formidable appearance he had a certain charm of manner. He had a trick of re-settling his spectacles on his nose which was curiously disarming – in some indefinable way, curiously civilized. It was a gesture which, if anyone had still thought in such terms, might have recalled an eighteenth-century nobleman offering his snuffbox. Winston had seen O'Brien perhaps a dozen times in almost as many years. He felt deeply drawn to him, and not solely because he was intrigued by the contrast between

O'Brien's urbane manner and his prizefighter's physique. Much more it was because of a secretly-held belief – or perhaps not even a belief, merely a hope – that O'Brien's political orthodoxy was not perfect. Something in his face suggested it irresistibly. And again, perhaps it was not even unorthodoxy that was written in his face, but simply intelligence. But at any rate he had the appearance of being a person that you could talk to if somehow you could cheat the telescreen and get him alone. Winston had never made the smallest effort to verify this guess: indeed, there was no way of doing so. At this moment O'Brien glanced at his wristwatch, saw that it was nearly eleven hundred and evidently decided to stay in the Records Department until the Two Minutes Hate was over. He took a chair in the same row as Winston, a couple of places away. A small, sandy-haired woman who worked in the next cubicle to Winston was between them. The girl with dark hair was sitting immediately behind.

(a) *1984* is largely written in the third person, but Orwell chooses to have access only to the mind of Winston Smith. What is the effect of this when Winston thinks about O'Brien?

(b) Since you, the reader, know no more about O'Brien than Winston does, write about the puzzles and problems that you have in understanding what O'Brien is like.

(c) When you read that Winston feels 'deeply drawn' to O'Brien and that he has 'a secretly-held belief' about him, what are your reactions to Winston?

(d) Winston feels that O'Brien has 'the appearance of being a person you could talk to'. What is Orwell inviting the reader to expect by writing this, and do you see any possibility that what is to come will cast an ironical light on these words?

4 Read the following passage from Dicken's *Little Dorrit* and answer the questions below. Mr Dorrit has spent many years of his life in the Marshalsea, a prison to which debtors are sent. It has been discovered that he is the heir to a fortune and, therefore, will be released. His daughter, Little Dorrit, is talking to Arthur Clennam. Mr Dorrit is asleep.

Little Dorrit had been thinking too. After softly putting his grey hair aside, and touching his forehead with her lips, she looked towards Arthur, who came nearer to her, and pursued in a low whisper the subject of her thoughts.

'Mr Clennam, will he pay all his debts before he leaves here?'

'No doubt. All.'

'All the debts for which he had been imprisoned here, all my life and longer?'

'No doubt.'

There was something of uncertainty and remonstrance in her look; something that was not all satisfaction. He wondered to detect it, and said:

'You are glad that he should do so?'

'Are you?' asked Little Dorrit, wistfully.

'Am I? Most heartily glad!'

'Then I know I ought to be.'

'And are you not?'

'It seems to me hard,' said Little Dorrit, 'that he should have lost so many years and suffered so much, and at last pay all the debts as well. It seems to me hard that he should pay in life and money both.'

'My dear child – ' Clennam was beginning.

'Yes, I know I am wrong,' she pleaded timidly, 'don't think any worse of me; it has grown up with me here.'

The prison, which could spoil so many things, had tainted Little Dorrit's mind no more than this. Engendered as the confusion was, in compassion for the poor prisoner, her father, it was the first speck Clennam had ever seen, it was the last speck Clennam ever saw, of the prison atmosphere upon her.

He thought this, and forebore to say another word. With the thought, her purity and goodness came before him in their brightest light. The little spot made them the more beautiful.

(a) Dickens chooses to have access to what Clennam thinks but he presents Little Dorrit through Clennam's impressions of her; what is the effect of this, and why do you think Dickens chose to write this way?

(b) Look at the conversation from Clennam's 'You are glad that it should be so?' down to 'And are you not?': what clues does Dickens give to how we ought to understand the feelings of the two speakers?

(c) How do you understand Little Dorrit's 'Yes, I know that I am wrong'? Is she wrong, or does Dickens intend us to see that it is not right for a man to 'pay in life and money both'?

(d) Is there any irony in Arthur Clennam seeing 'a speck . . . of prison atmosphere upon her'. Is the speck on Little Dorrit, or is the reader invited to see that she is right and he is wrong?

# CHAPTER 7

# CHARACTERS

## 7.1 CHARACTERS ARE FICTIONAL CREATIONS

Many of the questions in public examinations are about character. Whenever you write about characters in novels, you should remember that, because they are in novels, they are not just like real life people. The reason for this has already been given in the previous chapter: characters in novels have been specially created by authors. When authors create characters, they select some aspects of ordinary people, develop some of those aspects whilst playing down others, and put them together as they please. The result is not an ordinary person but a fictional character who only exists in the words of the novel.

Because characters in novels are specially made, you can always ask this question of them: how are these characters created? Whatever you write about a character will depend upon how the character has been created. If, for instance, you ask yourself what you feel about a character (a good question to ask), the answer will depend upon the way in which the author has made that character. But since to ask how a character is made is a big question, it is a good idea to break it down into a number of others. We will first ask about the range of characters, and then we will look at a number of questions you can ask about characters, the answers to which will help you to see how characters have been made and how they function in the novel.

## 7.2 THE RANGE OF CHARACTERS: THREE EXAMPLES

What is meant by the range of characters? The word 'range' refers to the fullness, or otherwise, which a character is given. If you think back to what was said about the access an author can allow the reader to have into a character's mind, you will see that you will understand more about a character into whose mind you are admitted than one whom you only know from the outside. The character into whose mind you can see is likely to be deeper, richer and more varied than one whose mind is closed to you. The matter can be put very simply by saying that some characters have more to them than others. Let us look at some examples.

There are some characters whom readers feel they know very well. They seem alive, independent and, in many cases, original. When they act, think and speak, they do so in a distinctive way, and it makes sense to ask: why did he or she do, think or say that? These characters have many sides to them; they have a rich inner life; they are capable of growing and changing; and readers can follow them through a very wide variety of experiences, including, in some novels, death itself. Readers feel they know these characters well because their authors have chosen to give them range, depth and richness.

George Eliot creates characters like this. In *Middlemarch* she creates Dorothea Brooke in a wonderfully rich way. This is how the novel begins:

> Miss Brooke had that kind of beauty which seems to be thrown into relief by poor dress. Her hand and wrist were so finely formed that she could never wear sleeves not less bare of style than those in which the Blessed Virgin appeared to Italian painters; and her profile as well as her stature and bearing seemed to gain the more dignity from her plain garments, which by the side of provincial fashion gave her the impressiveness of a fine quotation from the Bible – or from one of our elder poets, – in a paragraph of to-day's newspaper.

Look how much we are shown in two sentences: Dorothea has a special kind of beauty, her hands and wrists are finely formed, her clothes are plain yet her profile, stature and bearing gain dignity in contrast to them.

But, as you will have seen, there is no exploration of Dorothea's mind in that passage. When, however, we are shown what Dorothea's inner self is like, the impression that her character is rich and deep is further strengthened. In the following passage Dorothea is deeply unhappy; her husband resents her friendship with Will Ladislaw, but increasingly Dorothea looks to Will for companionship:

> It was another or rather a fuller sort of companionship that poor Dorothea was hungering for, and the hunger had grown from the perpetual effort demanded by her married life. She was always trying to be what her husband wished, and never able to repose on his delight in what she was. The thing that she liked, that she spontaneously cared to have, seemed to be always excluded from her life; for if it was only granted and not shared by her husband it might as well have been denied.

George Eliot explores Dorothea's innermost feelings and needs. Dorothea has a hunger for companionship, which is born of the fact that, though she tries, she can never get her husband to be pleased with her as she is. She feels that the one thing that she cares for in life is denied her. We are shown all this: Dorothea is known from the inside.

When you wish to show that authors have created rich and deep characters, it is a good idea to select one or two passages about them and examine the different ways in which they are shown to the reader. You can expect to find that the characters are viewed from the outside, that their speech is reported, that their thoughts are revealed, and that their feelings and needs are shown. Such characters are rich and complex not just because a lot is said about them but because they are presented in these different ways.

In some novels there are characters who are known from both the inside and the outside but who, nevertheless, are not as rich, varied or original as the ones written about above. They are characters who have a much more limited life. Their authors have given them a few characteristics, but they do not develop or change very much, and consequently they rarely surprise the reader. To use a metaphor from art, they are lightly sketched in with a few broad lines, but there is little light or shadow to them. This is not to say that they have very little purpose in the novels in which they appear. Quite often their presence is very important, but often the reader gains the impression that the author has put them there not because he or she is interested in them but because they serve a purpose in the total design of the novel.

Take, for instance, the case of Ida Arnold in Graham Greene's *Brighton Rock.* She is the woman who decides to prove that Pinkie, the boy who runs a gang of criminals, has murdered Fred Hale. Pinkie is a strange and deep character, but Ida is simple – she is friendly, wordly, good-natured and has a strong, simple idea of justice. Once her character has been established by Greene, he does not allow her to grow or change. What he wants is someone who is very different from Pinkie, and who will fight for her idea of justice. Even at the moment when she decides to investigate Fred's death, Greene makes it clear that there is nothing complex about her:

> Somebody had made Fred unhappy, and somebody was going to be made unhappy in return. An eye for an eye. If you believed in God, you might leave vengeance to Him, but you couldn't trust the One, the universal spirit. Vengeance was Ida's, just as much as reward was Ida's, the soft gluey mouth affixed in taxis, the warm handclasp in cinemas, the only reward there was. And vengeance and reward – they were both fun.

Ida is not only simple in herself, but Greene presents her simply. Ida is bent on revenge, but that is all Greene says. He could have shown someone who was worried about whether it was right to revenge a death, or someone who had to build up their own courage. But he does neither. He makes Ida work with the simple idea that since someone had made Fred unhappy, that someone should be made to suffer. Indeed, so simple is her idea of revenge that he makes her look upon it as 'fun'. It is possible for authors to present simple people in a full and rich way, as Dickens presents Joe in *Great Expectations,* but that is not Greene's purpose. He wants someone with a few characteristics who will have a place in the design of his novel – Ida Arnold is the result.

There are some characters that have only one feature. They never develop, rarely have any inner life, never surprise the reader ( if they do, it's only once), and they often repeat phrases. The reader is never puzzled about them, because there is nothing about them to cause puzzlement. They can, however, be delightfully funny, and many of them, in consequence, are memorable.

In Dickens's *Little Dorrit* there is a character who is known as Mr F's aunt. This old lady has two characteristics: she does not like Arthur Clennam, the central character, and she utters inconsequential sayings. Whenever she appears she says something that has nothing at all to do with what everybody else is talking about. The following incident occurs during tea:

> A diversion was occasioned here, by Mr F's aunt making the following inexorable and awful statement:
>
> 'There's mile-stones on the Dover Road!'

There is very little else to Mr F's Aunt; she is always very funny, and readers remember her with affection, because her remarks introduce a delightful note of absurdity into the novel. But she has no motives, no inner life, and she never grows, changes or develops.

Now, you should not understand from Dorothea Brooke, Ida Arnold and Mr F's Aunt that every character in every novel should be either very wide ranging, of limited range, or composed of just one or two characteristics. The point of the examples was that novelists create a very wide range of characters in terms of their fullness. You should not think of just three types but rather of a scale running from deep and rich characters to very simple ones. You will find rich characters who are less fully realised than Dorothea Brooke, and limited characters who have more to them than Ida Arnold. And the point to remember about any character, whether full or simple, is that the character is like that because that is how the author has made him or her.

## 7.3 THE RANGE OF CHARACTERS: HOW TO WRITE ABOUT THEM

There are a few terms that should give you some help in writing about the range of characters you will find in novels. The novelist E.M. Forster published a book, called *Aspects of the Novel,* in which he distinguished between round and flat characters. Round characters are full, complex and rich, such as Dorothea Brooke, whereas flat characters are simple ones, such as Mr F's Aunt. Another way of distinguishing between characters of a wide and those of a narrow range is to call one open and the other closed. These terms are more concerned with the capacity of characters to change; an open character can grow and develop, whereas a closed one is fixed and unchanging. Dorothea Brooke is clearly an open character, and Ida Arnold a closed one. Round and flat, and open and closed are used as technical terms. If you want to explore alternative ways of writing about the range of characters authors create, you can use words such as flexible and inflexible, surface and depth, and multi-faceted and one-sided. You must not, of course, simply label a character and leave it at that. You must discuss character and show the contribution he or she makes to the novel as a whole. For instance, Ida Arnold is important because she is wordly, but Greene shows that life can only be understood in religious terms.

When you write about characters in terms of their range, you should be careful to avoid three mistakes: the mistake of thinking that every character has a fixed range throughout the novel, the mistake of thinking that a simple character is not as good as a complex one, and the mistake of thinking that all the characters in one book will be in the same range. Some examples will help you here.

It is all too easy when reading a novel to decide that a particular character exists within a certain range and then become blind to the way even the most fixed ones can grow. There are some characters who are closed and flat for most of the novel, but then the novelist suddenly reveals new aspects to them. Jane Austen does this with Miss Bates, the pleasant, well-meaning but tiresomely talkative old maid in *Emma.* Emma, through whom we see much of the novel, is understandably bored by her, and while we may think that she is intolerant, we can understand that Miss Bates is trying company. Towards the end of the novel this changes. An outing is arranged to Box Hill. It is not successful; the characters feel ill at ease, slightly bored and disappointed. During a conversation Emma makes a joke at Miss Bates's expense. It is a personal one, and Miss Bates is hurt by it. Suddenly, she is revealed as a woman of feeling, and in her admission that she must be very tiresome to people there is a touching dignity:

> 'Oh! very well,' exclaimed Miss Bates, 'then I need not be uneasy. "Three things very dull indeed." That will just do for me, you know. I

> shall be sure to say three dull things as soon as ever I open my mouth, shan't I? – (looking round with the most good-humoured dependence on everybody's assent) – Do not you all think I shall?'
>
> Emma could not resist.
>
> 'Ah! ma'am, but there may be a difficulty. Pardon me – but you will be limited as to number – only three at once.'
>
> Miss Bates, deceived by the mock ceremony of her manner, did not immediately catch her meaning; but, when it burst on her, it could not anger, though a slight blush showed that it could pain her.
>
> 'Ah! – well – to be sure. Yes, I see what she means, (turning to Mr Knightley,) and I will try to hold my tongue. I must make myself very disagreeable, or she would not have said such a thing to an old friend.'

At this point we must adjust our view of her; she is not just a flat, closed character with no inner life and no capacity to change.

If you see more of a character, it is understandable that you should judge that character to be more interesting than one who is flat. The trouble is that there is a temptation to move beyond this and think of all full characters as necessarily better written than flat ones. It is true that the fuller a character is, the more opportunity an author has to explore a wide range of thoughts and feelings, but this is a very different question from the one of success. Dickens is a test case. Some readers complain that some of his central characters are closer to caricature. But it is possible to agree with this and yet argue that they are still vigorous and entertaining. They may be flat but they are marvellously effective.

Take the case of Mr Bounderby from *Hard Times*:

> He was a rich man: a banker, merchant, manufacturer and what not. A big, loud man, with a stare and a metallic laugh. A man made out of coarse material, which seemed to have stretched to make so much of him. A man with a great puffed head and forehead, swelled veins in his temples, and such a strained skin to his face that it seemed to hold his eyes open, and lift his eyebrows up.

Mr Bounderby is close to caricature; the picture of him is highly selective, and its elements are exaggerated. But Mr Bounderby is monstrously funny, because Dickens has created him with such relish and energy. And even the jokes are appropriate and have a bearing upon the meaning of the novel. Mr Bounderby is a manufacturer in a novel which is about the kind of life that is lived in an industrial town. Dickens suggests that this life crushes people and makes them less than fully human. We can see this in Bounderby. The joke about him is that he is a manufacturer who is presented as a factory-made article; he is 'made out of coarse material' which is 'stretched' and 'strained'. But the joke points to the way his humanity is diminished. Even the factory owner, who enjoys a better standard of living than his workers, is made less than fully human by life in an industrial society. Mr Bounderby remains a flat character, but he is superbly presented by Dickens.

Because authors create characters for different purposes, you should not be surprised to find characters of different ranges within one novel. If some characters are fuller than others, it is not necessarily a mistake. What you should be careful about is treating characters of different ranges in the same way. If one character is full and another limited or flat, they cannot be easily compared with each other. What you should do is think about why an author chose to create characters in different ways.

In Hardy's *Tess of the D'Urbervilles* there are two men who are created in quite different ways. This is odd, because both of them are major characters, and both of them have a dramatic effect upon the heroine – Tess. One of the men is Angel Clare, the son of a clergyman, and the other is Alec D'Urberville, the son of a rich northern family which has recently moved south. Angel Clare is a fully realised character. The reader is shown how he thinks and feels, and at the moments of crisis in the novel he is portrayed as someone who responds in a very complex way. The keynote to his character is established on his second appearance:

> He wore the ordinary white pinner and leather leggings of a dairy-farmer when milking, and his boots were clogged with the mulch of the yard; but this was all his local livery. Beneath it was something educated, reserved, subtle, sad, differing.

Hardy is keen to show that he is a character who has an inner life, hence words such as 'reserved, subtle, sad, differing'. Alec, on the other hand, is nearly all surface. Hardy presents him as a conventional, wild young man, who dresses in tweeds, curls his moustache, smokes in the presence of ladies, and talks in clichés such as, 'Well, my Beauty'. Only rarely is the reader shown what goes on in his mind, and while he changes quite dramatically, Hardy does not offer complex accounts of how and why he has changed.

Because both characters affect Tess, it is tempting to compare them, and indeed Hardy seems to invite comparisons by putting them both in parallel situations. For instance, they both take Tess on journeys by horse and cart. Nevertheless, it is very difficult to compare two characters who are drawn in such different ways. It is, however, useful to ask why Hardy has created two important characters who are so different in range. One suggestion is that he has done so because they appeal to different things in Tess: Angel is associated with Tess's capacity for inward thought, and Alec with her spontaneous actions. It could also be that Hardy felt that two fully developed characters would detract from the centrality of Tess. It does not matter which view you take, as long as you understand that Hardy has deliberately created two important but very different characters, and that this raises the problem of why he has done this.

## 7.4 QUESTIONS ABOUT CHARACTERS

It is important that you should be able to recognise whether a character is round or flat, but you should not confuse this with another kind of question. An author can create a character in a full or limited way, but the range of the character is a different consideration from *what the character is like.* You should, therefore, also think about how an author creates the personality, or individuality, of a character. You need to do this, because many questions in public examinations ask you to write about what a character is like. In answering a question like that you will be writing about the ways in which an author has made a particular character distinctive.

The best way in which you can approach thinking about the personality of a character is to ask questions about the characters you meet in books. These questions should be about the ways in which an author can make a character. What now follows is a set of questions with examples drawn from novels that are set at 'O' and 'A' level. Some questions will be more important than others, and some will not apply to every character. What you should do is recognise that you can ask questions about how an author has given a character a personality and then judge for yourself whether a particular question is appropriate.

## 7.5 TELLING AND SHOWING

There are two very general questions you can ask. The first is: what are we told about the character? Most authors find it necessary to tell their readers directly something about the characters they are creating. An author might tell readers that a character has grey hair, is fifty-five years old, is married to an architect, has had two children, looks after her mother and paints for a hobby. Authors need not tell their readers directly about the personalities of their characters. They might show readers a number of things in and through the events of the story, but it is very rare to find characters who are entirely created in this way. Most authors use direct telling to convey something about their characters. Look at how Scott Fitzgerald begins *Tender is the Night*:

> In the spring of 1917, when Doctor Richard Driver first arrived in Zurich, he was twenty-six years old, a fine age for a man, indeed the very acme of bachelorhood. Even in wartime days it was a fine age for Dick, who was already too valuable, too much of a capital investment to be shot off in a gun.

At the very beginning of his novel, Scott Fitzgerald decides to tell us things; we learn when Richard Driver arrived in Zurich, his age, and something of the value placed on him by others.

If a question asks you to write about what a character is like, one of the things you can do is look to see what the author tells you. There are only two problems you will have to bear in mind when you do this. One is when the novel is written in the first person. In that case it is the narrator who tells you things and not the novelist. You should, therefore, remember that what you are told is a personal view. The other thing to look out for is an ironical voice. If you miss the irony, you might take a statement literally when it was meant to be read as a judgement. With the exception of those two cases, however, you can treat what you are told as reliable and use it when you are writing about what a character is like.

The second general question has already been hinted at: what are we shown about the character? When an author shows a reader something, it is done indirectly. Something about a character can emerge from the way he or she speaks, reacts or thinks. The author will not say, for instance, 'Mr Brown was a hesitant man' but will show Mr Brown hesitating a number of times before making a decision. As you can see, showing the character's behaviour places much more responsibility on the reader to recognise the importance of what is going on.

Take, for example, Harper Lee's *To Kill a Mockingbird.* This is a first person novel written from the point of view of Scout, the daughter of the lawyer Atticus Finch. The novel shows the way she grows up and comes to an understanding of the kind of world in which she lives. At the start she recounts how, as children, they used to play a game of running up to the Radley House to touch the door. This was thought to be daring, because Boo Radley lived there, and he was the strange son of the Radleys who suffered from mental trouble. Towards the end of the novel she says this about the game: 'I sometimes felt a twinge of remorse, when passing the old place . . .' That is an important moment, but it is one which is shown and not told. The reader is left to see that the remorse she feels is a sign that she is becoming more mature and is recognising the moral significance of her actions. It is important to remember that, though telling and showing are discussed here in terms of character, the ideas are applicable to other aspects of novels such as story-telling and setting.

## 7.6 HOW CHARACTERS SPEAK

It is important to ask: how do the characters speak? In many novels the way a character speaks is an expression of that character. Authors frequently give characters personalities by making them repeat certain words, use many illustrations in their speech, talk a great deal or say very little, or speak in a very complicated or a quite simple manner.

George Eliot often gives a character such a distinctive way of speaking that a few sentences are all that is necessary for that character to be established. Listen to how Mr Casaubon, the scholarly clergyman from *Middlemarch*, speaks:

> Not immediately – no. In order to account for that wish I must mention – what it were otherwise needless to refer to – that my life, on all collateral accounts insignificant, derives a possible importance from the incompleteness of labours which have extended through all its best years. In short, I have long had on hand a work which I would fain leave behind me in such a state, at least, that it might be committed to the press by – others.

The style is the man; look how Mr Casaubon piles up the clauses of his sentences, and look how he says something and then stops to qualify what he has said by adding another remark. Even in the last sentence, when he begins by saying 'In short', he is not brief but wordily gropes his way to the end of his sentence. It is clear from those sentences that he is a dry, over-correct and lifeless man.

You will not find every character is as carefully drawn as Mr Casaubon, but you should always look to see if a character speaks in a way which expresses his or her personality. Sometimes it is useful to point to the grammatical features which establish a particular speaking style. Mr Casaubon builds up clauses; other characters might use very short sentences, employ lots of adjectives, or use many personal pronouns that refer to themselves.

## 7.7 THE APPEARANCE OF CHARACTERS

In many novels it is important to ask: what does the author tell us about a character's appearance? It is important to remember that not all novelists do. Dickens clearly enjoys painting verbal pictures of his characters, but Jane Austen is much less concerned about her characters' faces. She tells us, for instance, that Emma is pretty and looks healthy, but there is no hint as to what particular features make her pretty. It is, therefore, worth asking why some novelists create detailed pictures when others do not. If there is a detailed picture, the novelist will be able to control a reader's reactions, but if there is not, the reader may feel invited to use his or her imagination.

Look how D.H. Lawrence presents the central figure of *Sons and Lovers,* Paul Morel:

> Paul was now fourteen, and was looking for work. He was a rather small and finely-made boy, with dark brown hair and light blue eyes. His face had already lost its youthful chubbiness, and was becoming somewhat like William's – rough-featured, almost rugged – and it was extraordinarily mobile. Usually he looked as if he saw things, was full of life, and warm; then his smile, like his mother's, came suddenly and was very loveable; and then, when there was any clog in his soul's quick running, his face went stupid and ugly.

Lawrence tells us a great deal about Paul's appearance; he is 'small', 'finely-made', has 'dark brown hair', 'light blue eyes' and his face is becoming 'rough-featured' and 'rugged'. We are also told about the impression his looks give of his inner life. Throughout the passage Lawrence is directing us to see and feel; we are even told that his smile is loveable. It is worth noticing that physical appearance is rarely described on its own. When an author writes about the appearance of a character, he or she is usually telling or showing the reader something about the inner world of the character's personality. It is not surprising in the Lawrence passage that he goes on from saying that Paul's face was 'mobile' to tell us that he 'was full of life, and warm' – both of which are qualities of the inner self.

## 7.8 HOW CHARACTERS DRESS

Another question to ask about the appearance of a character is: how does the character dress? If the clothes of a character are not mentioned, you may assume that the author does not wish to make a point about them. Some authors, however, make clothes a significant part of a character's personality, important for the atmosphere of the book or essential to the development of the plot. If you look back to the passage from the beginning of *Middlemarch*, you will see that Dorothea Brooke's character emerges from the way in which she wears her clothes. Their plainness not only sets her beauty off, but they are also expressive of her seriousness about life. In Graham Green's novels clothes often contribute to the atmosphere of the books. Greene presents many seedy characters, whose shabby, dirty or old clothes are part of a general atmosphere of corruption, decay and failure. In L.P. Hartley's *The Go-Between* clothes play an essential part in the development of the plot. The central character is Leo Colston, a boy who spends the summer of 1900 with a wealthy school friend. The weather is very hot, and poor Leo is inappropriately dressed in warm, heavy clothes. A photograph records this:

> I am wearing an Eton collar and a bow tie; a Norfolk jacket cut very high across the chest, incised leather buttons, round as bullets, conscientiously done up, and a belt that I have drawn more tightly than I need have. My breeches were secured below the knee with a cloth strap and buckle, but these were hidden by thick black stockings, the garters of which, coming just below the straps, put a double strain on the circulation of my legs.

Leo, we are made to see, is enclosed, almost imprisoned, in his clothes: the jacket is cut very high, his buttons are done up, the belt tightly drawn, the breeches secured with a strap below the knee, and his legs covered with thick black stockings, held in place by garters. His hosts see that he is uncomfortable, and he is taken into Norwich by Marian, the daughter of the house, to be bought something more suitable. The new clothes are lighter and freer, they remind him of Robin Hood, and he claims, though he admits it's not entirely true, that he feels 'quite another person'. The clothes are part of his transformation from a reserved boy to someone who is allowed freedom and is encouraged to indulge in fantasies. That is one of the themes of the book. Because he develops an increasingly high opinion of himself, symbolised by his new clothes, he suffers a terrible reversal of fortune, from which he never recovers.

## 7.9 THE SOCIAL STANDING OF CHARACTERS

Close to the question about clothes is this one: what is the social standing of the character? If an author is interested in the relation between the different classes within society, he or she is likely to stress the social standing of characters. You should remember that not every author is interested in the workings of society, and that those that are will be interested in different societies and will have different attitudes towards them. Dickens, for instance, writes about town society, whereas George Eliot seems to be more interested in the society found in villages or small provincial towns. Dickens is more aware of the faults of society – its unfriendly nature, its pretence, the incompetence of its officials – but George Eliot, though by no means without criticism, appreciates tradition, the sense of belonging, and the way in which many classes tolerate each other. Mrs Gowan in *Little Dorrit* is a nasty blend of snobbery and cynicism. She keeps up the pretence that Mr and Mrs Meagles want their daughter to marry her unpleasant son: 'I know such people will do anything for the honour of such an alliance.' That is not true, and Mrs Gowan's insistence upon it shows that Dickens is aware of how social standing can give rise to dishonesty and deceit.

Quite different is George Eliot's portrait of churchgoing in *Adam Bede*. Church is important because it brings the whole rural community together:

> The women, indeed, usually entered the church at once, and the farmers' wives talked in an undertone to each other . . . Meantime the men lingered outside, and hardly any of them except the singers, who had a humming and fragmentary rehearsal to go through, entered the church until Mr Irwine was in the desk.

George Eliot then writes about the congregation: the blacksmith, the farm labourers, the farmers, the landlord of the inn, the sexton and the Squire. By showing all these characters of different social standing gathering together, she suggests the strong ties and the unity of a country village.

## 7.10 THE NAMES OF CHARACTERS

It is useful to ask: is there anything significant about a character's name? Often the answer will be no, but there are novels in which the names suggest the nature of the characters. Mr Rushworth in *Mansfield Park* is a silly man who rushes about the country and who rushes into the latest ideas. In *1984* the central character is Winston Smith. His name is clearly symbolic. Smith is the commonest surname in England, so the character can be seen as standing for the ordinary man; and Winston is the name borne by the great war leader Winston Churchill. The novel was written in 1948, so the boldness and determination associated with the name Winston would be very much in readers' minds. The name is thus important for the meaning of the novel. Orwell intends readers to see the central character as one who fights tyranny just as Churchill fought it. The terrible irony of the name is that whereas Winston Churchill won, Winston Smith did not.

## 7.11 THE COMPANY OF CHARACTERS

It is worth asking: in what company do characters appear? It is important to appreciate what this question is driving at. It does not matter whether you know that a character is a member of a family or of a larger group such as the workforce of a factory. What matters is how the author presents the character.

An interesting example is Hetty Sorrel from *Adam Bede.* In the early part of the novel we know she is living with the Poysers, but, nevertheless, George Eliot often presents her alone. Later in the novel she leaves home, and the feeling of her isolation grows as we see her lonely wanderings and are shown her thoughts:

> The horror of this cold, and darkness, and solitude - out of all human reach - became greater every long minute: it was almost as if she were dead already, and knew that she was dead, and longed to get back to life again.

Hetty Sorrel appears to be a lonely character because she is frequently shown to be alone, and the most powerful writing about her, of which the above extract is an example, is concerned with her feelings of utter solitude.

## 7.12 WHAT CHARACTERS DO

Finally, you can ask an important question: what do the characters do? The way in which a character is shown as acting or reacting is one of the chief ways in which authors establish personality. An author can make everything a character does important. Even if the action is one that is normally thought of as slight, it can be made significant. Jane Austen is particularly skilful in showing how everyday events can express the moral standing of characters. Mary Crawford's habit of riding the horse usually reserved for Fanny Price shows that she is selfish. At another point in *Mansfield Park,* Mrs Norris's character is revealed through her insistence that she must have a spare room in her house and therefore can't accommodate Fanny. Sometimes, however, the action that reveals what a character is like is dramatic. Jane Eyre has to decide whether to live with a man whom she cannot marry, Hetty Sorrel must cope with an illegitimate child, and Winston Smith must revolt against the state.

You must be prepared to find some characters' actions to be complex, because not every character reacts in the same way throughout the novel. In the case of such characters you must look at everything they do and balance one action against another. Authors sometimes want to show tensions within characters and therefore show them acting in contrary ways. Thus Tess in *Tess of the D'Urbervilles* is sometimes passive and sometimes forceful. She gives in to Alec's desire to kiss her and eventually agrees to marry Angel, yet she angrily shouts at the vicar who will not bury her child, strikes Alec, and, at the end, murders him. Although characters in books are not real people, they can be as puzzling. Therefore, you should be prepared to find their actions problematic.

## EXERCISES

1 Write about the characters in the novels you are studying in terms of their range. You may ask whether some are fuller than others and question why the author has made them this way.

2 Look through the questions that have been set out in the second part of this section and see how many of them are helpful in showing you what the characters in your books are like.

3 Read the following extract from Jane Austen's *Pride and Prejudice* and answer the questions on it. Mr Collins is a clergyman who is visiting the Bennet family.

> Mr Collins was not a sensible man, and the deficiency of Nature had been but little assisted by education or society; the greatest part of his life having been spent under the guidance of an illiterate and miserly father; and though he belonged to one of the universities, he had merely kept the necessary terms, without forming at it any useful acquaintance. The subjection in which his father had brought him up had given him originally great humility of manner, but it was now a good deal counteracted by the self-conceit of a weak head, living in retirement, and the consequential feelings of early and unexpected prosperity. A fortunate chance had recommended him to Lady Catherine de Bourgh when the living of Hunsford was vacant; and the respect which he felt for her high rank, and his veneration for her as his patroness, mingling with a very good opinion of himself, of his authority as a clergyman, and his rights as a rector, made him altogether a mixture of pride and obsequiousness, self-importance and humility.
>
> Having now a good house and very sufficient income, he intended to marry; and in seeking a reconciliation with the Longbourn family he had a wife in view, as he meant to choose one of the daughters, if he found them as handsome and amiable as they were represented by common report. This was his plan of amends – of atonement – for inheriting their father's estate; and he thought it an excellent one, full of eligibility and suitableness, and excessively generous and disinterested on his own part.

(a) What is the effect of Jane Austen directly telling the reader that Mr Collins 'was not a sensible man'?

(b) How does what we are told about Mr Collins's background – his family, university, and position as vicar of Hunsford – help us to understand him?

(c) Write about the way in which Jane Austen is interested in his character rather than his appearance.

(d) What is your judgement of Mr Collins?

4 Read the following extract, which is the opening of Hardy's *Far From the Madding Crowd.*

When Farmer Oak smiled, the corners of his mouth spread till they were within an unimportant distance of his ears, his eyes were reduced to chinks, and diverging wrinkles appeared round them extending upon his countenance like the rays in a rudimentary sketch of the rising sun.

His Christian name was Gabriel, and on working days he was a young man of sound judgement, easy motions, proper dress, and general good character. On Sundays he was a man of misty views, rather given to postponing, and hampered by his best clothes and umbrella: upon the whole, one who felt himself to occupy morally that vast middle space of Laodicean neutrality which lay between the Communion people of the parish and the drunken section – that is, he went to church, but yawned privately by the time the congregation reached the Nicene creed, and thought of what there would be for dinner when he meant to be listening to the sermon. Or, to state his character as it stood in the scale of public opinion, when his friends and critics were in tantrums, he was considered rather a bad man; when they were pleased, he was rather a good man; when they were neither, he was a man whose moral colour was a kind of pepper-and-salt mixture.

Since he lived six times as many working days as Sundays, Oak's appearance in his old clothes was most peculiarly his own – the mental picture formed by his neighbours in imagining him being always dressed in that way. He wore a low-crowned felt hat, spread out at the base by tight jamming upon the head for security in high winds, and a coat like Dr. Johnson's; his lower extremities being encased in ordinary leather leggings and boots emphatically large, affording to each foot a roomy apartment so constructed that any wearer might stand in a river all day long and know nothing of damp – their maker being a conscientious man who endeavoured to compensate for any weakness in his cut by unstinted dimension and solidity.

(a) What do you think is the significance of the name Gabriel Oak?

(b) What is the effect upon the reader of Hardy introducing Gabriel Oak's smile first?

(c) Write about the importance of clothes in the passage.

(d) What effects and expectations does Hardy create by the way in which he writes about Gabriel Oak in relation to church and 'public opinion'?

# CHAPTER 8

# SETTING

## 8.1 THE IMPORTANCE OF SETTING

A good question to ask about any book is: what do I remember? Sometimes you will find that what the characters said and did sticks in your mind, but you may also find that what you recall is a scene. Of course, when you remember a character, you may find that you cannot separate him or her from their scenes. It may be that you retain a vivid picture of someone in the countryside, or a group of people in a town. You may also have an impression of the atmosphere, mood or feel of the book. If you think about that impression, you will find that it is partly made up of scenes presenting, for instance, the weather, a town, the countryside or the inside of a house.

When you recall scenes in a novel, or remember an impression of the atmosphere, mood or feel, you will be thinking about what this section calls setting. Novels don't just consist of dialogue, or actions and insights into characters' minds; most authors set these against a background of scenes, and these scenes combine to create the atmosphere, mood or feel of the book. 'Setting', you will realise, is a broad word. It covers the places in which characters are presented; the social context of characters, such as their families, friends and class; the customs, beliefs and rules of behaviour of their society; the scenes that are the background or the situation for the events of the novel; and the total atmosphere, mood or feel that is created by these. All of them are examples of setting. Thus, you may find yourself having to talk about, for instance, the social setting of a novel, or the way in which landscape is used as a setting within the book.

When you study a novel, you should pay attention to setting, because it can make a contribution to the book. A successful setting is one which is appropriate to the section of the novel in which it appears and also, possibly, to the book as a whole. When you read a novel, you can ask the following questions about the way the author handles the setting. What does the setting reveal about the mood and emotions of the characters? What does the setting reveal about the situation of the characters? What does the setting reveal about the personality of the characters? What does the setting reveal about the theme of the book? Let us ask these questions of books that regularly appear on examination syllabuses.

## 8.2 SETTING AND THE MOOD OF CHARACTERS

In *Tess of the D'Urbervilles* Hardy makes the landscape and the seasons appropriate to the mood of Tess. Not only are the scenes through which she moves striking in themselves, they also reveal a great deal about her feelings.

The section of the novel called 'The Rally' deals with her attempts to overcome the disasters of her earlier life. The opening words of the section establish the mood of the season:

> On a thyme-scented, bird hatching morning in May, between two and three years after the return from Tantridge – silent reconstructive years for Tess Durbeyfield – she left her home for the second time.

These words are full of hope; there are sweet smells in the air, and new life is appearing. The words have a steady rhythm (you can scan them like poetry – 'Ŏn ă thýme-scĕntĕd, bírd hătchĭng mórnĭng ĭn Máy') that carries the reader on in hopeful expectation. But the words are not just about the newness of life in the spring, for the new life reflects Tess's new start. She has spent 'silent reconstructive years' and now she has launched herself once again into life. A few paragraphs later Hardy makes it clear that we should see a relation between the season and Tess's mood:

> The irresistible, universal, automatic tendency to find sweet pleasure somewhere, which pervades all life, from the meanest to the highest, had at length mastered Tess.

The desire to find pleasure runs through the whole of nature; it's there in natural things, and now it has mastered Tess. That is Hardy's reason for the relation between her mood and the month of May.

But that is not the only time in the novel when the mood of Tess is reflected in the setting. Tess does find 'sweet pleasure' during the summer she works as a dairy-maid at Talbothays. There she meets Angel Clare. Hardy shows how they gradually come to love each other by placing them in appropriate settings. At one point they meet early in the morning: 'They met daily in that strange and solemn interval, the twilight of the morning, in the pink and violet dawn . . .' The 'strange and solemn interval' is not only Hardy's way of telling the reader when they met, it is also his way of indicating the growth of their love. For them, love, like the sun, has not fully dawned. They are in a strange, and wonderful, interval between the first light of affection and the full beams of love.

As the summer unfolds, their love matures. Setting matches mood. One chapter begins:

> Amid the oozing fatness and warm ferments of the Var Vale, at a season when the rush of juices could almost be heard below the hiss of fertilization, it was impossible that the most fanciful love should not grow passionate.

These words make clear the relation between setting and events. The seasons and the landscape are not pleasant, incidental decorations of the novel, they shape and reflect the feelings of the characters; as the juices of the season flow, love grows passionate. It is not surprising that, by the end of the chapter, Angel Clare has openly declared to Tess that he loves her.

Angel courts Tess throughout the summer and autumn, eventually marrying her in December. On their wedding night he learns of her past and deserts her. From this point onwards both the weather and the landscape reflect Tess's sad mood; not only has Angel rejected her, but the whole of Nature seems to turn against her.

From the lush, fertile valley of the Great Dairies, where Angel courted her, Tess, in order to find work during a harsh winter, has to go to the bare hillsides of Flintcombe Ash. The name indicates the type of place it is – life there is as hard as flint, and nothing is left of pleasure but ashes. Hardy says of Flintcombe Ash that it is 'uncared for either by itself or its Lord', and we see that in this it reflects Tess who is no longer cared for by her lord – her husband, Angel. The weather is also pictured as harsh and uncaring:

> Each leaf of the vegetable having already been consumed, the whole field was in colour a desolate drab; it was a complexion without a feature, as if a face, from chin to brow, should be only an expanse of skin. The sky wore, in another colour, the same likeness; a white vacuity of countenance with the lineaments gone.

Here the landscape reflects not only Tess's mood but also her situation. The drabness of the scene reflects the drabness of her world without love, and the anonymous nature of the land (there is something very disturbing about a face that only consists of skin) is Hardy's way of showing us that nobody is taking an interest in Tess – to the world she is faceless and anonymous.

## 8.3 SETTING AND THE SITUATION OF CHARACTERS

The scenes at Flintcombe Ash are examples of setting showing the situation of a character. (The fact that it also shows mood proves that a scene can have more than one function.) Dickens, like Hardy, uses setting to show how a character is situated. In *Hard Times* the factory worker, Stephen Blackpool, dies by falling down a disused mine shaft. The way he dies reflects his situation as a worker in a hard and unfeeling industrial society. Dickens shows how a society in which everything is calculated and run for profit is, to put it simply, a death-trap for its members. This is the moment when two women discover what has happened to Stephen: 'Before them, at their very feet, was the brink of a black ragged chasm hidden by the thick grass.' The mine (it has the dramatic name of 'the Old Hell Shaft') is a symbol of industrial society. Both are black ragged chasms that are ready to swallow up their victims, and both are dangerous because their danger is hidden from view.

In *Great Expectations* Dickens also uses landscape to bring over the situation of Pip. In the third paragraph of the novel Pip realises who he is and how he is placed in the world. The bleakness of the landscape appropriately accompanies this realisation:

> . . . that dark flat wilderness beyond the churchyard, intersected with dykes and mounds and gates, with scattered cattle feeding on it, was the marshes; and that the low leaden line beyond was the river; and that the distant savage lair from which the wind was rushing, was the sea; and that the small bundle of shivers growing afraid of it all and beginning to cry, was Pip.

The setting of the dark and oppressive landscape shows that Pip is a lonely and frightened child in a hostile world; the wilderness is 'dark' and 'flat', the sky 'low' and 'leaden', and the wind rushes at him from the 'distant savage lair' of the sea. Soon characters rush at Pip. He meets the convict who frightens him with ghastly threats, and then he returns home to meet his equally hostile sister.

## 8.4 SETTING AND THE PERSONALITY OF CHARACTERS

Settings can reveal the personality of characters. One of the features of *Jane Eyre* is that two men propose marriage to the heroine. One of the men, Mr Rochester, is loved deeply by Jane; the other, Mr Rivers, is admired but hardly loved in a romantic way. The settings in which the proposals occur reveal a great deal about Jane's impressions of these two men. Mr Rochester proposes in an orchard on a warm summer eveing:

> No nook in the grounds more sheltered and more Eden-like; a very high wall shut it out from the court on one side; on the other a beech avenue screened it from the lawn. At the bottom was a sunk fence, its sole separation from the lovely fields: a winding walk, bordered with laurels and terminating in a giant horse-chestnut, circled at the base by the seat, led down to the fence. Here one could wander unseen. While such honeydew fell, such silence reigned, such gloaming gathered, I felt as if I could haunt such shade for ever.

The landscape reflects what Jane (and therefore, to some extent, the reader) feels about Mr Rochester. She sees him as a romantic, mysterious, larger than life figure, who is quite unlike the ordinary run of people. Hence the setting: it is cut off from the world in romantic isolation – she even compares it to the Garden of Eden! Here, with Mr Rochester, Jane feels she 'could haunt such shade for ever'.

But her view of Mr Rivers is very different; he is a man driven by a strong sense of duty, so will not allow himself to enjoy pleasures. Jane feels admiration, even awe, for his dedication to missionary work, but she finds him cold and aloof. There is a great contrast between the secluded, Eden-like orchard of Mr Rochester's proposal and the bleak, open moorland which Mr Rivers chooses for his offer of marriage. One detail of this setting is very important: 'we reached the first stragglers of the battalion of rocks, guarding a sort of pass, beyond which the beck rushed down a waterfall'. The landscape is spoken of in military terms – 'battalion', 'guarding a . . . pass' – with the river ('the beck') rushing as a waterfall. Military discipline, and cold water falling over hard rock: those are images that reveal Mr Rivers's personality. He is a man of iron self-discipline, and, like the waterfall, he is cold and hard. Further on Jane says he has 'no more of a husband's heart for me than that frowning giant of a rock, down which the stream is foaming in yonder gorge'. That makes it clear: Jane feels that Rivers is as hard as the rocks of the moor. The setting, in short, brings out what she feels he is like.

The questions that have just been answered are all about the relation between character and setting. As you may well have to answer such questions in public examinations, it is useful to think about how you should write about this relation. The first thing you should do is draw out the similarities between the setting and the character. If you can do this by drawing attention to particular words, your writing will be all the more impressive. For instance, the word 'brink' in the passage from *Hard Times* is crucial for the links between character and setting. The brink refers to the edge of the Old Hell shaft, but it also points to the 'brink' between life and death, and to the brink of disaster upon which the whole of industrial society is teetering. Stephen has plunged down it, but all people, metaphorically speaking, could plunge to their death down the pit of industrial chaos. The second thing you must do is to master words that will express the relation between character and setting. Setting could be said to reflect, represent, echo, picture or reveal character. Sometimes you can use words introduced in the poetry section by writing of how the setting is a mental landscape, an image or symbol. In using such words you will be showing that you understand that the setting has a function in relation to character.

## 8.5 SETTING AND THEME: THE AUTHOR'S VIEW

To ask whether the setting reveals anything about the theme of a book is to pose a slightly different question. You are not concerned with one scene but with how a particular setting, or series of settings, points to the theme of the novel. There are three ways in which the settings of a book can reveal something about the book as a whole: setting can reveal the author's view of the world, it can help to establish a distinctive world, and it can be the main source of interest in the book. Let us look at examples of all these.

There are some novelists who create settings for the purpose of giving their views about the world. Such a novelist creates landscapes, townscapes, interiors of houses and the weather in order to convey his or her particular feelings and views about life. A reader can look at these and see, to put it simply, what the author thinks about things. Graham Greene is an example. Not only do many of his novels establish a similar atmosphere through their settings, but this atmosphere reveals how Greene views the world. For Greene the world is a corrupt, seedy and oppressive place, hence his novels are full of rotting houses, dirty towns, stiflingly hot weather, dry, lifeless landscapes and grimy interiors. So distinctive are the settings of his novels that a word has been coined to characterise them – Greeneland. No matter whether the setting is England, as in *Brighton Rock*, Africa, as in *The Heart of the Matter*, or Latin America, as in *The Power and the Glory*, an atmosphere of seedy corruption prevails.

But for Greene this is not just atmosphere; the settings show us something. Greene is showing us that ours is a fallen world; that is, a world which is not at peace with its maker, God, and so is given over to corruption. The settings of his novels, then, present his religious view of the world. He fills his novels with seedy settings as a way of showing that the world has been cut adrift from God. People left to themselves will lead squalid lives is the basic point in Greene's novels; this is borne out in the settings.

There is a scene in *Brighton Rock* in which Pinkie marries Rose in order to prevent her from giving evidence against him. Both are catholics but they go to the registry office. Greene uses a civil wedding to show how squalid people can be when they fail to recognise God. This is evident in the setting. Here are two passages:

> In the great institutional hall from which the corridors led off to deaths and births there was a smell of disinfectant. The walls were tiled like a public lavatory. . . They sat down. A mop leant in a corner against a tiled wall. The footsteps of a clerk squealed on the icy paving down another passage. Presently a big brown door opened; they saw a row of clerks inside who didn't look up; a man and wife came out into the corridor. A woman followed them and took the mop.

Greene intends us to find these scenes very unpleasant. The setting shows us the squalid lives of people cut off from God. In such a world marriage is simply a civil arrangement carried out by council employees – 'a row of clerks inside who didn't look up'. Greene makes the scene seedy and corrupt by including details such as 'a smell of disinfectant', 'the walls . . . tiled like a public lavatory' and the mop leaning against the wall.

In that scene we have to make the link between the nastiness of the setting and the world adrift from God. Sometimes, though, Greene makes the connection clear. In *The Power and the Glory* he frequently uses the word 'abandoned' to sum up the condition of the world, and at one point – in an overcrowded jail – the priest realises that 'this place was very like the world: overcrowded with lust and crime and unhappy love, it stank to heaven . . .' That could be said of many of Greene's settings: as images of corruption they show his belief that the world is cut off from God.

You should not think that because Greene uses his settings to express a religious view of the world, other authors will do the same. Many of them use settings to give their views, but these views are not religious ones. For instance, in Conrad's *The Heart of Darkness* the journey up an African river is expressive of his dark and pessimistic view of man; the oppressive heat, the huge tracts of jungle, and the squalid trading outposts create an overwhelming sense of evil. For Conrad, the world is a forbidding place, and to understand it properly is to take a journey into the heart of darkness.

## 8.6 SETTING AND THEME: DISTINCTIVE WORLDS

Whilst Greene presents his view of Brighton and Conrad his view of Africa, there are some authors who create an entirely new world to express their views. Two novelists who do this – Aldous Huxley and George Orwell – are regularly set in public examinations. In *Brave New World* and *1984* we find distinctive worlds that have been specially created to reflect what the authors think about human life. In both these books the authors express their fears that people are losing their humanity because of political and scientific changes. If the word 'setting' is interpreted very widely, it could be said that the settings are more important than the stories.

What is memorable about *1984* is the setting. It is a world in which the state controls everything, even the thoughts inside people's heads. The effect of this, Orwell shows, is that all that we look upon as good is destroyed. This is evident in the setting. Everywhere there are terraces of rotting, nineteenth-century houses, which smell nauseously of cheap cooking; the wind carries dust from waste sites, and near the terrifying ministries – great buildings that dominate the skyline – there are mazes of barbed wire and machine gun nests. The language characters speak – it is called newspeak – is so narrow, inflexible and basic that most of the things that matter – beliefs, emotions, ideals – cannot be said in it. Everybody dresses in the same drab clothes, drinks revolting gin, and goes in fear of their children, who are likely to betray them to the authorities. Once someone falls into the hands of state, unspeakable torture is used to make the person conform. Taken together these create a distinctive world, which is the expression of Orwell's fear that what makes people human is being deliberately destroyed.

Huxley's *Brave New World* expresses the fear that science, and the way of thinking that goes with it, will make people less than human. The settings of his novel are an expression of that: babies are made in bottles, people are deliberately bred with specific levels of intelligence and then conditioned so they will be content, nobody ages, nobody forms lasting relationships, and if there is worry or anxiety, it is banished by the use of a drug called soma. It is this distinctive world, created by a number of scenes, that most readers find memorable. That is what Huxley intended: the settings make a complete world, and that world can be said to be the central theme of the book.

## 8.7 SETTING AND THEME: THE CENTRAL FEATURE

*1984* and *Brave New World* do have stories, though they are less interesting than the settings, but some books that are set in public examinations, particularly at 'O' level, are virtually all setting. That is to say, what is important about the book is the mood or atmosphere that the settings create. Quite often the atmosphere is of a particular time and place. Flora Thompson's *Lark Rise* is about growing up in a north Oxfordshire village in the 1890s. Two other very popular books are Laurie Lee's *Cider with Rosie* and Gerald Durrell's *My Family and Other Animals.* Both of these focus on the feeling of being alive at a particular time in a particular place: in *Cider with Rosie* it is the world of the child in deeply rural England during and just after the First World War, and *My Family and Other Animals* is concerned with what it is like to grow up in a remarkable family on the exotic Greek island of Corfu.

If you have to study these books, you will find that whilst there are memorable incidents – Laurie's first day at school, or the drive through Corfu chased by dogs – what you will probably remember is the mood of the settings. These books are more like a series of beautiful pictures than stories. Indeed, it would not be foolish to say that they are almost entirely setting. Here is a passage from *Cider with Rosie* about summer; from his bedroom window Laurie is watching the lake:

> Then suddenly the whole picture would break into pieces, would be smashed like a molten mirror and run amok in tiny globules of gold, frantic and shivering; and I would hear the great slapping of wings on water, building up a steady crescendo, while across the ceiling passed the shadows of swans taking off into the heavy morning. I would hear the cries pass over the house and watch the chaos of light above me, till it slowly settled and re-collected its stars and resumed the lake's still image.
>
> Watching swans take off from my bedroom window was a regular summer awakening. So I woke and looked out through the open window to a morning of crows and cockerels. The beech trees framing the lake and valley seemed to call for a Royal Hunt; but they served equally well for climbing into, and even in June you could still eat their leaves, a tight-folded salad of juices.

What Laurie Lee is interested in here is the setting. He looks at the reflections on the ceiling, listens to the noises of the swans, gazes at the beech trees and thinks about how he climbed into them and even ate their juicy leaves. He uses words to convey the experience of looking and hearing. Hence the careful way he talks about 'a molten mirror', 'tiny globules of gold', 'the great slapping of wings' and 'the lake's still image'. He even talks about what he sees as a picture; the reflection of the lake on his ceiling is called 'the whole picture', and the beech trees are said to be 'framing' the lake. The passage is typical of the book; the sights and scenes of the countryside are what interests the author.

You should write about how settings express the themes of books in ways similar to those outlined above for writing about the relation between character and setting; that is, show how the theme is evident in settings by looking at the words, and then writing about the relation between the two in an appropriate way. In order to do this, you will need to locate passages. Therefore, when you read you should look out for passages in which the setting expresses the book's theme. In doing this you will be acting upon the basic piece of advice this section offers – settings are not incidental but a significant part of the novel as a whole.

**EXERCISES**

1 Look at the novels you are studying to see if there are any occasions when the settings reveal something about a character's mood, situation or personality. If there are, try to write in detail about those passages.
2 Look at the novels you are studying to see if any of the settings reveal the theme of the book. If you can find some, try to write in detail about how they do this.
3 Read the following passage from George Eliot's *Adam Bede*, and answer the questions below.

Captain Donnithorne is visiting the dairy at the Old Hall Farm; there he meets Hetty Sorrel. A 'calenture' is an hallucination.

> The dairy was certainly worth looking at: it was a scene to sicken for with a sort of calenture in hot and dusty streets – such coolness, such purity, such fresh fragrance of new-pressed cheese, of firm butter, of wooden vessels perpetually bathed in pure water; such soft colouring of red earthenware and creamy surfaces, brown wood and polished tin, grey limestone and rich orange-red rust on the iron weights and hooks and hinges. But one gets only a confused notion of these details when they surround a distractingly pretty girl of seventeen, standing on little pattens and rounding her dimpled arm to lift a pound of butter out of the scale.
>
> Hetty blushed a deep rose-colour when Captain Donnithorne entered the dairy and spoke to her; but it was not at all a distressed blush, for it was inwreathed with smiles and dimples, and with sparkles from under long curled dark eyelashes; and while her aunt was discoursing to him about the limited amount of milk that was to be spared for butter and cheese so long as the calves were not all weaned, and the large quantity but inferior quality of milk yielded by the short-horn, which had been bought on experiment, together with other matters which must be interesting to a young gentleman who would one day be a landlord, Hetty tossed and patted her pound of butter with quite a self-possessed, coquettish air, slily conscious that no turn of her head was lost.

(a) George Eliot is trying to create a special atmosphere in the opening paragraph. What is it, and what words does she use?

(b) George Eliot speaks of 'these details' surrounding Hetty. What is she trying to tell us about Hetty by placing her in this setting?

(c) Is Hetty's behaviour in the second paragraph in accordance with what was suggested about her in the first?

(d) This is the first time Hetty Sorrel has been introduced: what do we expect from her in the rest of the novel, and what role does the setting play in our expectations?

**4** Read the following passage from Dickens's *Little Dorrit*, and answer the questions below.

Arthur Clennam has returned to London, the scene of his childhood, after being abroad for many years. It is Sunday.

> At such a happy time, so propitious to the interests of religion and morality, Mr. Arthur Clennam, newly arrived from Marseilles by way of Dover, and by Dover coach the Blue-eyed Maid, sat in the window of a coffee-house on Ludgate Hill. Ten thousand responsible houses surrounded him, frowning as heavily on the streets they composed, as if they were every one inhabited by the ten young men of the Calender's story, who blackened their faces and bemoaned their miseries every night. Fifty thousand lairs surrounded him where people lived so unwholesomely that fair water put into their crowded rooms on Saturday night, would be corrupt on Sunday morning; albeit my lord, their county member, was amazed that they failed to sleep in company with their butcher's meat. Miles of close wells and pits of houses, where the inhabitants gasped for air, stretched far away towards every point of the compass. Through the heart of the town a deadly sewer ebbed and flowed, in the place of a fine fresh river. What secular want could the million or so of human beings whose daily labour, six days in the week, lay among these Arcadian objects, from the sweet sameness of which they had no escape between the cradle and the grave – what secular want could they possibly have upon their seventh day? Clearly they could want nothing but a stringent policeman.
>
> Mr. Arthur Clennam sat in the window of the coffee-house on Ludgate Hill, counting one of the neighbouring bells, making sentences and burdens of songs out of it in spite of himself, and wondering how many sick people it might be the death of in the course of the year. As the hour approached, its changes of measure made it more and more exasperating. At the quarter, it went off into a condition of deadly-lively importunity, urging the populace in a voluble manner to Come to church, Come to church, Come to church! At the ten minutes, it became aware that the congregation would be scanty, and slowly hammered out in low spirits, They *won't* come, they *won't* come, they *won't* come! At the five minutes, it abandoned hope, and shook every house in the neighbourhood for three hundred seconds, with one dismal swing per second, as a groan of despair.

'Thank Heaven!' said Clennam, when the hour struck, and the bell stopped.

But its sound had revived a long train of miserable Sundays, and the procession would not stop with the bell, but continued to march on. 'Heaven forgive me,' said he, 'and those who trained me. How I have hated this day!'

(a) What impression of London is created by the first paragraph?

(b) Do phrases such as 'frowning as heavily' and 'the inhabitants gasped for air' suggest anything about the mind of Arthur Clennam?

(c) In the second paragraph Arthur Clennam thinks of 'sick people'; does this reveal anything about his feelings?

(d) From this passage, can you see how Dickens is going to treat life in London in the rest of the novel?

# CHAPTER 9

# PLOT AND STORY

## 9.1 EXPECTATION, INTEREST, SURPRISE AND RELIEF

You must never forget that the enjoyment of a good story is one of the basic pleasures of literature. This goes for both ordinary readers and examination candidates. There is, however, a difference between these two sets of people; all ordinary readers need to do is express the fact that they enjoyed the book, whereas candidates need to say *why*. (This is not to say, of course, that ordinary readers wouldn't gain more enjoyment if they did ask themselves why; in all probability, they would.) In order to write about why a story is enjoyable you will need to master some terms. They are: expectation, interest, surprise and relief.

Expectation occurs when an author leads you to think that some particular thing is going to happen. An author shows you something about a character and then places him or her in a situation in which certain things could happen. You will know that an author is leading you to expect something if you find yourself asking: I wonder what she will do, or I wonder if that is going to happen to him? Expectation is exciting and can create tension in the reader, because he or she will want to know whether what is expected will take place.

For example, Jane Austen's *Pride and Prejudice* is about marriage. In the early chapters Jane Bennet falls in love with Mr Bingley. Some expectation is created, because we anticipate that they will marry. However, her sister, Elizabeth, arouses much more expectation in us. In the third chapter a ball is held at which Elizabeth meets Bingley's friend, the proud and aloof Mr Darcy. Bingley tries to persuade him to dance with Elizabeth, but in her hearing he replies:

> She is tolerable, but not handsome enough to tempt *me*; and I am in no humour at present to give consequence to young ladies who are slighted by other men. You had better run to your partner and enjoy her smiles, for you are wasting your time with me.

That remark, not surprisingly, prejudices Elizabeth against him; it is an insult to be called 'tolerable'. Yet the reader is left wondering. Why does Jane Austen bring the two together in this dramatic way? Why does she make Mr Darcy speak so rudely and Elizabeth react so strongly? After all, isn't her witty, playful intelligence an interesting contrast to his silent and moody personality? In other words, expectations are aroused, and those expectations make the story enjoyable.

Expectation, you must remember, is created by the author and recognised by the reader. Therefore, when you write about it you should frequently refer to both. You should write about how an author raises expectations in a reader by, for instance, the use of conversation (as in that passage from *Pride and Prejudice*), setting, access to private thought and the placing of events. It is wrong to write, as some examination candidates do: 'There is a lot of expectation in this novel'. It is much better to write: 'The author arouses expectation in the reader . . .'

You can't have expectations about characters unless you are interested in them. Here, 'interest' means any way in which you respond to a character; it could be loathing, tenderness, pity or frustration. The only thing the word 'interest' rules out is indifference. Interest, in other words, covers feelings of approval and disapproval, liking and not liking, hatred and love. If you are interested in a character, you are concerned about what happens to him or her.

You may remember that in the section on character it was said that characters in books differ from people in real life. Nothing that has been said about interest denies that. You can only be interested in a character in the way in which the author allows you to be, and that, of course, depends upon how the character has been created. Look how Dickens directs our interest in this passage from *David Copperfield*:

> . . . I met Uriah in the street, who reminded me of the promise I had made to take tea with himself and his mother: adding, with a writhe, 'But I didn't expect you to keep it Master Copperfield, we're so very umble.'
>
> I really had not yet been able to make up my mind whether I liked Uriah or detested him; and I was very doubtful about it still, as I stood looking him in the face in the street. But I felt it quite an affront to be supposed proud, and I said I only wanted to be asked.

David says he does not know what he feels about Uriah. That is Dickens's way of directing us towards him. We are interested in the indecision. But it may be that we have already decided what to think. Look at the way Uriah writhes as he speaks and the way he openly claims to be 'umble'. We might recoil from him because he seems devious and falsely modest. But such reaction is, of course, a way of showing interest, and it has been directed by Dickens's writing.

Sometimes the characters in whom we are interested do not do what we expect; the result is surprise. Other things in a story may surprise us. There may be an unexpected event, or the appearance of a new character. Once we are surprised, we will alter our attitude to the characters and our expectations of the story. Not every story contains surprise, but when it does occur, it is often enjoyable because it forces us to think again about what we are reading. For instance, most readers of *Middlemarch* are surprised by the disclosure that the upright, puritanical banker, Bulstrode, is a man with a shady past. As soon as we discover this (it is done through the introduction of a new character), our attitude to him changes, as do our expectations of the novel. We wonder whether he will succeed in concealing the matter, and if he does not, how he will handle his guilt and public disgrace.

You may find that surprise presents you with the problem of whether or not you can believe what has happened. This is not a matter upon which it is easy to offer guidance, but you might bear the following points in mind. There are some novels in which surprising events take place, and you are supposed to accept them because they are crucial to the plot of the novel. Most readers of *Hard Times* are surprised that Mr Bounderby proposes to the young Louisa, and even more surprised that she accepts him. It should, however, be accepted because it creates a new set of problems which are central to the development of the novel. Moreover, Dickens does not invite the reader to question the characters' motives because he reveals very little of their inner thoughts about the matter. It is also worth remembering that different readers are bound to have different ideas on what cannot be believed. Some readers, for instance, find Angel Clare's rejection of Tess not only cruel but incredible, whilst others feel that it is the sort of thing somebody from Angel's background might do. The point you should remember is that surprises in novels can be difficult, and that, therefore, you should reflect this in your writing. It is a good idea to say that the behaviour of a character is both surprising and difficult to believe in. You can then review the arguments for and against accepting the behaviour as credible, but if, after that, you are still uncertain, you should say so. Some things in books are problematic, and nothing is to be gained from pretending that they are not. In many cases the most you can do is explore the problems honestly.

If expectation holds your interest, it is because you wish to be relieved from the tensions it creates. Relief is the relaxing of tension that you experience when you discover the outcome of the story. It is a simple and basic experience. You wanted to know something and now you do; you feared something and now you either know it has happened or not; you hoped for something to happen and now you have either been satisfied or disappointed. In all these cases you experience relief. And remember:

relief occurs whether the outcome is sad or not. One of its simplest forms is the discovery of what happens to a character. For instance, throughout *Oliver Twist* Oliver has only had his innocence to defend him from wicked characters. At the end of the novel it is discovered that he is not, after all, an orphan but has a family to care for him. Relief comes when the reader realises that Oliver will no longer be exposed to evil characters.

## 9.2 PLOTS AND CAUSES

So far, only stories have been discussed; what about plot? What is it that makes a plot different from a story? The most satisfactory answer is that a plot is concerned with causes – with the 'whys' of events – whereas a story is simply a sequence. From the reader's point of view, a plot is different from a story because it invites and answers the question as to *why* one event follows another. E.M. Forster put the point very clearly in *Aspects of the Novel* when he said that a story was 'the King died and then the Queen died' whereas a plot was 'the King died and then the Queen died *of grief*'. That '*of grief*' makes all the difference, because a reason is given for what has happened; we know *why* one event has followed another.

If, therefore, you want to think about the plot of a novel, you must ask the question: why have these events happened? If you find that too general, you can make it more specific by building into the question the recognition that plots exist in time. The following questions could then be put. Why did those things happen in the past? Why are these things happening now? What things are going to happen in the future and why will they happen? If you write about plots in the light of these questions, you will be making it clear that they are built upon causes.

It is very important to make clear in your writing that you understand about the causes of plots. Consider how the bad and the good candidate would write about the plot of *Hard Times*.

> Mr Gradgrind is a hard but well meaning man who has very strong ideas about bringing up his children. But by the end of the novel his daughter's marriage has failed and his son has become a thief. Mr Gradgrind ends the novel as a sad and disappointed man.

> Dickens presents Mr Gradgrind as a hard but well meaning man who has very strong ideas about the upbringing of his children. But these ideas prove to be disastrous, with the result that his daughter's marriage fails, and his son becomes a thief. These failures make Mr Gradgrind a sad and disappointed man at the end of the novel.

The differences between the bad and good candidate are that one does not see the events as a plot, whereas the other recognises that Mr Gradgrind's views are the *cause* of his children's unhappiness, and that their unhappiness brings him misery.

There are, of course, many different kinds of cause in the plots of novels. (This should warn you not to assume that you can understand the plot until it is well under way.) Nevertheless, there are two causes which occur in many novels: past events shape future ones, and characters aim to achieve things. It is a good idea to look at these very common causes in more detail.

## 9.3 PLOTS AND PAST EVENTS

Nobody can change the past. What's done is done. Those two statements express what some novelists show – that characters can't escape from the past, be the past what they have done themselves or what other people have done. The plot of Hardy's *The Mayor of Casterbridge* can be summed up very simply as the failure of a man to live down his past. At the beginning of the novel Henchard gets drunk and in a grotesque auction sells his wife. As soon as he realises what he has done, he tries to find her, but when he fails to do so, he vows not to drink for twenty years and to lead a better life. These events happen in the first two chapters. Chapter three shows that many years have passed, and Henchard is Mayor of Casterbridge – but then his wife returns. The rest of the novel is the record of his doomed attempts to escape from his past. He suffers disappointment and failure, usually as a consequence of his one foolish deed – the selling of his wife. Hardy shows that characters act the way they do because of the influence of past events.

The weight of past events is not quite so heavy in Lawrence's *Sons and Lovers*, but, nevertheless, much of what happens later to the central character, Paul Morel, results from the unhappy marriage of his parents. When the romance of marriage has faded, Mrs Morel seeks her emotional companionship in her sons and not her husband. At first, William, the eldest son, is the object of her affection, but after his death she turns to Paul. Lawrence shows that the failure of his parents' marriage has a deep effect upon Paul. His relation with Miriam and Clara are blighted by his mother, who resents him loving anybody but her. The past that affects him is not a specific event, as in *The Mayor of Casterbridge*, but a failed relationship.

## 9.4 PLOTS AND THE AIMS OF CHARACTERS

When we read of characters who aim to do things, it is easy to see that what they hope to achieve will be a cause of the plot. No matter how different novels are in setting and tone, many of them share the common factor of a central character who attempts to achieve something. For instance, Jocelin, the Dean of the Cathedral in William Golding's *The Spire* wants to beautify the building by erecting a spire; Howard Kirk, the sociology lecturer, who is the central character of Malcolm Bradbury's *The History Man*, wants more power and influence; and the hero of Sir Walter Scott's *Ivanhoe* wants to win back the affection of his father and his place in society.

You should be prepared to think about the aims of a character in a broad way. Jane Austen's *Emma* links the aims of the heroine to the more important, and unconscious, aim of self-knowledge. Emma, in her attempt to find suitable marriage partners for her friends, persuades, prompts and plans, but her efforts are all unsuccessful. The reader sees that the reason for this is Emma's lack of self-knowledge. Yet as she stumbles from one failure to another, it dawns upon her what she really wants for herself. Thus, it can be said that even if she were not aware of it, she was aiming at self-knowledge, and her actions can be said to lead to that end.

There are many different kinds of plot. It is, therefore, impossible to cover every one, though there are some popular ones that you are likely to meet at 'O' and 'A' level. It is a good idea to be aware of what they are and to have some idea as to what to look out for in the examination. Four kinds of plot will be looked at: the plot based upon a journey, the plot based upon a character coming to a discovery about life, the plot based upon the structure and workings of society, and the plot based upon mysteries and secrets.

## 9.5 PLOTS BASED ON JOURNEYS

Some of the earlier English novels are either based upon a journey or upon the life of a central character who, so to speak, journeys through a number of experiences. Such books are often called picaresque novels, after the Spanish word for rogue. Originally, the Spanish picaresque novel dealt with the adventures of roguish servants, but the term has now become extended to cover any character who has a series of adventures on a journey or through life. The novels you are likely to come across are: Daniel Defoe's *Moll Flanders* and Henry Fielding's *Joseph Andrews* and *Tom Jones*.

These novels have simple plots: Moll Flanders journeys through life, and Joseph Andrews and Tom Jones make individual journeys. What the plots make possible are very lively individual episodes. There is a superb moment in *Moll Flanders* when Moll (the novel is written in the first person) tells of how she robbed a child. The writing is vivid and detailed, and the reader finds pleasure in seeing how Moll honestly comes to terms with the feelings the episode arouses in her. In *Joseph Andrews* there is a marvellously funny scene in which Joseph, having been robbed and left naked, meets a coach. Fielding uses the episode to satirise the occupants whose false ideas of good manners are stronger than their charity. Their reluctance to allow the coachman to pick him up is shown to be due to their distorted values.

Another great quality of these novels is the attractive energy of the central characters, particularly Moll Flanders. Moll has an indestructible quality; she passes through life experiencing crime, marriage, and living in the country, London and America. Throughout she is tough, sane and likeable.

## 9.6 PLOTS BASED ON DISCOVERIES

Many novels show the central characters making discoveries about life. In some novels ideals are shattered, in others false ideas are recognised and replaced by truer ones. In most the connection between events is the growth in understanding that emerges from one event and then shapes the following one. James Joyce's *Portrait of the Artist as a Young Man* tells how young Stephen Dedalus grows up in Ireland. As he moves from one stage in his life to another he learns to question Ireland's cultural and religious traditions. In Harper Lee's *To Kill a Mockingbird* the focus is on how Scout gradually becomes aware of the tensions and prejudices of the racially torn southern states of America. In L.P. Hartley's *The Go-Between* the plot concerns a boy, on the edge of adolescence, discovering the conflicts of adult sexuality.

When you write about plots that deal with characters growing towards understanding, you should bring out the pleasure the reader can feel when witnessing a character's development. Difficult as it is to explain, there is great pleasure in following through a plot which unfolds because the central character is gradually learning more about life. In *Great Expectations* wealth turns Pip into a snob. The reader can see that this snobbery leads Pip to neglect good and kind Joe. There may be pain in this for the reader, but this leads on to the pleasure of seeing him gradually wake up to the fact that, for all his wealth, he is not a true gentleman, and Joe is. The pleasure we feel is not just a case of being pleased when Pip sees things clearly; there is also a pleasure in recognising that that is how a mind might grow and respond to life.

You should also bring out the point that such plots can't be appreciated unless the reader responds in sympathy to the characters. George Eliot allows her readers to do this. In *The Mill on the Floss* she brings the reader very close to the wild and much misunderstood Maggie, who suffers a great deal from her unfeeling brother. But the novel is about how they both discover life, so when Tom is sent to school, George Eliot invites the reader to pity him in his life of grinding misery and to understand that this affects his later life.

A final point to look out for in plots that are concerned with growth is the place of the reader in relation to events. One of the pleasures of these novels is seeing something before a character does. In *Emma* the reader sees that Mr Elton is courting Emma and not Harriet Smith long before the unseeing Emma does. There is, then, much humour leading up to her moment of discovery that she has been mistaken. This should help you to see that plots dealing with discovering life need not always be dark and sombre: *Emma* is a deep and serious book but it is also an amusing one.

## 9.7 PLOTS BASED ON THE WORKINGS OF SOCIETY

Most plots deal with society in one way or another. There are, however, some novels in which one of the central concerns of the plot is to explore how a particular society works. Such plots might show why some characters prosper while others do not, how newcomers establish or fail to establish themselves in a society, how societies gradually change, or why there are rivalries between families, institutions or classes. The point about plots based on the workings of society is that characters behave as they do because of the way society runs.

The novel that achieves this in a quite outstanding way is *Middlemarch*. George Eliot presents the many social levels of a Midlands town in the early 1830s. She explores the relations between the rising middle class, the Vincy family, and the relative newcomer, the banker, Bulstrode. She shows how attempts to bring the railway affect the people, and how leading citizens differ in their politics. Individual events are looked upon in a social light. When the rich Peter Featherstone dies, his funeral is attended by his immediate family, but the upper classes only watch it from a distance.

The young doctor, Lydgate, is a good example of a character whose actions are shaped by the way society runs. He is an intelligent, well-educated man of high ideals who wants to bring new medical ideas to the town. His interest in the new hospital is shared by Bulstrode, but because Bulstrode is not very popular in the town, Lydgate also arouses suspicion.

This suspicion affects his day to day medical work. The people of Middlemarch are accustomed to old-fashioned ways of medicine, and when Lydgate, on what he thinks are good scientific grounds, refuses to prescribe pills, they become hostile. Lydgate is not a success, and the hostility he has aroused because of his new ideas does not help him when he is suspected of helping Bulstrode to kill off a blackmailer. Lydgate is a very interesting example of how a man with high ideals fails to bring improvement because he does not understand how society works.

When writing about plots that centre on the working of society, you should try to show what attitude the author takes. In the case of Lydgate, George Eliot's is a very subtle one. She seems to admire his desire to improve health but she also likes the sensible, rather conservative townsfolk who don't like new ideas. There is a very interesting passage which shows Lydgate's keen thrill in discovering medicine, but against that are ones which show that he is naive in expecting provincial people to respond readily to his ideas.

Above all, plots based upon the workings of society, or ones in which a picture of society is at least fairly central, give the feeling of the wholeness of life. In *Middlemarch* there are many different kinds of character and many human interests. In its wonderful sweep the novel deals with love, marriage, money, religion, social improvement, politics, the family, work, leisure, the arts and intellectual fashions.

## 9.8 PLOTS BASED ON MYSTERIES

There can be no denying that novels in which some things remain mysteriously hidden from the characters and the reader have an enormous popular appeal. The fact is that we like mysteries. A simple case is the detective story – we want to know 'who dunnit'. It is true that detective stories need more than the mystery of who committed the crime if they are to maintain their appeal, but this is not to deny that there is pleasure in being held in suspense. In Sir Arthur Conan Doyle's Sherlock Holmes stories (some of which do appear on 'O' level syllabuses) there are wonderfully atmospheric settings and an absorbing central character, but the problems and the intricate solutions they require generate a great deal of pleasure, simply because the reader wants the mystery to be solved. The same can be said about the novels of Wilkie Collins: the pleasure of *The Moonstone* and *The Woman in White* grows from the mystery created by crimes as well as atmosphere and characters.

There are, however, novels which are not detective stories, but which, nevertheless, have plots that depend upon mysteries. Dickens, for instance, enjoys enticing his readers with mysteries. Quite often readers find themselves asking: who is this character? Why is he or she in this state? What is the relation between these characters? Why has this character appeared so suddenly in the novel? Why aren't we told anything about this character's past? In *Little Dorrit*, for instance, there is a watch, which had belonged to Arthur Clennam's father, on which are engraved the initials D.N.F. They stand for 'Do Not Forget', but for much of the novel what it is that must not be forgotten remains a mystery. In addition, at the beginning of the novel Little Dorrit herself is employed by Arthur's mother, but nobody knows why. Arthur is puzzled – and so is the reader. The point about such mysteries is that they depend upon the idea of plot as a sequence of events connected by a set of causes. The plot based upon a mystery works by allowing the reader to see that there must be a cause behind the events while keeping the cause concealed. The formula is: there must be a cause, but it is mysteriously hidden.

When you write about plots based on mysteries you will find yourself using the terms introduced to discuss stories. Mysteries arouse the reader's expectations and increase the tension of the book, while the unravelling of the mystery creates surprise and relief.

It is worthwhile asking yourself whether the mystery is central to the theme of the novel. *Great Expectations* has a plot which contains a good deal of mystery, as well as showing how the central character discovers about life. Quite often the reader is prompted to ask: who is this character? In the case of one character, the answer is very much to do with the theme of the book. Pip wants to be a gentleman, but because of his early association with the criminal, Magwitch, he feels he is tainted by crime. This is particularly painful for him, because the beautiful Estella, whom he loves, is very scornful of criminals (at one point she calls them 'wretches'), and he feels ashamed and unworthy of her because of this. But there is a mystery: who is Estella? As the intricate plot unfolds, Pip feels Estella is increasingly superior to him, but then the truth emerges; Estella, far from being a character untainted by crime, is intimately associated with it – she is Magwitch's daughter. The identity of Estella, one of the mysteries of the plot, is thus part of the book's central theme – Pip's desire to be a gentleman.

## 9.9 HOW PLOTS ARE CONSTRUCTED

There is one more aspect of plots that you may be asked about in examinations – how they are constructed. Much of what has already been said is relevant to this problem. For instance, a plot can be made by the author following the adventures of the central character. Plots can also be built upon an author's presentation of a whole society. Three further points about the construction of plots should be made. They are: the way in which a plot is introduced in the beginning of a novel, the problem from which a plot grows, and the way a plot can be built on contrasts.

Because plots emerge in the early stages of a novel, it is a good idea to attend closely to the opening chapters. They are often the place where an author signals what kind of plot is to follow. The dramatic event of Henchard selling his wife at the start of *The Mayor of Casterbridge* is Hardy's way of signalling that this event is going to shape the development of the plot. But an author need not start with a dramatic event. Sometimes a scene at the start of the novel points to the mood, if not the specific events, of the plot. In Graham Greene's *The Power and the Glory* the opening chapter creates a sinister, death-laden atmosphere. In the first paragraph waiting vultures, the bust of an ex-President and sharks establish a mood of death waiting to pounce. Into this world comes a man who is trying to take a boat out of the country. Later it is learnt that he is a priest fleeing from the military authorities. The mood of death and the man trying to escape are thus the seeds from which the plot grows.

The priest trying to escape yet feeling he has a duty to minister to his people is the problem behind the plot of *The Power and the Glory.* You can see from this that the word 'problem' is used to indicate any source of conflict from which a plot grows. It is always a good idea to put the problem of the plot to yourself. You can ask: what is the problem from which this plot grows? In answering that question, you will be getting to grips with the central point of the novel. The problem, for instance, of *The Spire* is whether in building the spire Jocelin will come to see the motives which compel him to action. There is a danger that you will over-simplify plots if you ask about the problem from which they grow. You should remember that you are talking about the problem from which the rest of the plot grows, and that, therefore, you are not saying that the problem is all there is to the novel.

Some authors deliberately construct their plots on a number of contrasts. Here 'contrasts' stands for any structural device whereby elements in a novel, perhaps characters, perhaps settings, are drawn together so that the reader can see them in a relationship. Authors do this to give shape to their novels and also to reveal to the reader how they judge the life they are presenting. *The Power and the Glory* is built upon a stark (perhaps too stark?) contrast between the characters of the priest and the lieutenant. Greene invites the reader to think of them together by refusing to give them names (a fact which invites the reader to see them as the representatives of conflicting outlooks – the religious and the secular) and by giving to each the qualities usually associated with the other: the priest is worldly and sensual, whereas the lieutenant is strict and puritanical. The contrasts upon which *Middlemarch* is built are subtle and complex. Throughout the book the reader is invited to see how a number of characters react to love, marriage, success, failure and the prospect of death. These contrasts allow George Eliot to pass judgement, but she refuses to treat such an opportunity in a simplistic way. For instance, Fred Vincy tries to borrow money from Bulstrode and Caleb Garth; Bulstrode refuses but Garth lends him some. Fred has no luck and can't repay the loan. George Eliot invites the reader to see that Bulstrode is sensible not to lend money, but at the same time it is difficult not to think of Bulstrode as hard and Garth as kind. The contrast leaves the reader with a problem: is it better to be sensible but cold or foolish and generous?

## EXERCISES

**1** Write about the pleasure you have gained from the stories you have studied, paying attention to the way they provide expectation, interest, surprise and relief.
**2** Write summaries of the plots of novels you are studying, showing that the author is interested in why the events follow each other in the order they do.
**3** Write as clearly as you can about the problems behind the plots of the novels you are studying.
**4** Write about how authors have constructed the plots of their novels, paying attention, where appropriate, to the way a plot is introduced and whether, and how, it is built upon contrasts.

# CHAPTER 10

# THEMES

## 10.1 THE IMPORTANCE OF THEMES

The previous chapter has emphasised *how* novels are made. There are two reasons for this emphasis. The first is that it is a mistake to think of them as just like ordinary life. The second is that many questions at 'O' and 'A' level ask you to write about *how* characters are presented and plots developed. The questions, in other words, often invite you to show that you understand that a novel is a work of art which is specially shaped and moulded by the author.

But it is also necessary to ask what a novel is *about*. If that question is put to some people, the answer given will be a brief summary of the story. Such an answer is not good enough at 'O' and 'A' level. The kind of answer that you must learn to give is that a novel is also about the significant themes that emerge in and through the plot. Two words in that sentence, 'significant' and 'theme', need explaining. 'Significant' stands for the fact that readers find characters and events in a novel to be humanly important, or, to put it another way, the reader sees a meaning in what is happening. Yet another way of putting this point is to say that what is written matters, matters because it reveals something about people. 'Theme' means what the novel can be summed up as saying. Another way of putting it would be to talk of the 'ideas' of the book. You can also think of the book from the point of view of the author and write of his or her concerns or interests. Let us briefly look at two examples.

One of the themes of *Hard Times* is the importance of imagination and compassion in education. Sissy Jupe, the girl who was brought up in the imaginative world of the circus, is seen to have an inner strength and a natural concern for people, whereas Tom Gradgrind and Bitzer, both of whom have been taught only to weigh and calculate, are either shown to be weak when faced by temptation or heartless and unfeeling in their treatment of people. One of the themes of *1984* is that human qualities such as imagination, affection, joy and love of art and nature can't survive when the state controls all aspects of life. Winston Smith tries to rediscover human qualities, but the state roots them out, replacing them with an unthinking loyalty to Big Brother.

Whenever you write about novels, you should try to look beyond character, setting and plot to what it is about – its themes or issues. The themes of a novel, you should remember, are there because the author intended them to be. They are the author's interpretation and judgement of life, expressing, to use two useful words, his or her view or vision of things. You should avoid writing about themes as if they were separate strands in the novel, for they can't be isolated in that way. A theme emerges *in* and *through* the dialogue, development of character, setting and plot. One way of saying what makes up the theme of a novel is to say that it is the significance of all those elements.

To say that a novel is *about* something is not to deny that it is a specially made world in words. In fact, the best way to think about the themes of a novel is to ask *how* a novelist creates them. That is what this chapter does. What follows is a guide to a number of different ways in which a novelist can create themes. If you can see that a novelist can create significant meanings in these ways, you will be better able to see the themes of the books you are studying. The following will be briefly examined: the titles of novels, how an author presents his or her interests, how an author treats a common theme, the way an author uses symbols, the way an author stresses important words, the author's use of moral words, the way an author shapes a novel, the use of important speeches, the use of important events, and the special treatment of ordinary, everyday occurrences. This list does not cover every single way in which an author creates his or her themes. For instance, it has already been said that the settings of a novel can express its themes.

## 10.2 THE TITLES OF BOOKS

When you are thinking about the themes of a book, it is worth asking yourself: why did the novelist give the book this name? It could be that the novelist has chosen the title in order to tell the reader something important about the book. In some cases the central themes of the book are present in the title. This is the case with *Pride and Prejudice*, which is about Darcy's pride and Elizabeth Bennet's prejudice. *Middlemarch* is about life in a Midlands town; George Eliot provides a sub-title – *A Study of Provincial Life.* A very interesting title is *Mansfield Park.* Why did Jane Austen name the book after the home of the Bertrams and not, as she might have done, after the heroine, Fanny Price, or the moral qualities the heroine displays – patience, sensitivity and loyalty? The fact that Jane Austen chose the name of the house indicates that one of her central interests is the whole way of life that is represented by Mansfield Park – a life based on tradition, a strict idea of manners, a demanding moral code, and an education that passes on such values to the next generation. This traditional way of life is shown to be under threat from people like the Crawfords, who seem to live for nothing but the pleasure of the moment, and, even more seriously, from the shallowness of those who have inherited it – the Bertram children. Jane Austen, then, gave the book its title as a way of indicating that what she was interested in was a tradition of country living rather than just the individual lives of the central characters.

It is worth noticing that examiners at both 'O' and 'A' level do set questions in which they ask why a book was given the title it has. They could, for instance, set a question such as this: why did Dickens call his book *Great Expectations*? (You should note that this kind of question can also be set on drama; examiners might ask why plays such as *Measure for Measure, The Rivals* or *The Crucible* have these titles.)

## 10.3 HOW AUTHORS SHOW THEIR INTERESTS

It has already been stated that one way of saying that a book has themes is to say that the author takes an interest in certain aspects of life. But this raises the problem of how that interest is shown. Here are two suggestions: authors show their interest by writing in detail and by devoting a great deal of space to some things. To these a negative one can be added: authors' interests are sometimes evident in what they leave out. The deatil in which George Eliot and Henry James write about how their characters change, grow and make up their minds shows that their interests include moral and psychological development. The point about space also applies to them; many pages of their novels are devoted to minute analysis of their characters' minds. The space a novelist devotes to some topics is revealing also in the case of *1984.* Students are often puzzled by the lengthy section from 'the book' – a supposedly forbidden work that explains the workings of society. The space given to it shows Orwell's interest in political theory. Once you see that, you can ask whether elsewhere in the book Orwell is directing your attention to the political ideas that lie behind the way society runs.

It is, of course, difficult to be confident about whether the omission of something is important. It is, nevertheless, worth noticing. For instance, in Lawrence's *The Rainbow* there is very little about the kind of society in which the characters live. The characters are explored inwardly and they are written about with considerable emotional force, but the impression the reader is left with is of a world of individuals rather than a society. The fact that Lawrence has not stressed that factor shows that his interest lies in another direction.

## 10.4 COMMON THEMES

Some themes crop up in very many novels. There are, for instance, numerous novels that deal with love, growing up, or conflict. If a novel is clearly about one of these popular themes, the question you should ask is: what exactly is this author's approach to this theme? It's not good enough to say 'this novel is about growing up'. What you must show is how an author handles that theme. When you come to write about the approach of a particular author, you must guard against assuming that the author treats a common theme in a similar way to other authors. You will have to look through all the relevant sections of the book and ask yourself whether the author has a particular viewpoint.

An example will help. Many books deal with love, but what exactly is the approach of Jane Austen to it? In many books the author recognises that young men and women actively court each other. In fact, the way men court women is a central feature of a number of novels. If, however, you look at Jane Austen, you will see that she does not seem to approve of this. The men that actively and openly court women are seen to be untrustworthy and even wicked, whereas those couples who naturally grow together without any artificial plotting or planning are seen as being truly in love and capable of making lasting relationships. Henry Crawford from *Mansfield Park* and Mr Knightley from *Emma* exhibit these differences. Henry Crawford sets out to woo Fanny as a game, but later, when he finds he does love her, he persuades his sister Mary to lend Fanny a necklace which, in fact, belongs to him. Fanny is quite unaware of this little plot, but when the truth is known, she is shocked. She speaks strongly to Mary about it:

> Do you mean then that your brother knew of the necklace beforehand? Oh! Miss Crawford, *that* was not fair.

We can feel her anger in the 'Oh!', and 'fair' is a strong word; Fanny is accusing Henry of being deceitful. To deceive people into loving, Jane Austen suggests, is wrong. By contrast, Mr Knightley makes no attempts to court Emma; all he does is ask her, and since she has decided already that no one must marry Mr Knightley but she, he is accepted. In a conventional sense it is not like most proposals, yet we feel it is real love. Although it is not conventional, Jane Austen's view is deeply romantic:

people need not plot and plan, because true love will grow naturally and will flower into marriage.

## 10.5 THE FUNCTION OF SYMBOLS

Novels, as well as poems, employ symbols. A repeated symbol, or one used at an important moment, can give expression to a central theme of the novel. It is, therefore, a good idea to ask this question: is there a repeated symbol in this novel, and what is its significance? In asking such a question you should, of course, not ignore other elements in a novel. Symbols are important if they work alongside the characters and the settings.

L.P. Hartley's *The Go-Between* is a novel that employs symbols. The symbolism begins with a diary that Leo Colston is given in 1900. Young Leo is full of hope for the twentieth century, and he associates his hope with the figures of the zodiac that appear on the diary cover. When he goes to spend summer with a school friend of his in Norfolk, he interprets those whom he meets, and himself, in terms of the zodiac figures: the beautiful Marian, the elder sister of his friend, is the Virgin; the man she is to marry, a soldier called Hugh, is the archer; and the local farmer, Ted, is the water-carrier. Leo so looks up to them that he regards them as gods, and they call him Mercury – the messenger of the gods. Leo is also fascinated by the temperature; each day he goes to see if the mercury in the thermometer has risen any higher. Seeing himself as the messenger of the gods and associating himself with the ever-rising temperature increases his hope and belief in the twentieth century. But without realising what is happening to him, he becomes the one who helps Marian and Ted to carry on a secret love affair by carrying messages between them. When they are discovered together, he suffers a nervous breakdown; his hopes for the century are destroyed, and he remains an emotional cripple for the rest of his life. Hartley, then, uses the symbols to express the theme of hope destroyed.

You could not understand *The Go-Between* unless you saw the pattern of symbols. There are, however, some novels that don't depend upon such a highly developed scheme – and some people think they are all the better for it. For instance, the superb opening of Dickens's *Bleak House* presents London wrapped in a thick fog which penetrates every area of life. This fog that obscures and confuses is a symbol of the Court of Chancery, a maze with no exit, but, unlike the symbols in Hartley, it is not part of a rigid scheme of symbols running through the novel.

The fog in *Bleak House* is near to being the case of a symbol used at an important moment. Another example of a moment that has a symbolic force is to be found in *Mansfield Park*, when Fanny Price is thinking about which necklace to wear with the little gold cross that her brother, William, has given her – the one that Edmund, whom she loves, has given her, or the one from Mary Crawford, which Edmund feels she ought to choose instead of his for the sake of politeness. But when she tries to thread Mary's necklace 'the one given her by Miss Crawford would by no means go through the ring of the cross'. It is an ordinary, everyday moment, but, nevertheless, it is charged with symbolic significance, for it is an indication that she is not fitted to the Crawfords' way of life. Her world, symbolised by the cross from her brother, won't fit in with the Crawford necklace, so she turns to the one from Edmund which, happily and symbolically, fits.

## 10.6 IMPORTANT WORDS

Authors can give expression to the themes of novels by stressing certain words. Words used carefully can focus the meaning of a novel and take the reader to the heart of the author's concerns. If the meaning of a novel is focused in a particular word, you will often find that it is used in the climax. When, therefore, you come to the climax of a novel you can ask: is there an important word here that focuses the central theme of the book?

Such a word is 'heart' in *Hard Times.* The novel has started with Mr Gradgrind saying, 'Now what I want is, Facts'. Education, he believes, should banish feeling and emotion and concentrate on nothing but facts. A model pupil in his school is Bitzer. Gradgrind brings his own children up this way, but the results are disastrous. Tom, his son, robs a bank and has to escape, but at the climax of the novel Bitzer prevents this. Gradgrind, who now sees that his ideas about education have been wrong, appeals to the very thing his method of education has neglected – feelings:

> 'Bitzer,' said Mr. Gradgrind, broken down, and miserably submissive to him, 'have you a heart?' 'The circulation, Sir,' returned Bitzer, smiling at the oddity of the question, 'couldn't be carried on without it.'

What Mr Gradgrind means by 'heart' is sympathy, understanding, mercy and pity, but for Bitzer 'heart' can only mean one thing – the organ that pumps blood round the body. The word is the key to the book. Gradgrind's system of education ignored the heart by reducing the meanings of words to nothing but their factual content, but now that he can see the ghastly product of his own system he sees that feelings are important and that words shouldn't be reduced to a factual minimum. Dickens, therefore, focuses the theme of the book in the different way in which Bitzer and Gradgrind use the word 'heart'.

## 10.7 MORAL WORDS

Moral words work in a similar way. The point about a moral word is that it carries a judgement with it; that is to say, we can tell whether we should approve or disapprove simply by attending to the meaning of the word. For instance, we know that the word 'spiteful' means something which is bad, and the word 'generous' something which is good, because both words carry a judgement with them. Authors often invite us to judge characters by giving them moral words in their speech. A shallow character might be given rather trivial words, whereas a deep character would be given serious ones. Therefore, you can ask: do the way characters use moral words indicate how the author is asking us to judge them?

There is a very clear case of this in *Mansfield Park*. When Fanny learns that Henry Crawford has eloped with Maria she is deeply shocked. Her shock is expressed in very strong moral words:

> The horror of a mind like Fanny's, as it received the conviction of such guilt, and began to take in some part of the misery that must ensue, can hardly be described. At first, it was a sort of stupefaction; but every moment was quickening her perception of the horrible evil.

Look at the words used – 'horror', 'such guilt', 'misery', and 'horrible evil' – all of them very strong moral words, which show the depth of Fanny's character. But Jane Austen carefully shows that Mary Crawford's reaction is very different. Edmund reports them to Fanny:

> She said – 'I wanted to see you. Let us talk over this sad business. What can equal the folly of our two relations?'

Mary Crawford uses no stronger moral words than 'sad business' (hardly a moral term at all) and 'folly', which is a very weak term, standing for no more than a silly mistake.

Throughout the novel Edmund has been captivated by the beauty of Mary Crawford, but these words make him see sense; nobody who talks like that can have any depth. From then on his affections for Mary cool. Thus one of the central themes of the book – Edmund's growth away from infatuation – is focused in the way he is shocked by Mary's use of the word 'folly'. Eventually he turns to Fanny, who, we have already seen, has judged the elopement as a 'horrible evil'.

## 10.8 THE CONSTRUCTION OF PLOTS

Since a novelist could write a novel in many different ways, the fact that a particular one has been chosen might tell you something about its appropriateness to the theme. You can ask of every novel: does the fact that the novelist has chosen to write the novel this way tell me anything about its themes? In the very best novels the way it is written, that is, the way it is constructed, plotted or ordered, is an expression of its themes. An example will make this clear.

In *Middlemarch* the way the novel is written is an expression of one of its themes. Throughout, George Eliot tries to show us how characters think and feel, so that we will be sympathetic. No matter who the character is, George Eliot asks us to understand what it feels like to be that character. This way of writing the novel is, in fact, an expression of her belief that people should always consider what other people are feeling. Take the case of Dorothea Brooke. The crisis of the novel occurs when Dorothea finds Will Ladislaw, the man she loves, holding hands with Rosamund, the wife of Lydgate. Will is not having an affair with Rosamund, but poor Dorothea does not know this. So hurt and shocked is she that she spends the night lying on the floor of her room, and it's only with the dawn, a symbolic moment, that she comes to this realisation:

> Was she alone in that scene? Was it her event only? She forced herself to think of it as bound up with another woman's life – a woman towards whom she had set out with a longing to carry some clearness and comfort into her beclouded youth.

What Dorothea sees is what George Eliot expresses in the way she writes the novel – that we should always consider what other people are feeling. Thus, it can be said that the way *Middlemarch* is written is an expression of one of its most important themes.

## 10.9 IMPORTANT SPEECHES

One of the clearest guides to the themes of a novel is what the characters say. Since some characters say a great deal, you will have to learn to detect those speeches that are particularly important. (This does not mean you should ignore the others.) You can only do this if you know a novel well, but when you are acquainted with a novel, you will be able to see that particular speeches focus the main concerns of the plot.

This is the case with Emily Brontë's *Wuthering Heights*. Throughout the novel there is a deep yet very puzzling relation between Cathy and Heathcliff. They are together a great deal as children. Cathy can't bear to see Heathcliff beaten, and yet their relation is very strange. For instance, it is not, in any conventional sense, a romantic one. They do use the word 'love', but it does not have its usual romantic and sexual meaning. It is because this relation is puzzling that the reported speeches of Cathy are so important. At one point she says this to Nellie, her nurse:

> My love for Heathcliff resembles the eternal rocks beneath: a source of little visible delight but necessary. Nelly, I *am* Heathcliff. He's always in my mind: not as a pleasure, any more than I am always a pleasure to myself, but as my own being.

That is the closest we ever come to understanding their relation; Catherine says she *is* Heathcliff. The love she talks of, then, is for somebody who is herself – 'as my own being'. Of course, no reader can just take what Cathy says as true, but when that speech is seen alongside other aspects of their relation, it is difficult not to see it as expressing the truth. Her words, then, focus what goes on in the rest of the novel.

## 10.10 IMPORTANT EVENTS

Novels are concerned with what happens as well as with what is said. Events, therefore, can express the themes of books. This is particularly the case with the climax of a novel. Many nineteenth-century novels contain what can be called 'big moments' in which, for instance, difficult decisions are taken, discoveries made, or mysteries revealed. One of the pleasures of reading such novels comes when the author handles the climax well. The reader enjoys the achievement of the author in making the events express the themes of the book. When, therefore, you reach a climax (or it could be a turning point) you can ask: does this event express the themes of the book?

Dickens plans the climaxes of his novels very carefully. He handles them theatrically; that is to say, they have the vividness and impact of a play. At the end of *Little Dorrit* Mrs Clennam, who has sat in her room throughout the novel, dramatically rises from her chair and runs through London to the Marshalsea Prison to beg forgiveness from Little Dorrit. This astonishing scene focuses on one of the main themes of the novel. Dickens has shown how difficult it is for characters to change their views and so escape from convention, habit or circumstances. For instance, Mr Dorrit physically escapes from the Marshalsea but mentally he lives in it for the rest of his life. Nobody in the novel has been as fixed in views or physical position as Mrs Clennam. She is hard, unforgiving and self-righteous in her outlook and never leaves her room. The fact, then, that she rises to her feet and runs out of the house to beg forgiveness for what she has done wrong is not only a spectacular change, it is also very significant for the theme of the novel. If somebody as fixed in her views as Mrs Clennam can change, then the novel, while stressing how difficult change can be, is not entirely gloomy or without hope.

An even more theatrical climax is the exposure of Mr Bounderby in *Hard Times.* He has always boasted that he is a self-made man who has risen from the very lowest level of society – a ditch. Throughout the novel a mysterious lady of a neat and respectable appearance occasionally appears, looking at the buildings owned by Mr Bounderby. The climax of the novel occurs when it is discovered that this woman is his mother, and that his upbringing, far from being squalid, was a very comfortable one. Dickens sets this discovery in Bounderby's house. People crowd in from the street to see what is going on, and some of them, as in a theatre, stand on chairs 'to get the better of the people in front'. This theatrical exposure of Bounderby is important because it shows that he is a hypocrite. Dickens uses it to hammer home the theme of his book – that the industrial world is run by hypocrites, who have beliefs about how to progress in society which are false.

## 10.11 THE TREATMENT OF ORDINARY EVENTS

But not all the significant events in a book have to be dramatic. An author can write about an ordinary, everyday event in such a way as to bring out that it is very important. A book's theme can be present in the seemingly ordinary, and it is often the experience of readers that they enjoy the way an author brings out the depth of meaning that can be found in everyday doings.

Nobody handles the everyday better than Jane Austen. She can show the moral significance of events that seem very ordinary indeed. Take, for example, the outing to Sotherton, which happens in the first half of *Mansfield Park.* Sotherton is the home of Mr Rushworth, the silly young man to whom Maria Bertram is engaged. The visitors explore the extensive grounds of the house and arrive at a locked gate. Since most of them want to go through it, Mr Rushworth hurries back to the house to fetch the key, leaving, among others, Maria and Henry Crawford. Maria is impatient; the locked gate gives her, she says, 'a feeling of restraint and hardship'. They are significant words, and Henry Crawford understands what they really mean. What Maria is talking about is the restraint and hardship of being engaged to be married to the silly Mr Rushworth. The gate, therefore, to which only Mr Rushworth has the key, is a symbol for marriage. What Henry Crawford suggests is that she can avoid her feelings of 'restraint' by climbing round the side of it:

> And for the world you would not get out without the key and without Mr. Rushworth's authority and protection, or I think with little difficulty pass round the edge of the gate, here, with my assistance; I think it might be done, if you really wished to be more at large, and could allow yourself to think it not prohibited.

That is an invitation to adultery. To go round the gate with the 'assistance' of Henry would be to escape from 'the authority and protection' of Mr Rushworth. In addition, she could do so with 'little difficulty', and she is tempted with the thought that she would be 'more at large' if she could look upon what she was doing as 'not prohibited'. These words apply to the act of adultery – an adultery that becomes real when they elope – as well as they do to the perfectly ordinary event of finding a way round a locked gate. Jane Austen uses an ordinary incident to bring out the theme of marriage and adultery, which is central to the novel.

## 10.12 WRITING ABOUT THEMES

Whenever you are asked to write about the themes of a book (and remember that the word 'theme' need not be used in such a question), you should write about the author's view of life. At 'O' and 'A' level most of the questions do no more than ask you to show that you understand the viewpoint of the author. Occasionally, however, you are invited to say what you think about the author's views. If your opinion is being sought for, you must remember that nobody can tell you what to think about the author; that is up to you. There are, nevertheless, two pieces of advice that you can follow.

The first is to understand what you are being asked. An author has a view of life; you are asked to say what that is, and to say what you think of it. For instance, you can recognise that Jane Austen believes that love should be allowed to grow naturally, but you should then ask yourself whether you believe that is true. Now although nobody can tell you what your view is, you can anticipate such questions by thinking about the issues as you study your books. The best way of doing this is to start with a simple question: do I agree with this? You can ask this each time you recognise one of the main issues of the novel. The second piece of advice is to be honest. Don't be afraid either to agree, disagree or come down in between. If the examiner wants *your* view – give it. This does not mean that you should simply state it. As with all literary matters, you will need evidence, but such evidence should back up what *you* think.

## EXERCISES

1 Consider how appropriate are the titles of the novels you are studying.
2 By looking at what authors concentrate on and what they leave out, try to see what the central interests of their novels are.
3 Look at the novels you are studying to see if there are any symbols that express the theme of the book. If there are, write about them.
4 Can you see why the novelists you are studying have written the books the way they have?
5 Write about the central speeches and events of the novels you are studying, bringing out how they express their themes.
6 Try to sum up what are the themes of the novels you are studying and work out in writing your reactions to what the novelists are saying.

# PART III

# STUDYING DRAMA

# CHAPTER 11

# THE CONVENTIONS OF DRAMA

## 11.1 THE IMPORTANCE OF CONVENTIONS

What would you make of a cowboy film if you'd never seen one before? A number of things might surprise you: when there was a fist fight there would be loud, cracking noises, and chairs would break in pieces if anyone was hit with one; the goodies would be handsome men who rode white horses, and the baddies ugly men on black ones; and when anyone rode a horse, you would see them starting, and then, in the next shot, arriving at their destination, the journey taking, so it seemed, a couple of seconds. If, however, you knew what to expect in a cowboy film, none of these things would surprise you. The reason for this is that you would recognise and accept the conventions of cowboy films.

What is a convention? A convention is an agreement between author and audience that an idea will be presented in a particular way. A convention itself may not directly reflect the real world but it, nevertheless, stands for something that does, or might, happen in it. For instance, fist fights are tough, and this toughness is brought out by the convention of the loud cracking noises. In actual fact, punches don't sound like that, but in a film we accept the convention and appreciate the point it is making – that fighting is hard, painful and unpleasant. Conventions, then, allow an audience to accept what is going on as real, although it knows that the events are happening in a studio or on a stage.

An audience is usually so used to most conventions that it hardly notices them. The stage itself is a convention; the audience see an open space over which actors move but know that it represents, and so treat it as, a living room, a battlefield, a court of law or a boat. The audience knows that actors are real people, yet it regards them as kings, generals, peasants and prime ministers. It knows, too, that a play is meant to portray the action of weeks, months or even years, and it accepts that a great deal of time has passed even if the performance only lasts two or three hours. When a character dies, the audience feels pity and sadness, yet knows the actor playing the part will come back at the end and take a bow.

Shakespeare jokes about conventions in *A Midsummer Night's Dream.* A group of humble working men rehearse a play, which they hope will be performed at the Duke's wedding, but they don't understand the basic conventions of drama. Moreover, they think the audience won't understand them either. Two of the things they don't understand are that actors aren't really dead when they die on stage, and that actors can represent animals. The well-meaning Bottom suggests that a prologue should explain these difficulties to the audience:

> Write me a prologue and let the prologue seem to say, we will do no harm with our swords, and that Pyramus is not killed indeed; and, for the more better assurance, that I, Pyramus, am not Pyramus, but Bottom the weaver.

His suggestion about the lion is even funnier; the actor should show half his face to show them he is a man and should say:

> Ladies, – or, fair ladies, – I would wish you, – or, I would request you, – or, I would entreat you, – not to fear, not to tremble: my life for yours. If you think I come hither as a lion, it were pity of my life: no, I am no such thing; I am a man as other men are.

Bottom stumbles across the point about conventions: audiences *know* the lion is not real in the same way that they *know* actors don't really die. They know because they understand conventions.

Understanding drama, then, includes understanding its conventions. Whilst you are not likely to be as badly off as Bottom, you will find that some things in plays, particularly Shakespearian ones, will puzzle you because you don't understand their conventions. In addition, you won't pick up the significance of what is going on unless you recognise the conventions that are being used. The aim of this chapter is to introduce you to some of these. Three sorts of convention will be examined: conventions about how a play is constructed, conventions about the language of a play, and conventions about the actions of plays. Many of the examples will be taken from Shakespeare, but other playwrights will be discussed when they use the same conventions.

## 11.2 CONVENTIONS OF CONSTRUCTION: ACTS AND SCENES

You may notice two aspects of how plays are constructed: they are divided into sections called acts and scenes, and time passes within them at different rates. Both of these depend upon conventions.

The longer divisions of a play are called acts, and acts are sometimes further divided into scenes. Modern plays are often divided into two or three acts, whereas the plays of Shakespeare and his contemporaries are usually divided into five. Modern plays can have many scenes or the acts can be undivided: Shakespearian plays usually have numerous scenes. *Antony and Cleopatra,* for instance, has thirty-eight. In Shakespeare's plays all scenes start with the entrance of characters and close with the characters leaving the stage. When you read one of his plays, you will notice the 'Enter' at the beginning of the scene and the 'Exit' at the end, though you should remember that on stage the flow of action does not seem interrupted as it does on the page.

Can anything be learnt from these conventions? In the case of modern plays, it is a good idea to see if the act divisions correspond to the important stages in the action of the play. Peter Shaffer divides *The Royal Hunt of the Sun* into two acts, both of which have twelve scenes. The first act, called 'The Hunt', shows how Pizarro's army captures the Inca king and massacres the natives; the second, called 'The Kill', is concerned with the relation between Pizarro and the king and climaxes in the king's murder. Thus the convention of dividing a play into acts is made to serve the meaning of the play: Pizarro's army first hunts the Sun King and then it kills him. Of any modern play you can ask: why has the playwright divided the acts and scenes in this way? In answering that question you should see if the act divisions correspond to the development of the plot.

In Shakespeare, acts do not correspond to important stages in the action. There is, then, little point in studying how he divides his plays into five acts. Most of the plays consist not of an action in five sections but a two-fold movement: events gather pace till a crisis breaks, and from then on the play mounts to its conclusion. What this does mean is that act three – usually scene one and/or scene two – is the crisis of the play. Whenever you study a Shakespeare play, you should pay particular attention to these scenes. *Julius Caesar* has a two-fold movement: the growth of the plot to kill Caesar, and the campaign against those who killed him. The turning point – the crisis – is act three scenes one and two; in scene one Caesar is killed and in scene two Anthony skilfully turns the crowd against the plotters.

## 11.3 CONVENTIONS OF CONSTRUCTION: THE PASSING OF TIME

It is a convention that a long period of time can be represented in a play that only takes two or three hours to perform. This means that the structure of a play – the way it is put together – must convey the passing of time. This is usually done in two ways: time is assumed to have passed *between* scenes or acts, or time can pass quickly within a scene. In general, modern plays follow the first way, and Shakespeare – and his contemporaries – both.

It is now a convention that playwrights indicate the passage of time between acts and scenes by stating that so many days, say, have passed in the stage directions. In the theatre this information is printed in the programme. For instance, act two of Arthur Miller's *The Crucible* begins: *The Common room of Proctor's house, eight days later.*

Shakespeare does not employ that convention, so he indicates that time has passed between scenes by making characters refer to it. One of the most notable examples of this is in *The Winter's Tale,* when Shakespeare introduces the figure of Time, who announces that sixteen years have passed. In another play, *Twelfth Night,* Viola disguises herself as a man in order to join the court of Orsino. She states her intention to do this in act one scene two, and at the beginning of act one scene four a courtier, Valentine, says that Orsino 'hath known you but three days', so we know that time has passed.

That convention rarely bothers anyone studying or watching a play, but time passing within a scene can seem strange. Christopher Marlowe's *Dr. Faustus* closes with a scene in which Faustus waits in dread and horror for the Devil to take him off to hell. His speech lasts fifty-seven lines, and begins:

> Ah, Faustus,
> Now hast thou but one bare hour to live . . .

Fifty lines later, an hour has passed; the clock strikes, and Faustus despairingly cries:

> Oh, it strikes, it strikes! Now body turn to air,
> Or Lucifer will bear thee quick to hell.

When you read the scene, the quick passing of time might seem odd. It is a convention that you must accept: in plays time can be elastic. In the case of *Dr. Faustus*, however, Marlowe creates such mental agony in the fifty-seven lines that enough emotion to last an hour has been generated. In other words, the emotional tension of the scene helps us to accept the convention.

The convention that time is elastic in plays can be used by playwrights to indicate what is dramatically important. In general, a great deal of time is devoted to important events. For instance, although the action of *Julius Caesar* must take a few months, over half the action takes place in less than twenty-four hours – the night before and the morning of Caesar's death. By devoting so much time to the plot against Caesar, Shakespeare indicates the importance of that event and the issues it raises. Reading the play, we can see that we are meant to concentrate on Cassius's methods of organising the plot, Brutus's motives for joining in, and Caesar's attitude to danger.

There is one other way of indicating the passing of time that affects the structure of a play – the convention of the flash-back. This convention has been used very effectively in modern plays. It allows the playwright to contrast past and present, and to show how the present is to be understood in the light of the past. In *Death of a Salesman* Arthur Miller presents the pathetic contrast between the hopeful and confident young Willy Loman and the tired and defeated wreck he becomes. At the end of the play the audience are shown that Biff, the son upon whom Willy built his hopes, is hostile to his father because, in the past, he discovered that Willy was having an affair with a woman in Boston. Playwrights use flash-backs because these devices can offer a psychological explanation for a character's behaviour. Therefore, it is worthwhile asking of any play in which flash-backs occur: what is the playwright showing about the characters by using the convention of the flash-back?

## 11.4 CONVENTIONS OF LANGUAGE: VERSE AND PROSE

The most important conventions for you to master are those concerned with the words of plays. The following ones will be examined: the use of prose and verse, the way characters speak of themselves in the third person, the way in which rulers are spoken of, the distinction between 'you' and 'thou', the soliloquy, and the aside.

It is a convention in many plays that characters speak in verse and prose. Some characters always use one or the other, but many use both. Shakespeare, Marlowe, Jonson and Middleton write in both verse and prose, and though playwrights such as Congreve, Sheridan, Wilde and Shaw usually stick to prose, the convention has not died out. In this century T.S. Eliot, who is regularly set in public examinations, has written drama in verse. When you study a play that is written in both verse and prose, you should ask two questions: why do some characters speak in verse and others in prose? What effects do verse and prose create?

In Shakespeare and his contemporaries the important characters usually speak verse, whereas the minor ones use prose. Quite often an important character has a high social standing, whilst a minor one has not. The opening scene of *Julius Caesar* shows Marullus and Flavius dissuading a crowd from celebrating Caesar's triumphant return from war. They are tribunes (that is, representatives of the people), so they speak in verse. The citizens, however, are given prose, both because they are minor characters and members of the lower classes.

The distinction between prose and verse is, however, not always as clear as that. In *Julius Caesar* there is an important character of high social standing, called Casca, who speaks prose for much of the time. The reason for this is that he is a blunt, plain speaking man. Prose, in other words, is given to him because it suits his down to earth character. Nevertheless, even the blunt Casca speaks in verse during the storm. Shakespeare has probably given him verse because it is better at producing the tense and frightening atmosphere of a terrible thunderstorm. Verse and prose, then, can be used to indicate character and produce atmosphere.

This leads to the second question about the effects of each. Verse is usually more dramatically effective than prose because it uses all the resources of language – its figures of speech, rhythms, and sounds. Indeed, when you are writing about verse in plays, it is often appropriate to use the terms introduced in the poetry chapters of this book.

A very fine example of the different effects of verse and prose is act three scene two of *Julius Caesar,* when Brutus and Antony speak to the crowds about the death of Caesar. Shakespeare has a problem in this scene: he must show that Antony is more impressive than Brutus, or else the audience will not believe that the crowd who supported Brutus at the beginning of the scene could be crying for his death at the end of it. Shakespeare solves the problem by giving Brutus dry prose and Antony eloquent verse. This is an extract from Brutus:

> If there be any in this assembly, any dear friend of Caesar's, to him I say that Brutus's love to Caesar was no less than his. If then that friend demand why Brutus rose against Caesar, this is my answer: Not that I loved Caesar less, but that I loved Rome more.

Brutus offers cold, reasonable prose. He sounds as if he is conducting a hypothetical argument. Look, for instance, how both his sentences start with the word 'if'. His thoughtful, controlled prose, moving from question to answer, stirs very little emotion. By contrast, look at Antony's verse about Caesar's robe:

> I remember
> The first time ever Caesar put it on;
> 'Twas on a summer's evening in his tent,
> That day he overcame the Nervii.
> Look, in this place ran Cassius' dagger through:
> See what a rent the envious Casca made:
> Through this the well-beloved Brutus stabbed;
> And as he plucked his cursed steel away,
> Mark how the blood of Caesar followed it,
> As rushing out of doors, to be resolved

If Brutus so unkindly knocked or no;
For Brutus, as you know, was Caesar's Angel.

Look at the drama of the end-stopped lines; one begins with the arresting 'look' and ends with the grim picture of a dagger running through the robe. The horror of Caesar's death is thus dramatically expressed within one line. Look, too, at the image of Brutus knocking upon the door of Caesar's body, and, in a run-on line, Caesar's blood, eager to greet the friend, rushing out of doors. There is in that image a horrible contrast between what Brutus is doing (note how the word 'stabbed' forms the dramatic climax of the line) and the happy picture of a man gladly running to see his friend. Note, too, how the leisurely rhythms of the nostalgic opening – the lingering stresses on 'ever' and 'summer' – give way to the insistent monosyllables of the murder – 'look', 'rent', 'stabbed' and 'mark'. No wonder the crowd are moved to anger and revenge.

T.S. Eliot uses the contrast between verse and prose in *Murder in the Cathedral.* When the knights have murdered Thomas, they explain why they have done it. Eliot, by giving them prose, shows that they are narrow, unimaginative and worldly men. They don't really understand what they have done, so all they can offer as explanations are unemotional, everyday reasons. One, for instance, tries to persuade the audience that Thomas was a psychological case, who, in effect, committed suicide. Eliot contrasts this lack of feeling with the words of the priest who mourns the death of Thomas. The priest, of course, is given verse to express his overwhelming grief and bewilderment.

## 11.5 CONVENTIONS OF LANGUAGE: CHARACTERS TALKING ABOUT THEMSELVES

If you look back to Brutus's speech quoted above you will see that he refers to himself in the third person. This is a convention that often puzzles people who are new to Shakespeare. If you can recognise what is going on, you may be able to appreciate that it is a way of speaking that can make the occasion and the character impressive and grand. For instance, when Caesar refuses to listen to requests he talks about his firmness in the third person:

Be not fond,
To think that Caesar bears such rebel blood
That will be thawed from the true quality
With that which melteth fools . . .

Caesar is saying that he will not give into the things that persuade fools to change their minds. Speaking of himself in the third person helps him to create an impressive and grand sense of firmness, because it presents the idea that even Caesar himself is looking on with admiration at such a determined decision.

Another convention that can confuse students is that of a ruler being referred to by the name of his country. These lines occur in *King Lear*:

Call France. Who stirs?
Call Burgundy.

It is the King of France and the Duke of Burgundy who are being called, not the lands of France and Burgundy. The convention is an important one, for it tells you something of the importance of a king. In a very important sense a king *is* his country. He is the representative of it, and his character affects it. Thus the victory of Henry V in the play of that name is celebrated as a victory of England over France. One of the things you must accept in Shakespeare is the important position of the king. The convention of referring to him by the name of his country is a way of establishing that importance.

## 11.6 CONVENTIONS OF LANGUAGE: 'YOU' AND 'THOU'

The distinction between 'you' and 'thou' does not usually raise problems. It is, however, an important one to understand because it indicates the emotional tone of the scene. The distinction is that 'you' is used when the occasion is formal and a speaker wants to remind listeners of the social difference, but 'thou' when the speakers are equal and the mood is friendly and intimate. There is a striking example in the second scene of *Hamlet*, where the new king, Claudius, wants to be friendly to Laertes, the son of his chief minister. His speech to him is full of 'thees' and 'thous' and ends:

Take thy fair hour, Laertes, time be thine,
And thy best graces spend it at thy will.

'*Thy* fair', 'time be *thine*', '*thy* best graces' and '*thy* will'; we can feel that Claudius is going out of his way to appear friendly. When, however, he turns to Hamlet, the tone changes:

How is it that the clouds still hang on you?

That is chilly. The way he holds back the word 'you' till the end of the line indicates that Claudius wants Hamlet to see that he is not going to treat him either as an equal or a friend. From the very start of the play, therefore, the tension between them has been established. Whenever you come across a change from one form of address to the other, it is a good idea to ask: is it important that the characters are using 'you' or 'thou'? You will usually find that the change tells you something important about the attitudes of characters to each other.

## 11.7 CONVENTIONS OF LANGUAGE: THE SOLILOQUY

A soliloquy occurs when a character is either alone or isolated upon the stage and speaks aloud his or her thoughts. It is a convention in Shakespeare to place soliloquies at the beginning or at the end of a scene, although he doesn't always do this. Macbeth begins act one scene seven with his troubled thoughts about killing the king, and Viola ends act two scene two of *Twelfth Night* with her reflections on the tangle she has got herself in. An exception is Leontes, who, in *The Winter's Tale,* has two soliloquies in the middle of act one scene two.

Soliloquies are usually of two kinds: the public and the private. In a public soliloquy a character openly addresses the audience. It is interesting that it is often the villain who does this. Iago in *Othello* and Richard III in the play of that name openly talk about what they are going to do. There is something rather disturbing about the way they buttonhole an audience and share their wicked plans with them. This is particularly disturbing in the case of Richard III, who is charmingly honest about what he wants to do:

> Plots have I laid, inductions dangerous,
> By drunken prophecies, libels and dreams,
> To set my brother Clarence and the king
> In deadly hate the one against the other:
> And if King Edward be as true and just,
> As I am subtle, false, and treacherous,
> This day shall Clarence closely be mewed up.

Richard reveals everything: the plots he has laid, the goodness of King Edward, and his gleeful expectation that Clarence will soon be in jail. It is that glee, that relish, that audiences find charming. This is something you should remember when you write about public soliloquies. Because characters talk to us, and, in the case of Richard, reveal their delight in evil, it is easy to be taken in by them. Therefore, you should bring out in your writing that an audience can know that a character is wicked and yet find him or her attractive.

A private soliloquy creates a very different effect. The audience is not addressed but listens in to, or overhears, the innermost thoughts of a character. The audience does not share the thoughts but is aware of hearing the private questioning that is going on in a character's mind. You should, of course, write about such soliloquies in a different way from the public ones. Listen, for instance, to Hamlet angrily questioning himself:

> Am I a coward?
> Who calls me villain? breaks my pate across?
> Plucks off my beard, and blows it in my face?

Because you are not being addressed, it would be wrong to find answers to these questions. Hamlet is puzzled, and what you should do in your writing is reflect his bewilderment. You could point to the way question follows question with no pause for an answer, and to the way in which Hamlet feels himself to be attacked. Hamlet is a mystery to himself, and it is the purpose of the soliloquy to express that. You should respond to that mystery in your writing.

Public and private soliloquies create different effects and are appropriate to different dramatic situations. Iago's public soliloquies in the early part of *Othello* show that he is a manipulator of other characters, and their confident, controlled manner is very different from the chaotic anguish of Othello's private soliloquies later in the play. In Miller's *Death of a Salesman* Willy's increasingly pathetic mental collapse is appropriately expressed towards the end of the play by a private soliloquy in which he talks to his brother, Ben, whom Willy wrongly imagines is present. Whenever you have to write about a soliloquy, then you should ask: in what ways is it appropriate to the character's situation? What dramatic effect does it create?

## 11.8 CONVENTIONS OF LANGUAGE: THE ASIDE

The aside is the convention in which a character momentarily turns away from the character to whom he or she is either listening or speaking and addresses the audience directly. Because it is always public, it establishes a relation between character and audience. Whenever you come across an aside, you should ask what the effect of this relation is. You will probably find that two effects are very common: sympathy for the character and humour.

In the first scene of *King Lear* the old king divides his kingdom up between his daughters by asking them to declare their love for him. The youngest, Cordelia, refuses to please her father by playing what she sees as a hypocritical game. Her refusal is quite harsh, but it has also been the experience of audiences that they feel sympathy for her. This is not just because she is honest. It is, in part, due to the fact that throughout the scene she speaks openly to the audience in a series of asides. After a particularly oily speech from one of her hypocritical sisters, Regan, she declares to the audience:

> Then poor Cordelia!
> And yet not so; since I am sure my love's
> More ponderous than my tongue.

Audiences, as we have seen in the section on public soliloquy, like being talked to. The spectacle of an anxious and honest girl opening her heart generates a sympathy which persists even when she coldly speaks to her father.

The aside has become an important convention in English comedies. Comedy is often built on misunderstanding, and audiences, who usually know what is going on, find it very funny when characters appeal to them about the confusion they are in. Audiences enjoy being in the know, so feel very superior when they are spoken to by a confused character. Goldsmith frequently uses this device in his delightful play *She Stoops to Conquer.* At one point Marlow and Hastings arrive at their intended destination, the home of Mr Hardcastle, but, because of a trick, they believe it to be an inn. Hardcastle, of course, knows nothing of this, so can't understand why they treat him as little more than a servant, and they are puzzled by his over-friendly behaviour:

*Hardcastle*: . . . Here, Mr. Marlow, here is our better acquaintance!
*Marlow* (*aside*): A very impudent fellow this! (*Drinks*) But he's a character, and I'll humour him a little. Sir, my services to you.
*Hastings* (*aside*): I see this fellow wants to give us his company, and forgets that he's an innkeeper, before he has learned to be a gentleman.

The asides allow us to laugh at all the characters. Hardcastle is trying to be a genial host, but to Marlow he is 'a very impudent fellow'. But because we know that they have been tricked, we knowingly laugh at their astonishment at his behaviour.

The last set of conventions that need to be examined are those concerned with the actions of plays. The three that often cause difficulties are: the chorus, disguise, and songs and dance.

## 11.9 CONVENTIONS OF ACTION: THE CHORUS

A chorus is an individual, or group, who speaks directly to the audience about the action of the play. *Henry V* and *Dr. Faustus* both start and end with chorus figures talking about the play, and *Henry IV part two* begins with a chorus figure who is called Rumour. The convention of the chorus seems strange because it makes drama a mixed medium. On the stage are actors who are representing characters, but they are joined by another figure who openly advertises the artificiality of the stage by refusing to be a character like the others and talking directly to the audience about what is going on. Odd as this may seem, it is something that you will have to accept. But not everything about a chorus is confusing. Unlike many characters, the chorus can be believed. When the chorus in *Romeo and Juliet* tells us that the play is about 'the fearful passage of their death-marked love', we have no reason for not believing him. In addition, the chorus is openly helpful; the one in *Henry V* is there to assist the audience to imagine the battlefield of Agincourt.

The most interesting chorus figures are those who serve the function of chorus and character. This begins to happen in Shakespeare when a character, so to speak, steps out of his or her role to make a direct comment on the action of the play. It is as if Shakespeare decides that something needs to be said, so one character is made to change from his or her role to that of a public commentator on events. At the end of *Twelfth Night* the twins, Viola and Sebastian, appear on stage together. Since the whole play has depended upon the fact that they are identical, somebody must make this point to the characters and the audience. Shakespeare selects Orsino:

> One face, one voice, one habit, and two persons,
> A natural perspective, that is and is not.

What he says is not expressive of his character, but is a chorus-like comment on what everybody can see.

It is, however, in a modern play, *A Man for all Seasons,* that the full development of the chorus figure who is also a character can be seen. Robert Bolt creates the Common Man, who opens and closes the play, as well as commenting on the action in between. But he is also a character, or, rather, a number of characters: steward, boatman, publican, jailer, foreman of the jury and, finally, executioner. He is both apart from and part of the action. In so far as he is apart from it, he is close to the audience; an ordinary person who, like the audience, views the lives of kings and cardinals. Indeed, we are meant to see him as ourselves. At the end of the play he says: 'If we should bump into one another, recognise me.' In the play he becomes characters, and though the audience can't have that same relation with him, it might see in him the kind of roles its members might have played in history.

## 11.10 **CONVENTIONS OF ACTION: DISGUISE**

Some students who are new to Shakespeare notice how much disguise is used. They also notice that characters hardly ever see through it. That is the convention that you will have to accept. What is important about disguise is the dramatic opportunities it presents. In Shakespeare it makes two effects possible: characters can say what they would otherwise be unable to hear.

In *As You Like It* Orlando is too shy to court Rosalind openly, but when Rosalind has disguised herself as a man she playfully suggests to him that she will pretend to be Rosalind so he can court her. This Orlando feels able to do, so he can say what he never dared to say and she can hear what she never expected to hear. Their playful courtship is lively; he can be open and straightforward, and she can willingly accept his proposals:

> *Rosalind:* But come, now I will be your Rosalind in a more coming-on disposition; and ask me what you will, I will grant it.
> *Orlando:* Then love me, Rosalind.
> *Rosalind:* Yes, faith, will I, Fridays and Saturdays and all.
> *Orlando:* And wilt thou have me?
> *Rosalind:* Ay, and twenty such.

A more serious use of disguise comes in *Henry V*, when the king, on the eve of the battle of Agincourt, disguises himself and wanders through his camp, talking to his soldiers. Because he is disguised, he can hear what otherwise he would never hear – what the soldiers really think of him. He can also express what he feels – his ordinary human emotions. He does this in prose, the language of the soldiers:

> For, though I speak it to you, I think the king is but a man as I am. The violet smells to him as it doth to me; the element shows to him as it doth to me: all his senses have but human conditions.

A very important idea in the play is that of brotherhood. When, before the battle, Henry speaks of the army as 'a band of brothers', he can do so because they have spoken to him and he has spoken to them about what he feels. This is made possible by the convention of disguise. Whenever there is disguise, you should ask yourself: what does disguise allow the characters to say and hear?

## 11.11 CONVENTIONS OF ACTION: SONGS AND DANCE

Shakespeare's plays are full of dance, music and song. They are not there just to entertain, though they do, but to point to important meanings.

Dancing was thought of as very important in Elizabethan England because it was an expression of peace and harmony between people, and even of the peace and harmony of the universe. When, therefore, Shakespeare closes his comedies with dancing he is using this convention to indicate that the characters are in perfect harmony with one another. *As You Like It* and *Much Ado about Nothing* both conclude with dances.

Music in Shakespeare is an expression of harmony. Cordelia speaks of her father, the mad King Lear, in these words:

O you kind Gods,
Cure this great breach in his abused nature!
Th'untuned and jarring senses, O! wind up
Of this child-changed father.

His madness is seen as a lack of harmony – 'untuned' and 'jarring' – and hopes for his restoration are expressed as the tuning of a musical instrument – 'O wind up'. When he does come round from madness, it is to the accompaniment of music.

Many of Shakespeare's songs are very appropriate to the scene in which they occur and also to the meaning of the play as a whole. In one scene of *Twelfth Night* the drunken Sir Toby and Sir Andrew ask the clown, Feste, for a song. He sings a plaintive one about love, which includes these lines:

In delay there lies no plenty,
Then come kiss me, sweet and twenty.
Youth's a stuff will not endure.

The words are sadly appropriate to the listeners; both are getting old, and Sir Andrew, in spite of his wooing of Olivia, is unlikely to find a wife. There is no 'plenty' at all in his 'delay'. And beyond this scene, the play enforces the idea that, because youth will not endure, happiness must be taken while it offers itself. When Olivia falls in love, she is determined to have the man whom she loves (she does not know it is Viola), and when Sebastian is approached by her, he seizes the opportunity to wed her. And even Feste, although he does not fall in love, takes every opportunity to earn money by his singing. The words of the song are thus deeply appropriate to the whole play.

Whenever you find dance, music or song in Shakespeare, you should ask yourself whether it tells you anything about the meaning of the scene or the play as a whole. You will find that they are conventions that reveal to you the significance of the action.

## EXERCISES

1 Below is act I scene 4 of *Twelfth Night.* Read the scene carefully and answer the following questions on it.

Viola has disguised herself as a young man – Cesario – and is serving in the court of Orsino, the Duke. He is in love with Olivia, but she does not welcome his attentions because of the recent death of her brother.

*A room in the Duke's palace*
*(Enter Valentine, and Viola in man's attire)*

*Valentine:* If the Duke continue these favours towards you, Cesario, you are like to be much advanced. He hath known you but three days, and already you are no stranger.

*Viola:* You either fear his humour or my negligence, that you call in question the continuance of his love. Is he inconstant, sir, in his favours?

*Valentine:* No, believe me.

*Viola:* I thank you. Here comes the Count.

*(Enter Duke, Curio and attendants)*

*Duke:* Who saw Cesario, ho!
*Viola:* On your attendance, my lord, here.
*Duke:* Stand you awhile aloof . . . (*Curio and attendants withdraw*)
Cesario,
Thou knowest no less but all: I have unclasped
To thee the book even of my secret soul.
Therefore, good youth, address thy gait unto her,
Be not denied access, stand at her doors,
And tell them, there thy fixéd foot shall grow
Till thou have audience.
*Viola:* Sure, my noble lord,
If she be so abandoned to her sorrow
As it is spoke, she never will admit me.
*Duke:* Be clamorous and leap all civil bounds
Rather than make unprofited return.
*Viola:* Say I do speak with her, my lord, what then?
*Duke:* O, then unfold the passion of my love,
Surprise her with discourse of my dear faith:
It shall become thee well to act my woes;
She will attend it better in thy youth
Than in a nuncio's of more grave aspect.
*Viola:* I think not so, my lord.
*Duke:* Dear lad, believe it;
For they shall yet belie thy happy years,
That say thou art a man: Diana's lip
Is not more smooth and rubious; thy small pipe
Is as the maiden's organ, shrill and sound –
And all is semblative a woman's part.

I know thy constellation is right apt
For this affair. Some four or five attend him,
All if you will; for I myself am best
When least in company. Prosper well in this,
And thou shalt live as freely as thy lord,
To call his fortunes thine.

*Viola:* I'll do my best,
To woo your lady. (*aside*) Yet, a barful strife!
Whoe'er I woo, myself would be his wife.

(a) Why is the scene up to the entrance of the Duke in prose?

(b) Try to account for why some characters use 'you' and others 'thou'.

(c) Bearing in mind that the audience knows Viola is disguised as a man but that Orsino does not know this, write about the way Orsino speaks to Viola in the speech beginning 'Dear lad, believe it . . .' (line 29).

(d) What is the effect of the aside at the end of the scene?

2 Look at the plays you are studying to see if their construction tells you anything about their meaning. If any of them are by Shakespeare, see if act three scene one or two is the turning point of a two-fold movement.

3 Look at how verse and prose are used in the plays you are studying. Can you say why the playwright has used one or the other?

4 Write about any conventions of action such as a chorus, disguise or music that are used in the plays you are studying.

# CHAPTER 12

# THE LANGUAGE OF DRAMA

## 12.1 LANGUAGE AND DRAMATIC ACTION

All literary works employ conventions; in this respect drama is no different from poetry or novels. All literary works also make meanings with words. But this raises a question: what is distinctive about the language of drama? Poetry uses words in verse, and novels use them in prose. Since drama uses both, is it enough to say that an understanding of verse and prose is all that is needed to understand drama? It is true that the poetry used in drama can be looked at in the way Part I suggests poetry can be studied, and some of the things said in Part II on novels apply to drama, but more is needed. Drama is not something just read or heard, it is acted out before an audience. It follows that there must be something about the language of drama that makes it different from non-dramatic poetry or prose.

The difference can be put this way: the language of drama suggests, or invites, action. The words of a play should invite embodiment in action, whether that action is the movements of an individual actor or the placing of a group of actors on stage. When, therefore, you read a play, you must learn to see how the words, so to speak, cry out for accompanying actions. To help you to do this, three characteristics of dramatic language will be discussed: the way words invite actors to make movements, the way they indicate to the actor the mood of the scene, and the way they suggest grouping on the stage.

## 12.2 LANGUAGE AND MOVEMENT

A question you should always bear in mind when you read a play is: do these words invite movement? Some words, of course, do not, but unless there are others that invite the actors to make movements, the text of the play will be undramatic and dull.

Sometimes the words of a play invite a specific gesture. In *Twelfth Night* Viola, disguised as Cesario, goes to see Olivia. Olivia is wearing a veil, but the bold Viola asks: 'Good Madam, let me see your face.' Olivia is a little shocked, but she agrees:

> . . . but we will draw the curtain, and show you the picture. Look you, sir, such a one I was this present: is't not well done?

Olivia employs the image of a curtain hanging before a picture; the picture is her face, and the curtain her veil. The words invite the actress to lift the veil. At the word 'draw' she could take hold of the veil, start to lift it at 'show', and by the time she says 'Look you' her face must be visible.

That is a very simple example. Most of the speeches that invite action are more complex in that, though it is clear the words need to be acted out, a wide range of actions carried out in a number of ways are possible. It is important for you to remember this. Shakespeare is not asking actors to behave mechanically; his words need to be given bodily expression, but in most cases a variety of movements and gestures are appropriate. This is why the plays act so well, and why new productions are always possible; the words ask to be acted out but leave the actor free as to exactly how it should be done.

Let us look at an example. At the end of *Henry IV part two* Falstaff, the riotous companion of the youthful Prince Hal, hears that the old king is dead and that, consequently, Hal is the new monarch. Overjoyed with the news, he and Pistol rush to London to greet the new king in the expectation that their life of drunken merriment will continue. As Hal goes by, Falstaff confidently greets him from the crowd:

> *Falstaff:* God save thy grace, King Hal! my royal Hal!
> *Pistol:* The heavens thee guard and keep, most royal imp of fame!
> *Falstaff:* God save thee, my sweet boy!
> *King:* My lord chief justice, speak to that vain man.
> *Lord Chief Justice:* Have you your wits? know you what 'tis you speak?
> *Falstaff:* My king! my Jove! I speak to thee, my heart!
> *King:* I know thee not, old man. Fall to thy prayers.
> How ill white hairs become a fool and a jester!
> I have long dreamed of such a kind of man,
> So surfeit-swelled, so old, and so profane;
> But, being awaked, I do despise my dream.
> Make less thy body hence, and more thy grace,
> Leave gormandizing, know the grave doth gape
> For thee thrice wider than for other men.
> Reply not to me with a fool-born jest,
> Presume not that I am the thing I was,

For God doth know, so shall the world perceive,
That I have turned away my former self;
So will I those that kept me company.

The curt order 'Fall to thy prayers' tells the actor who is playing Falstaff what to do. The action is in the words – he must fall to the ground. It is as if a stage direction has been incorporated into the text of the play. It is, however, up to the actor as to *how* he falls. Does he immediately kneel, or does he stand in a state of shock and then slowly crumple, one knee at a time, to the ground? Does he fall to the ground himself, or does he need the help of Pistol? And how does Hal deliver the line? Does he point to the ground or does he move forward and force Falstaff to grovel before him?

There are other words that invite movement but don't specify what it should be. There could be a gesture in the words about Falstaff's 'white hairs'. Does the king gesture to the crowd to attend to him and then point to the head of the man who is pathetically kneeling before him? When he speaks of dreaming 'of such a kind of man', is he talking confidentially to the Chief Justice, publicly to the crowd, or reproachfully to the fallen Falstaff? Whichever way the actor chooses, there will be appropriate gestures; he could place his hand upon the Chief Justice's arm, extend his arm to the crowd, or point an accusing finger at his former friend. The line 'Reply not to me with a fool-born jest' offers interesting opportunities to the actor. Does the king see that Falstaff is about to speak? If so, does he make a dismissive gesture as he delivers the words, indicating that the humiliated Falstaff must not even open his mouth? Or does he angrily step forward and shout at Falstaff while gesturing towards himself at the words 'to me'? The lines about God and all the world knowing and perceiving surely invite Hal to make gestures expansive enough to match the huge claim that he is making, and the words 'I have turn'd away my former self' could be accompanied by a sharp turn, a gesture of putting something behind him, or a movement to a different place on the stage.

The point you should grasp is that the words richly suggest movement, and you should try to convey this in your writing. You can do this by pointing to the possibility of gestures in the words, or, as in the above paragraph, giving a few examples of what the actor might do. Whatever you say, you must not forget that it is the words of the play that invite action. You have, therefore, to show the dramatic opportunities that lie in them.

## 12.3 LANGUAGE AND MOVEMENT: THE MEANING OF PLAYS

Some of the actions suggested by the words have more than a particular importance. Words can invite actions which are significant for the whole meaning of the play. This, in fact, is true of the above scene. Throughout *Henry IV part one* and *part two* there is a tension between the need for order in society and the necessity – and pleasure – of games. Henry IV himself is worried that his son seems to spend all his time in the pursuit of pleasure and fears what the country will be like when Hal becomes king. The dismissive gestures which put Falstaff in his place are, therefore, central to the meaning of the play; when Falstaff falls to his knees, we know that Hal is a changed man, and that law, justice and order will not be neglected in England.

Another example of an action which reveals something central to the meaning of a play is to be found in *Macbeth.* Macbeth is given a soliloquy before he kills Duncan. Left alone, his mind starts to play tricks on him. In the air, or upon a table, he thinks that he sees a dagger. Aware that he might be having an hallucination, he questions its reality:

> Is this a dagger, which I see before me,
> The handle towards my hand? Come, let me clutch thee –
> I have thee not, and yet I see thee still.

Those words invite the actor to reach out for what Macbeth thinks is before him. It is a dramatic moment; Macbeth either grasps the air, or, if the director wishes, he can place his hand firmly on the table to find nothing but its hard surface. But the moment has significance beyond the scene; Macbeth is a man who wants things. Earlier, when the witches have finished speaking, he demands to know more: 'Stay, you imperfect speakers, tell me more.' And later, when he has become king, he longs to know more about the future. Above all, Macbeth wants the throne. Just as he clutches desperately at the imaginary dagger so he burns with desire for the throne of Scotland. In short, the dramatic gesture of reaching out reveals the very nature of the man and the central theme of the play – Macbeth is a bold, ambitious and ruthless man who clutches at those things he wants. When you write about an action suggested by the words that is central to the play, you should adopt the practice used here: write about the lines in detail and then relate it to other aspects of the play that bring out the same characteristics.

## 12.4 LANGUAGE AND MOVEMENT IN NON-SHAKESPEARIAN DRAMA

It is one of the very important features of Shakespeare's dramatic writing that there are movements in the words. What, however, of the other plays you are likely to find in public examinations? If you look at post-Shakespearian drama, you will find the words dramatists use still invite action, although it might not be quite so striking. Let us look at two examples.

In the opening scene of Congreve's *The Way of the World,* Mirabell and Fainall are rising from the card table. Fainall has been winning but he does not take up Mirabell's suggestion to 'play on to entertain you'. This is part of what Fainall says:

> No, I'll give you your revenge another time, when you are not so indifferent; you are thinking of something else now, and play too negligently; the coldness of a losing gamester lessens the pleasure of a winner.

Is there a light, dismissive gesture in the opening 'No', and could the words 'when you are not so indifferent' suggest that Fainall either leans forward or points his finger for emphasis? His remark that Mirabell is 'thinking of something else now' could be accompanied by a pointed finger or a wide sweep of the arm to suggest that thoughts are elsewhere. The final remark about 'the coldness of a losing gamester' might be said with a small flourish associated with words which have the self-evident truth of a proverb – the kind of gesture that is made when the speaker is effectively saying, 'we all know that.' Congreve's words, then, do suggest movement, although it is not dramatic or even immediately obvious. Yet that is appropriate; Congreve is writing about characters who are rich and leisured, but who do not lead momentous lives like kings and queens.

The second example is from a modern play, *A Man for all Seasons.* At one point Sir Thomas More deliberately picks a quarrel with the Duke of Norfolk. He shows that the nobility of England, because they have given in to the king, are men without honour. More, however, will not give in. This is part of the speech, including Robert Bolt's stage direction:

> Well, as a spaniel is to water, so is a man to his own self. I will not give in because I oppose it – *I* do – not my pride, not my spleen, nor any other of my appetites but *I* do – *I. (He goes up to him and feels him up and down like an animal.)* Is there no single sinew in the midst of this that serves no appetite of Norfolk's but is, just, Norfolk? There is! Give *that* some exercise my lord!

Bolt's stage direction is unnecessary; it is clear from the words that More must feel, or playfully thump, Norfolk as he speaks these lines. And in the words before it is clear that the emphasised 'I's must be accompanied by a gesture indicating More's true, inner self; perhaps he points towards his heart with both hands, or places one of his hands, palm down, in the centre of his chest.

The gestures in Congreve and Bolt are much weaker than in Shakespeare, yet they are there. In some plays, however, the words don't suggest action. In Tom Stoppard's *Rosencrantz and Guildenstern are Dead* some actions are given in stage directions, and one character, the player, is given words that invite sweeping, theatrical gestures, but the two main characters entertain the audience not by embodying words in actions but by the rapid and witty nature of their dialogue. Near the end of the play they discover that Hamlet, whom they are taking to England, will be executed on arrival. This is what Guildenstern says about this:

> Let us keep things in proportion. Assume, if you like, that they're going to kill him. Well, he is a man he is mortal, death comes to us all, etcetera, and consequently he would have died anyway, sooner or later. Or to look at it from the social point of view – he's just one man among many, the loss would be well within reason and convenience. And then again, what is so terrible about death?

It is difficult to see that those words are dramatic in the sense defined above. Of course, it is possible for an actor to invent accompanying actions, but that is different from the words suggesting or inviting movement. The words are entertaining, because a man trying to be rational about death is likely to sound absurd, but it is hard to see them requiring performance. Some think this is a fault; others say that an audience should just enjoy the wit of the words. You should make up your own mind, remembering that the theatre offers a variety of pleasures – big actions and clever dialogue – but bearing in mind that unless dramatic language is in some way distinctive it fails to be dramatic at all.

## 12.5 LANGUAGE AND MOOD

An important characteristic of dramatic language is the way it indicates the mood of a scene. It does this, so to speak, by incorporating stage directions into the dialogue. Quite often in Shakespeare at moments of high tension a character will remark upon how a speech has been delivered. Such remarks, of course, direct the actor to deliver the lines in a particular way. Let us look at two examples.

In *Much Ado about Nothing*, the young soldier, Claudio, who is to marry Hero, has been deceived into believing that she has been unfaithful to him before marriage. Claudio decides to denounce her at the wedding. This is from the speech he delivers before he leaves the church:

> O Hero, what a hero hadst thou been,
> If half thy outward graces had been placed
> About thy thoughts and counsels of thy heart!
> But fare thee well, most foul, most fair! farewell,
> Thou pure impiety and impious purity!

Claudio, who is deeply puzzled and angry, delivers these emotional words to the girl whom he once loved. Many readers have been shocked by their unfeeling harshness. He accuses her of being utterly deceitful and goes so far as to use the word 'foul' of her. If, however, the reader looks at the later part of the scene, something interesting emerges. Leonato, who is heart-broken, speaks of *how* the lines were delivered:

speaking of her foulness
Washed it with tears.

That indicates both how the lines should be delivered and how distressed Claudio is. The reader, therefore, should remember that though the words are harsh, they come from a man who weeps as he speaks. The emotional mood is one of distress and regret, as well as outrage.

In *Othello* there is a highly dramatic scene in which Othello, convinced that his wife has been unfaithful, enters her bedroom with the intention of killing her. But, like Claudio, his mood is not a simple one. He is outraged by her imagined adultery but, at the same time, he is overwhelmed by her beauty and his love for her. The actor playing Othello must portray a man suffering the terrible tension between loathing and love. In order to indicate the mood of the scene and manner in which the actor should deliver the lines, Shakespeare gives these lines to Desdemona:

And yet I fear you, for you are fatal then,
When your eyes roll so:

Alas, why gnaw you so your nether lip?
Some bloody passion shakes your very frame.

These lines are directions to the actor built into the text; he must roll his eyes, gnaw his bottom lip and shake. Those are the outward expressions of the terrible emotional conflict that is consuming Othello.

You will not find very many passages in which the words indicate the mood of the scene. Nevertheless, when you are writing about plays, you should bear in mind that dramatic language is different from the language of poetry or that of novels. One way of bringing out the difference is by discussing how the words occasionally indicate to actors how their parts should be performed.

## 12.6 LANGUAGE AND GROUPING

A very important characteristic of dramatic language is its ability to indicate how actors should be grouped upon stage. If the above point about language and mood can be looked upon as instruction to actors, this point can be seen as advice to directors. In Shakespeare there are no detailed stage directions telling a director where to place and group actors. All the director has – and all you have – is the text of the play. Once a play is looked at in detail, it is apparent that Shakespeare built into the language of his plays directions on where to stand. You will find that these directions do much more than tell you where actors might stand, they bring out the significance of the action. Let us look at two examples.

*Richard II* is about the fall of one king, Richard, and the rise of another, Henry IV. At the start of the play Richard banishes Henry, but after Richard has seized the property of Henry's dead father, Henry returns to England with an army. They meet first at Flint Castle; Richard is inside, Henry outside with his army. The text of the play makes it clear that Henry and his army should be placed on the stage, whilst Richard should be on a balcony above it. This is what Henry says:

> See, see, King Richard doth himself appear,
> As doth the blushing discontented sun
> From out the fiery portals of the east . . .

The gesture in the words 'See, see' and the image of the sun both point to Richard being in a physically higher position than Henry. The picture is at once glorious and troubled. The rising sun is a majestic image expressive of hope, yet the sun is blushing and discontented. As the scene develops, it is the troubled aspect of the image that dominates. Richard, the sun king, sees that he can't resist Henry so he agrees to descend. These are his words: 'Down, down I come' express one of the central actions of the play. in the ascendent. Using the image of the mythical Phaeton, who guided the sun across the sky, Richard descends to the level of Henry. The words 'Down, down I come' express one of the central actions of theplay. Richard's fortunes are declining, so his descent from a higher to a lower level is symbolic of his fall. The words not only indicate position on stage but also invite the actor to perform an action which is central to the meaning of the play.

In the second scene of *The Winter's Tale* Shakespeare indicates how characters should group themselves. This grouping, as we shall see, is expressive of the mood of the scene. Hermione, the Queen, is shortly to have a baby. It is, therefore, not surprising that she does not want to play with her lively son, Mamillius. The grouping of the scene is immediately suggested in the first words from Hermione:

> Take the boy to you: he so troubles me,
> 'Tis past enduring.

She is speaking to her attendant ladies. One of them replies by inviting Mamillius to join them:

Come my gracious Lord,
Shall I be your playfellow.

The conversation that follows shows that Mamillius has left his mother and is sitting with the ladies. There are, thus, two groups: Hermione, and the ladies. When Hermione feels she is ready to play with Mamillius again she calls him from the ladies:

Come, sir, now
I am for you again: pray you, sit by us,
And tell's a tale.

There follows a delightful dialogue between Hermione and her son. He says he will tell a tale of 'sprites and goblins', but from his mother's next remark, 'Nay, come, sit down, then on', it is clear that he is not sitting next to her. Then he says he doesn't want the ladies to hear the tale, so Hermione says:

Come on, then
And give't me in mine ear.

It may be assumed that after that line there are two groups on the stage: Hermione with her son, and the ladies. But Mamillius's story gets no further. Leontes, believing that Hermione has committed adultery with Polixenes, bursts into the room with a group of lords. This creates a third group. He demands the boy and tells the lords to

Bear the boy hence, he shall not come about her,
Away with him!

It is clear from the dialogue that follows that there are three groups on stage: the angry Leontes and his lords, the ladies, and the now isolated Hermione. The loneliness of Hermione is brought out in the language of Leontes. There is surely a condemnatory gesture in these lines spoken to the lords:

You, my lords,
Look on her, mark her well . . .

All eyes are directed at her lonely figure. The women are of no comfort to her; indeed, so overcome are they that it is Hermione who has to comfort them:

Do not weep, good fools,
There is no cause . . .

Her words are moving. In spite of her increasing loneliness, she comforts her weeping attendants. Soon they are all dismissed.

The sudden change from light-hearted merriment to anger and the increasing isolation of Hermione are all expressed in the groupings suggested by the words. The grouping, therefore, can be said to express the emotional mood of the scene. Whenever you have to write in detail about a scene from Shakespeare (there are questions on individual scenes at both 'O' and 'A' level), you should follow the practice outlined above of seeing how Shakespeare groups characters by indicating their positions in the words of the play. A good question to ask of any scene is: are there indications in the words of where characters stand? It is not sufficient just to mention groups. You should go on to show that the grouping suggested by the words is expressive of the mood and meaning of the scene, or even the play as a whole.

## EXERCISES

1 Read the following extract from act 2 scene 3 of *Twelfth Night* and answer the questions below. Sir Toby Belch, Sir Andrew Aguecheek and the Clown (Feste) are drinking and singing till late into the night. Maria, a servant, has been trying to stop them making so much noise, but the din they have been making has awoken the stern steward, Malvolio. At this moment, a song has just finished, and Sir Toby addresses the outraged Malvolio.

*Sir Toby:* . . . Art any more than a steward? Dost thou think because thou art virtuous, there shall be no more cakes and ale?

*Clown:* Yes, by Saint Anne, and ginger shall be hot i'th' mouth too.

*Sir Toby:* Th'art i'th' right. Go, sir, rub your chain with crumbs. A stoup of wine, Maria!

*Malvolio:* Mistress Mary, if you prized my lady's favour at any thing more than contempt, you would not give means for this uncivil rule; she shall know of it, by this hand.

*(Exit)*

*Maria:* Go shake your ears.

What actions and groupings do these words suggest? You might like to think about how the following lines could be acted:

(a) 'Art any more than a steward?'
(b) 'Th'art i'th' right. Go, sir, rub your chain with crumbs.'
(c) '. . . she shall know of it, by this hand.'
(d) 'Go shake your ears.'

2 Read these two extracts from Goldsmith's *She Stoops to Conquer* and answer the questions below. In the first, Mrs Hardcastle is complaining about the life they lead in their old mansion and Mr Hardcastle is defending it. In the second, Mr Hardcastle is talking to his servant about how they should serve at table when their important guests dine.

*Mrs. Hardcastle:* Ay, your times were fine times, indeed; you have been telling us of them for many a year. Here we live in an old rambling mansion, that looks for all the world like an inn, but that we never see company. Our best visitors are old Mrs. Oddfish, the curate's wife, and little Cripplegate, the lame dancing-master: and all our entertainment your old stories of Prince Eugene and the Duke of Marlborough. I hate such old-fashioned trumpery.

*Mr. Hardcastle:* And I love it. I love everything that's old: old friends, old times, old manners, old books, old wine; and, I believe, Dorothy, you'll own I have been pretty fond of an old wife.

---

*Mr. Hardcastle:* You, Diggory, whom I have taken from the barn, are to make a shew at the side-table; and you, Roger, whom I have advanced from the plough, are to place yourself behind my chair. But you're not to stand so, with your hands in your pockets, Roger; and from your head, you blockhead, you. See how Diggory carries his hands. They're a little too stiff, indeed, but that's no great matter.

What actions and groupings do these words suggest? In the first extract, you might like to think about how the following lines could be acted:

(a) 'Here we live in an old rambling mansion . . .'
(b) '. . . and all our entertainment your old stories of Prince Eugene and the Duke of Marlborough.'
(c) 'And I love it.'

In the second extract, you might like to think about how the following lines could be acted:

(a) 'You, Diggory, whom I have taken from the barn . . .'
(b) '. . . are to place yourself behind my chair.'
(c) 'But you're not to stand so . . .'
(d) 'See how Diggory carries his hands.'

CHAPTER 13

# CHARACTER AND PLOT

## 13.1 CHARACTERS AND WORDS

Many of the questions on drama in public examinations deal with character. They ask you to say what a character is like, show how he or she changes, discuss the way one character differs from another, and judge the importance of a character in the play as a whole.

What, then, can you say about characters in plays? The most important thing to remember is that you can only learn about a character from the words of the play; that is, from the dialogue. A playwright, unlike a novelist, can't tell you things *directly*; all he or she has to work with are the words characters speak. How then can these words be looked at? This chapter deals with four ways in which characters are created. They are: the way characters speak, what they say about themselves, what one character says about another, and the way characters are contrasted with each other. You will see from that list that it provides you with four different approaches to character. Whenever you are studying a character in a play, you can take one of these approaches to see if it helps you to understand what he or she is like.

## 13.2 CHARACTERS AND SPEECH

The first way is the most important; what makes one character different from another is the distinctive way in which they speak. The first question, then, you should ask about characters is: do these characters speak in an individual way? What you should find is that the playwright has given to each character (or, at least, the important ones) a distinctive manner of speech. For instance, characters could speak in very short sentences, they could repeat words, they could be very formal, they could use long words, they could say a lot when only a little is necessary, and so on. Let us look at some examples.

In Bernard Shaw's *St. Joan,* Joan goes to see Charles, the Dauphin, to tell him that she has a mission to drive the English from France and have him crowned in Rheims Cathedral:

*Joan:* Gentle little Dauphin, I am sent to you to drive the English away from Orleans and from France, and to crown you in the cathedral at Rheims, where all true kings of France are crowned.

*Charles: (triumphant to the court)* You see, all of you! She knew the blood royal. Who dare say now that I am not my father's son? *(To Joan)* But if you want me to be crowned at Rheims, you must talk to the Archbishop, not to me. There he is *(he is standing behind her)*!

*Joan: (turning quickly, overwhelmed with emotion)* Oh, my lord! *(She falls on both knees before him, with bowed head, not daring to look up.)* My lord: I am only a poor country girl; and you are filled with the blessedness and glory of God himself; but you will touch me with your hands, and give me your blessing, won't you?

How does Joan's speech reveal her character? Look at her first words: 'Gentle little Dauphin'. There is kindness and simplicity in that expression. There is also simplicity in the rest of that speech, yet it is a simplicity which is direct and purposeful. Look, for instance, at the way in which one difficult task directly leads to another; she will drive the English from France *and* (the task is as simple as uttering that ordinary word) crown him at Rheims. Her directness and simplicity are also evident when she speaks to the Archbishop. Look at the confidence behind her request for a blessing. In a few lines, then, Shaw has shown Joan to be kind, simple, direct and purposeful.

He also gives the Dauphin words that reveal his character. Look at the childish glee with which he says: 'You see, all of you! She knew the blood royal.' Those are the words of a man who feels he has to assert himself. But he is also something of a coward. After that outburst, he pathetically tells her she should speak to the Archbishop about the coronation. From his one speech we can see that he lacks confidence and is cowardly.

The second example is from Shakespeare. Alexander Pope, the eighteenth-century poet, said that even if all the names of Shakespeare's characters were to be lost, it would still be possible to work out who said what. His point was that Shakespeare gives each of his characters a unique way of speaking. Although there are some servants and messengers who don't seem to have any individuality, the point is generally true. If you want to know what a character in Shakespeare is like, look at the words he or she speaks.

In *Hamlet* there is a character called Polonius. He is the chief minister of state, who claims that he is very good at finding things out. At one point he explains to the king and queen that he has found out why Hamlet is behaving strangely:

> My liege and madam, to expostulate
> What majesty should be, what duty is,
> Why day is day, night night, and time time,
> Were nothing but to waste night, day and time.
> Therefore, since brevity is the soul of wit,
> And tediousness the limbs and outward flourishes,
> I will be brief. Your noble son is mad.
> Mad I call it, for to define true madness,
> What is't but to be nothing else but mad?

What do these lines reveal about Polonius? It is clear he is a busy man, whose mind overflows with ideas. Look at the examples he gives: majesty, duty, day, night and time. Notice, too, that he is liable to become confused. The order changes from day, night and time to night, day and time. When he comes to the point he says he will be brief, but here another characteristic emerges: his practice contradicts his intention. Instead of coming to the point he elaborates the metaphor. He moves from 'wit' (it means intelligence) to talk of 'limbs'. At last, he makes his point: 'Your noble son is mad'. But he feels that needs elaborating, so in two further lines he explains that to be mad means to be mad! We can see, then, what Polonius is like. He is busy, energetic, and his mind is full of ideas, but he is easily confused, frequently contradicts himself, and is given to repetition.

Whenever you have to answer a question about what a character is like, you should follow the practice outlined above. Since the way characters speak is the most important way of creating distinctive character, you should find one or two passages from the play and discuss the language used. Your aim should always be to show that the style of speaking creates character.

## 13.3 CHARACTERS ON THEMSELVES

The point about speech revealing character is that words can tell you what someone is like no matter what it is they are saying or to whom they are talking. Very occasionally, though, a character says something about him or herself. You should, therefore, always be prepared to ask this question: do any of the characters in this play comment upon themselves? For instance, in *The Winter's Tale* Hermione says this of herself:

> I am not prone to weeping, as our sex
> Commonly are; the want of which vain dew,
> Perchance shall dry your pities: but I have
> That honourable grief lodged here, which burns
> Worse than tears drown.

The speech reveals a great deal about her. She has been accused of adultery and treason but she remains calm. She is aware that onlookers might judge her harshly, so she tells them it is not in her character to weep, although deep within her there is the terrible, burning pain of grief. The lines are important; Hermione is noble, self-controlled and strong yet she seems to lack warmth. Her speech helps us to see that though outwardly rather cold she is someone who can be deeply hurt.

The big problem with such speeches is whether we can believe them. In the case of Hermione we can, because nothing that she says or does elsewhere in the play denies it. The same is true of Richard III. In his opening public soliloquy he announces that he is going to be a villain, and a villain is what he becomes. In addition to the fact that nothing in the rest of the play denies it, we can also rely on the convention of the soliloquy. No matter how untrustworthy a character is when talking to others, when addressing the audience he or she is usually honest. Some characters are not to be believed. We can see that when Willy Loman talks about his success in selling, he is not telling the truth, because if he were, the family would be much better off. You must, then, learn to question what characters say about themselves. You can do this by comparing what they say to their actions in the rest of the play, and to what others say about them.

## 13.4 CHARACTERS SPEAKING ABOUT EACH OTHER

This leads on to the third way of establishing character – what one character says about another. You can ask: do characters make comments upon other characters? When the Common Man in *A Man for all Seasons* speaks directly to the audience about Sir Thomas More, we believe him because he is acting as a chorus. When Biff in *Death of a Salesman* says that Willy was 'never anything but a hard-working drummer who landed in the ash-can', we believe him, because everything in the play points to the sad truth of that statement. In *King Lear* a gentleman says of Cordelia that she

> redeems nature from the general curse
> Which twain have brought her to.

Although it is only one view, everything in the play confirms the truth of his words.

However, one character's speech about another can express no more than an individual point of view. One of the problems in *Antony and Cleopatra* is whether Antony is a great lover or a once great man infatuated by a wily woman. This view is given right at the beginning of the play when Philo calls him:

> The triple pillar of the world transformed
> Into a strumpet's fool . . .

To Philo he was a great soldier and statesman who is reduced to playing around with a woman who is no more than a prostitute ('strumpet'). It would be foolish both to accept or reject that view until the play has been studied in great detail. You should, then, attend to what one character says about another but always ask whether or not it is true.

## 13.5 **CHARACTERS CONTRASTED**

Examination questions are often built around the fact that some playwrights deliberately contrast one character with another in order to bring out what each is like. It's always worthwhile asking: are any of the characters in this play contrasted? The contrasts can be of different kinds. Some characters are contrasted because they have a lot in common, others because they are very different. For all their difference, Brutus and Cassius share many ideals, whereas, to pick an extreme example, Ariel and Caliban in *The Tempest* are opposite to each other in almost every way.

It is important to understand why the playwright contrasts characters. Usually a contrast brings out something important about the meaning of the play as a whole. For instance, the vivid contrast between 'Captain' Jack Boyle and Juno Boyle in Sean O'Casey's *Juno and the Paycock* brings out the difference between those who never face tragedy and those who do. Jack is idle, irresponsible and concerned with little else but drink, whereas Juno is sensible, determined and sensitive to the terrible times through which they are living. The contrast between them is brought out in their attitudes to the 'political' killings. Jack dismisses them as nothing to do with him: 'That's the Government's business, an' let them do what we're payin' them for doin'.' But Juno thinks otherwise: 'Sure, if it's not our business, I don't know whose business it is.'

The contrast in their attitudes is focused in the difference between Jack's 'them' and Juno's 'us'; he shuffles off responsibility, she sees it as theirs. Whenever you write about contrasts between characters, you should examine how their language creates differences. You should then be able to show that these differences, as in the case of *Juno and the Paycock,* are central to the play's meaning. O'Casey is concerned with how people react to the troubles of the civil war: Jack ignores them, whereas Juno chooses to face the horror and recognise her responsibility.

## 13.6 CHARACTERS WITHOUT DISTINCTIVE PERSONALITIES

The discussion above has shown that the four ways of creating character can be used as approaches to the study of character. Sometimes, however, you may not be able to discover characters who have distinctive personalities. There may be three reasons for this: they could be 'stock' characters, they may change to serve the plot, or the playwright may not be interested in them as personalities at all. Let us examine each of these.

A stock character in a play is like a flat character in a novel; that is, someone who has only one or two features rather than being fully rounded. One of the conventions of English drama is that there are a number of stock characters whom the audience can recognise. Here are some: the bashful lover, the domineering wife, the henpecked husband, the lovesick young man, the bold girl who will go to any lengths to get a husband, the stern father who will not allow his daughter to marry, the clever servant who gets his dim-witted master out of trouble, the revenger who seeks to right wrong by murder, the malcontent who shuns and is shunned by society, the fop who follows fashion, the rake who leads a riotous life, the fool, the jester who is clever and witty, the soldier who boasts about his deeds, the melancholy man who is never cheerful, and the priest who thinks up a clever plan to put everything right. Let us look at one example – the bashful lover.

The plot of *She Stoops to Conquer* requires that Marlow is a bashful lover, who is overcome with shyness when he meets the girl he wishes to court. Hardcastle says that he is 'one of the most bashful and reserved young fellows in the world'. That is Goldsmith's way of preparing the audience. When Marlow is left alone with Kate Hardcastle, he never looks up, and speaks hesitantly. But it is also part of the convention of the bashful lover that he is bold with serving women. Kate, therefore, has to dress as one in order to attract his attentions. She is not disappointed. Marlow never does anything unexpected; Goldsmith makes him conform to the stock figure of the bashful lover. There is, then, no need to say anything about his character other than that he conforms to the convention of a stock theatrical type.

In the case of Shakespeare, you will have to be careful. Many of his characters have, as it were, grown from stock types, but in their growing they have developed an individuality that makes them distinctive. Orlando in *As You Like It* is a bashful lover but he also vigorously defends Rosalind to others, is quick-witted when talking to Jaques, has a strong sense of family loyalty, is kind to his old servant, and, when roused, has a temper. None of these qualities are part of the conventional bashful lover. Even a character such as Brabantio in *Othello*, who comes very close to the stock figure of the angry father who won't let his daughter marry, is given an unexpected depth of feeling. At the end of the play it is revealed that he was so distressed by his daughter's marriage that he died of grief. When the audience knows that, it sees him not just as the conventionally angry father but as a man of deep feeling.

Sometimes a character is made to do a number of things in order to help the progress of the plot. The result is that when you study them, you find they don't make sense as individuals. The phrase that is often used of them is 'psychological inconsistency'. The point, however, is that they are consistent in a *dramatic* sense, not a psychological one. Quite often such characters don't cause problems in the theatre; it's only when the play is studied that their psychological inconsistency is noticed.

Such a character is the Duke in Shakespeare's *Measure for Measure*. Shakespeare uses the Duke to do a number of things: he leaves Vienna, gives power to a young lawyer called Angelo, returns in disguise, prepares for death a man who has been condemned by Angelo, works out a plan to save the young man from death, helps Mariana to take the place in bed of Isabella, a young nun with whom Angelo wishes to sleep, and, at the end, stages his return, exposes Angelo and marries Isabella. It is difficult to make consistent psychological sense of the Duke. (For instance, since the Duke knew that Angelo had refused to marry Mariana because her dowry was too low, why did he leave such an untrustworthy person in charge?) But we don't have to. Shakespeare is using the Duke to serve the demands of the plot. His interest in him can be said to be opportunist; that is, he uses him to do very many different jobs as the opportunities arise. Without him the plot would not work.

The third reason why you may not be able to find characters in a play is that there aren't any. Instead of characters a dramatist may create symbolic figures or mouthpieces for ideas. Marlowe's Dr Faustus is more of a symbolic figure than a character. It is true that he is proud, adventurous and self-centred, but these don't give him a personality. Rather, they are symbolic of human pride, discontent and selfishness. At the end of the play the chorus invites the audience to see him not as a particular character but as an example from which to learn:

> Regard his hellish fall,
> Whose fiendful fortune may exhort the wise
> Only to wonder at unlawful things,
> Whose deepness does entice such forward wits,
> To practise more than heavenly power permits.

The language sets him forward as an example. The audience is to 'regard' his fall, which will 'exhort the wise' to only 'wonder' rather than 'practise' 'unlawful things'. Faustus is a warning to those who don't take that advice.

Oscar Wilde was interested in clever dialogue. Therefore, his 'characters' are mouthpieces for it. In *The Importance of being Earnest* the young men and women can hardly be said to have personalities. What matters about them is their dialogue. For instance, Gwendolen says: 'I never travel without my diary. One should always have something sensational to read in the train.' That is delightfully funny because it combines a primness of manner – 'one should always . . .' – with an open admission about the sensational nature of her diary. Likewise, Jack Worthing's remark, 'It is a very ungentlemanly thing to read a private cigarette case', is funny because it links what is socially important – being a gentleman – with something as trivial as looking at the initials inside a cigarette case. In neither case does the remark express the personality of the speaker. Wilde is interested in the wit of the dialogue not the creation of individual characters.

If you are unsure whether a character in a play should be treated as an individual or not, you should try asking why they do what they do. If you feel it makes sense to ask that question, then the character has a distinct individuality. If the question yields no answer at all, it is likely that the 'character' should be described in terms of his or her dramatic function. You must remember that in the greatest plays it may seem right to ask the question, but satisfactory answers are not easily had. For instance, nobody knows why Hamlet delays in his revenge, but few would doubt that it's a proper question to ask.

## 13.7 DRAMATIC PLOTS

As soon as you ask what a character does in a play, you are asking a question about plot. The plot of a play can be defined as all the actions of all the characters, and the reasons for them. But since plot has already been discussed in Chapter 9, and since many of the things said there apply to plays, there is no point in repeating them. What you should pay attention to are the different parts of dramatic plots. But before they are discussed, a question must be answered: is there anything distinctive about dramatic plots? The answer is yes. What is distinctive is related to what was said above about the language of drama: the plot of a play must act out, or embody, what the play is about. What makes a play a play is not its ideas, issues or themes, but the fact these are presented to the audience in the words and actions of the characters. In drama, audiences not only hear about issues, they see them acted out before them.

For instance, one of the ideas in J.M. Synge's *The Playboy of the*

*Western World* is the Irish people's love of heroes. Synge presents a young man, Christy Brown, who arrives in a remote part of Ireland with the story that he has murdered his father. The people regard him as a hero when they hear what he has done, because he has done what few dare to do. But Synge has to *show* the audience that this is an important element in the plot. He does this by introducing a group of girls who bring him gifts:

> *Sara:* And asking your pardon, is it you's the man killed his father?
> *Christy:* I am, God help me!
> *Sara:* Then my thousand welcomes to you, and I've run up with a brace of duck's eggs for your food to-day. Pegeen's ducks is no use, but these are a real rich sort. Hold out your hand and you'll see it's no lie I'm telling you.

Handing over gifts acts out the theme of the play. Honouring a hero is not a mere idea, it is publicly acted out in Sara's words and actions.

If you have to answer an examination question about the plot of a play, you should look for moments such as that one and try to bring out how the very actions of the play embody the basic ideas of the plot. The question you should always bear in mind is: are there moments in this play when the basic issues of the plot are acted out? You will not, of course, be able to do this unless you can see what the plot is about. If you are in doubt, you can look through the play scene by scene to see *why* one event follows another. If you do this a number of times, you should discover what the play is about.

In order to answer some examination questions you will need to recognise how different elements of plots work. The rest of this chapter helps you to do this by discussing six aspects of plots. They are: the way a plot begins, how the placing of scenes develops the plot, the pace at which a plot develops, the way playwrights handle expectation and surprise, the climax of a plot, and the way a plot is wound up at the end of a play.

## 13.8 HOW PLOTS BEGIN

Drama is the most immediate and intense form of literature. It is immediate because it is performed and intense because, in most cases, it is short. At the beginning of a play, therefore, the playwright must bring the issues of the plot quickly and clearly into focus. A good question to ask about the opening of a play is: can I see the plot emerging in the opening words and actions? Terence Rattigan's *The Winslow Boy* is a good example. The play begins with Ronnie Winslow alone on the stage. He looks nervous and is very worried when he hears someone coming into the room. It is Violet, the elderly maid, who enters. She is surprised, though pleased, to see him.

She sees that he is anxious, so asks: 'What's the matter with you? What have they been doing to you at Osborne?' Ronnie replies sharply: 'What do you mean?' An attentive audience will see from that that his worries are connected with the Osborne naval college, and when, a few lines later, he hears his parents and rushes into the garden, the audience will guess that he is ashamed of something. Later the entire plot of the play is brought to light – Ronnie has been expelled for stealing a postal order – but already Rattigan has made the audience aware that it must be something like that. The plot, then, emerges in the opening lines of the play.

## 13.9 **SCENES, SUB-PLOTS**

Once the play has begun, it is important to ask this question: why has the playwright made one particular scene follow another? If you remember that the playwright has created the plot, you will realise that there must be a reason for arranging the scenes in a particular order. The most useful answers that can be given are that the playwright is either inviting the audience to see the links between two scenes, or that one scene has raised expectations that the next scene might fulfil. Some examples will help.

Playwrights often invite audiences to see the connection between two scenes when plays have sub-plots. A sub-plot is a separate piece of action which is less important than the main plot; it might use a different set of characters though it could also use some from the main plot. In many cases sub-plots echo the themes of main plots, which is why playwrights invite audiences to see the connection between scenes. *Dr. Faustus* starts with three scenes in which Faustus decides to practise black magic, summons Mephistopheles, and agrees to sell his soul in exchange for twenty-four years of pleasure. And then in the fourth scene the sub-plot is introduced; Faustus's servant, Wagner, asks a clown to wait on him and summons two devils. The fourth scene reflects the preceding three. Both Faustus and Wagner want power and both want an assistant, and though Faustus is learned and Wagner only a servant, there is a disturbing relation between the two. The sub-plot is an ironical reflection on the main one, because although Faustus dreams of power he fritters his power away, like Wagner, on playing tricks. The two scenes show that they are not very different from each other.

There is an interesting case of one scene raising expectations which the next fulfils in *Twelfth Night.* At one point Viola is in a dilemma because she loves Orsino, who, in turn, loves Olivia, who, because she is misled by disguise, loves Viola. Viola can't see a way out of the problem, but in the very next scene Shakespeare introduces her twin-brother, Sebastian. When the audience learns that Sebastian, whom Viola thought was dead, looks just like her, it realises that there is somebody for Olivia to marry. The fact that Shakespeare moves so quickly from one scene to another indicates that he wants the audience to see the possibility of a happy ending; hence the quick fulfilment of expectation.

## 13.10 THE PACE OF PLOTS

If you have to answer a question on a play's hold over an audience (these questions are usually put in terms of a play's tension or dramatic interest), one of the issues you must discuss is pace. Pace is the speed of events, and the point about it is that it always varies throughout a play. Even in Samuel Becket's *Waiting for Godot,* a play in which two tramps wait for Godot, there are marked variations of pace, and though Godot never comes, the action changes from being quiet and leisurely to quite hectic.

There are two things you should look out for when you are considering pace: why the pace of a play changes and the appropriateness of pace to action and atmosphere. In the fourth act of *Antony and Cleopatra* there are many short scenes; within 280 lines soldiers hear strange noises, which they interpret as bad luck for Antony, both armies prepare for battle, the deserter Enobarbus becomes convinced of Antony's generosity and dies, a battle takes place, another battle takes place, Antony turns on Cleopatra, and Cleopatra tells her servants to inform Antony that she is dead. After such hectic activity, the pace slows dramatically; in a scene of 140 lines Antony attempts suicide, and in another of 90 lines they meet for the last time, and he dies. In other words, instead of seven separate pieces of action in 280 lines, there are two in 230. Why does Shakespeare slow down the pace? The answer is that he wants to concentrate on the death of Antony. The change from hectic activity to the simple gravity of death focuses the audience's mind and makes it see Antony's death as both touching and grand.

The pace of the opening scenes of *Macbeth* is in keeping with the action and atmosphere of the play. Once Macbeth has met the witches, he desires the crown. Scene then follows scene at a quite relentless pace until Duncan is murdered. The pace of the play is deeply appropriate to its action and atmosphere. The Macbeths desire power, and their desire is enacted in the swift succession of short scenes. The speed of events creates a tense, concentrated atmosphere.

## 13.11 EXPECTATION AND SURPRISE

Another way in which a playwright holds the interest of an audience is by raising their expectations. It is always a good idea to ask yourself at any point in a play: what expectations is the action of the play raising? As soon as that question is asked, you may see that drama appeals to something very primitive in us: we want to know what is going to happen next. When we see what the main concerns of a plot are, we want to know how it will work out. That 'how' is important; not only do we want to know what will happen to the characters, we also want to know how the playwright will make it happen. This is particularly the case in comedies. In *The Importance of being Earnest* there are two young men, neither of whom is called Ernest, who love two young women, both of whom want to marry someone called Ernest. Wilde has raised expectations that this problem will be resolved, but it is not until, at the end, he focuses attention on the governess, Miss Prism, that he sorts it out. The audience will be relieved that the problem has been resolved and will admire the skill with which Wilde has handled the plot to produce a satisfying end. In more serious plays expectation arouses foreboding. We know that *Death of a Salesman* is not likely to end happily (the title tells us that), so as the plot unfolds, our expectations are touched with a sense of oncoming disaster.

Most plays raise expectation, but sometimes a playwright works another way – by surprise – which, of course, is the failure to fulfil expectation. It can happen both in the middle and at the end of a play. The first act of *The Winslow Boy* (it is a two-act play) closes with Sir Robert Morton, a famous lawyer, interviewing Ronnie about the alleged theft of the postal order. The Winslows hope he will agree to act as their barrister. The pace increases as Sir Robert asks him about every detail of the case. Ronnie becomes increasingly confused, and Sir Robert concludes by saying he should stop wasting everybody's time and confess that he is liar and a thief. Ronnie runs to his mother and bursts into tears, and his father says Sir Robert's treatment of the boy is 'outrageous'. Then, very casually, Sir Robert asks that all the papers be sent round to his office in the morning. Everyone is surprised (including the audience), because it had looked as if Sir Robert believed Ronnie had stolen the postal order. But Rattigan has a further surprise – it is the last line of the act: 'Oh, yes. The boy is plainly innocent. I accept the brief.'

Surprises are often sprung on an audience at the end of a play. An audience watching *The Playboy of the Western World* is surprised at the beginning of act three by the appearance of Christy's father, whom Christy claims to have killed. But Synge provides more surprises. When father and son meet, Christy again attacks his father, but this time, instead of looking upon him as a hero, the people of the village are horrified and want to turn him over to the law. And then, in the last minutes of the play, father appears again – battered but still alive!

## 13.12 CLIMAX

A successful climax should do two things: it should fulfil the expectations created by the plot (or overturn them by surprise), and it should fulfil them by embodying them in a piece of dramatic action. The climax of *Measure for Measure* does both. The returned Duke stages a kind of trial in which the crimes of Angelo are exposed. This fulfils the expectations of the audience; throughout the play it has seen his moral decline, and, like Isabella, demands justice. But the play is also about mercy. The Duke insists that Angelo should die, but Isabella, although she believes Angelo has executed her brother, is persuaded to beg for mercy. In the words of the play, she lends 'a knee'; that is, she kneels and begs for the life of the man whom she thinks has wrongly condemned her brother. The point is that Shakespeare does not simply make her ask for mercy, he makes her kneel. That dramatic action embodies the theme of the play – the relation between justice and mercy. That is what all good climaxes should be like.

## 13.13 HOW PLOTS END

There are two things you should look out for at the end of a play: whether the end finishes off the action of the play, and how, in Shakespeare, the ends of plays reflect beginnings.

Some plays leave no questions to puzzle an audience. At the end of *The Importance of being Earnest*, for instance, it never occurs to anyone in the audience to ask whether the young couples will be happy. The play has fulfilled all its expectations so nothing is left to puzzle or intrigue the audience. But at the end of *The Playboy of the Western World* questions remain. Christy returns with his father, though their relationship has changed, with the son now dominating. The last words of the play, like the first, are given to Pegeen, the daughter of the landlord, who has grown to love Christy: 'Oh, my grief, I've lost him surely. I've lost the only Playboy of the Western World.' These words raise questions: will she marry the weak Shawn to whom she was engaged at the start, and if she does, will she be happy with him?

It is a good exercise asking yourself whether the end of a play finishes the action completely or leaves questions. You will find that the more serious a play is, the more questions are left to worry you. It is usually only in the happiest, lightest and most artificial plots that the action is neatly and smoothly finished off at the end.

Shakespeare makes the ends of his plays mirror the beginnings. He seems to do this for two reasons: to make the audience aware of the form of his art and so find pleasure in the symmetry of beginnings and ends, and to show the audience how much, or how little, things have changed in the course of the play. For instance, *Romeo and Juliet* begins with a street quarrel between the servants of the Montagues and the Capulets, the leading families of Verona. The play ends with both families reconciled and united in grief for their dead children. Thus, although there is personal tragedy, there is a change in atmosphere from the beginning to the end. But it is more difficult to see change in *Macbeth*. The play begins and ends with a battle. Moreover, in both battles the cause of the trouble is the Thane of Cawdor. At the beginning he is a rebel helping Norway; at the end Macbeth, as well as being a tyrannical king, is also the Thane of Cawdor. Peace is restored and the play ends with rejoicing, but the end mirrors the beginning so clearly that it is not wrong to wonder whether anything has really changed.

## EXERCISES

**1** Write about how the playwrights you are studying create characters. You can ask yourself whether the major characters are given a special way of speaking.

**2** Bearing in mind the point about what makes a plot dramatic, write about the plots of the plays you are studying.

**3** In the light of what has been said about how characters are created through the way they speak, read the following extract from Shakespeare's *Richard III* and then answer the questions below. Two murderers have been sent to kill the Duke of Clarence.

> *Second Murderer:* What, shall we stab him as he sleeps?
> *First Murderer:* No, he'll say 'twas done cowardly when he wakes.
> *Second Murderer:* Why, he shall never wake until the great Judgement Day.
> *First Murderer:* Why, then he'll say we stabbed him sleeping.
> *Second Murderer:* The urging of that word 'judgement' hath bred a kind of remorse in me.
> *First Murderer:* What, art thou afraid?
> *Second Murderer:* Not to kill him, having a warrant; but to be damned for killing him, from the which no warrant can defend me.
> *First Murderer:* I thought thou hadst been resolute.
> *Second Murderer:* So I am – to let him live.
> *First Murderer:* I'll back to the Duke of Gloucester and tell him so.
> *Second Murderer:* Nay, I prithee stay a little. I hope this holy humour of mine will change; it was wont to hold me but while one tells twenty.

*First Murderer:* How dost thou feel thyself now?

*Second Murderer:* Faith, some certain dregs of conscience are yet within me.

*First Murderer:* Remember our reward when the deed's done.

*Second Murderer:* Zounds, he dies! I had forgot the reward.

*First Murderer:* Where's thy conscience now?

*Second Murderer:* O, in the Duke of Gloucester's purse.

*First Murderer:* When he opens his purse to give us our reward, thy conscience flies out.

*Second Murderer:* 'Tis no matter, let it go. There's few or none will entertain it.

*First Murderer:* What if it come to thee again?

*Second Murderer:* I'll not meddle with it; it makes a man a coward. A man cannot steal, but it accuseth him; a man cannot swear, but it checks him; a man cannot lie with his neighbor's wife, but it detects him. 'Tis a blushing shamefaced spirit that mutinies in a man's bosom. It fills a man full of obstacles. It made me once restore a purse of gold that, by chance, I found. It beggars any man that keeps it. It is turned out of towns and cities for a dangerous thing, and every man that means to live well endeavours to trust to himself and live without it.

*First Murderer:* Zounds, 'tis even now at my elbow, persuading me not to kill the Duke.

*Second Murderer:* Take the devil in thy mind, and believe him not. He would insinuate with thee but to make thee sigh.

*First Murderer:* I am strong-framed; he cannot prevail with me.

*Second Murderer:* Spoke like a tall man that respects thy reputation. Come, shall we fall to work?

*First Murderer:* Take him on the costard with the hilts of thy sword, and then throw him into the Malmsey butt in the next room.

*Second Murderer:* O excellent device: And make a sop of him.

By looking very closely at the way the two murderers speak, what do you learn about the character of each? You might like to think about the significance of the second murderer's use of 'judgement' and 'damned', and about how the first murderer speaks of 'reward' and 'purse'. You might also ask yourself why the second murderer is given a long speech, and why it is the first murderer who suggests the manner of killing Clarence.

4 Here is the closing scene of Arthur Miller's *The Crucible.* Read it carefully and then answer the questions below. The play is about the trials for witchcraft in Salem. John Proctor has falsely signed a confession that he has served the devil. The Judge, Danforth, intends to display the confession publicly, but Proctor refuses because he does not want his name to be

ruined. Parris and Hale are clergymen, Elizabeth is Proctor's wife.

*Danforth:* Then explain to me, Mr Proctor, why you will not let –

*Proctor (with a cry of his soul)*: Because it is my name! Because I cannot have another in my life! Because I lie and sign myself to lies! Because I am not worth the dust on the feet of them that hang! How may I live without my name? I have given you my soul; leave me my name!

*Danforth (pointing at the confession in Proctor's hand)*: Is that document a lie? If it is a lie I will not accept it! What say you? I will not deal in lies, Mister! *(Proctor is motionless.)* You will give me your honest confession in my hand, or I cannot keep you from the rope. *(Proctor does not reply.)* Which way do you go, Mister? *(His breast heaving, his eyes staring, Proctor tears the paper and crumples it, and he is weeping in fury, but erect.)*

*Danforth:* Marshal!

*Parris (hysterically, as though the tearing paper were his life)*: Proctor, Proctor!

*Hale:* Man, you will hang! You cannot!

*Proctor (his eyes full of tears)*: I can. And there's your first marvel, that I can. You have made your magic now, for now I do think I see some shred of goodness in John Proctor. Not enough to weave a banner with, but white enough to deep it from such dogs.

*(Elizabeth, in a burst of terror, rushes to him and weeps against his hand.)*

Give them no tear! Tears pleasure them! Show honour now, show a stony heart and sink them with it! *(He has lifted her, and kisses her now with great passion.)*

*Rebecca:* Let you fear nothing! Another judgement waits for us all!

*Danforth:* Hang them high over the town! Who weeps for these, weeps for corruption! *(He sweeps out past them. Herrick starts to lead Rebecca, who almost collapses, but Proctor catches her, and she glances up at him apologetically.)*

*Rebecca:* I've had no breakfast.

*Herrick:* Come, man.

*(Herrick escorts them out, Hathorne and Cheever behind them. Elizabeth stands staring at the empty door-way.)*

*Parris (in deadly fear, to Elizabeth)*: Go to him, Goody Proctor! There is yet time!

*(From outside a drumroll strikes the air. Parris is startled. Elizabeth jerks about toward the window.)*

*Parris:* Go to him! *(He rushes out the door, as though to hold back his fate.)* Proctor, Proctor!

*(Again, a short burst of drums.)*

*Hale:* Woman, plead with him! *(He starts to rush out the door, and then goes back to her.)* Woman! It is pride, it is vanity. *(She avoids his eyes, and moves to the window. He drops to his knees.)*
Be his helper! – What profit him to bleed? Shall the dust praise him? Shall the worms declare his truth? Go to him, take his shame away!

*Elizabeth supporting herself against collapse, grips the bars of the window, and with a cry):* He has his goodness now. God forbid I take it from him!
*(The final drumroll crashes, then heightens violently. Hale weeps in frantic prayer, and the new sun is pouring in upon her face, and the drums rattle like bones in the morning air.)*

(a) What is the significance of Proctor tearing the paper which bears his signed confession?

(b) Write about the dramatic significance of Proctor saying that he can hang.

(c) Write about the dramatic impact of Elizabeth not preventing her husband going to the gallows.

(d) Do you think this is a successful conclusion? (You might like to think about the relation between Proctor's concern for his name and his willingness to be hanged.)

# CHAPTER 14

# TRAGEDY AND COMEDY

## 14.1 THE TERMS

Many of the plays set in public examinations are described as tragedies or comedies, and many of the questions ask candidates to discuss the tragic or comic qualities of a play. You must, therefore, understand what these terms mean. The word 'tragic', for instance, means a certain kind of literary art and not, as it does in the newspapers and television, any kind of disaster. (Snooker players failing to pot the black, as well as serious accidents, are called 'tragic' by journalists and commentators.) In understanding the terms, you will see that they are broad. This means that it is sometimes difficult to say whether a play is tragic or comic. Hence, you must learn to use the terms flexibly and avoid treating them as laws to which plays must conform.

Nevertheless, tragic and comic plays do have certain recognisable features. Let us look at them in turn.

The following aspects of tragedy will be examined: the plot that ends in disaster, the tragic hero or heroine, the fall of the hero, the sense of inevitability, the impact of suffering upon the audience, the sense of waste, the way the audience is caught up in the play, and the feelings of the audience at the end of a play.

## 14.2 TRAGEDY, CHAOS AND DEATH

Tragic plots offer a bleak vision of life; they concentrate on failure, conflict and disaster. In most tragedies two aspects of this vision are stressed: chaos and death. Chaos (it could also be called disorder) is both personal and communal; in some plays the central character goes to pieces, in others society disintegrates, while in many both fall apart. Othello descends into a personal chaos when he is misled into believing that his wife is unfaithful.

At one point he actually uses the word, though the tone is a loving one. His wife, Desdemona, has just exited, and, looking after her, he playfully says:

> I do love thee, and when I love thee not
> Chaos is come again.

The terrible irony is that it does. When Othello is misled, he becomes a psychological wreck who, at one point, collapses in helpless rage. Nobility and dignity give way to the chaos of an inhuman thirst for revenge.

In *Macbeth* the nation is thrown into disorder. Shakespeare presents this by showing the murders of Lady Macduff and her family, and through the imagery. Look at the following lines about Scotland:

> It cannot
> Be called our mother, but our grave.
>
> good men's lives
> Expire before the flowers in their caps . . .
>
> Meet we the medicine of the sickly meal . . .

These images are of death and disease. They show the state into which Scotland has fallen under the tyranny of Macbeth. There are many other lines. Shakespeare shows Scotland howling in pain, fearful and becoming accustomed to death.

In *King Lear* the chaos is both personal and communal. Lear gradually loses control of himself and, as he descends into madness, first his family, then the nation, and finally nature plunge into chaos. The central third act shows a mad Lear (personal chaos), having been shut out of his daughter's home (communal chaos), raving in a storm (universal chaos).

Chaos usually ends in death – the great shadow that hangs over all tragedy. At the end of Shakespeare's tragedies there is often a stark comment on the triumph of death. *Hamlet* closes with the entry of Fortinbras, who sees the bodies of Hamlet, Leartes, Claudius and Gertrude. He solemnly addresses death:

> O proud Death
> What feast is toward in thine eternal cell,
> That so many princes at a shot
> So bloodily hast struck.

The image is horrific; death is pictured as a hungry hunter, who, in order to have a feast, has struck down princes. Shakespeare uses such a horrible image in order to bring home the power and presence of death. At the end of many tragedies the audience is left staring the reality of death in the face. Indeed, some people say that the tragic vision of life arises from the fact that all life ends in death.

## 14.3 TRAGIC HEROES AND HEROINES

Tragedies usually centre on one character – a man of exceptional qualities in a high position. Lear is King of Britain, Coriolanus the greatest soldier of Rome, Hamlet a prince. These men inspire wonder and awe in others, so whatever happens to them has grandeur and significance. Because they are both remarkable and occupy high positions, it is understandable that their tragedy will affect the whole nation. The central character is called the 'hero'. The title indicates the character's importance; a hero is larger than life, almost god-like, and is at the centre of myths and legends.

At this point two questions arise. Can the central character be a woman? Can the character occupy a low position in society? Though tragedy is dominated by men, this does not mean there are no tragic women. Juliet and Cleopatra are clearly tragic, and so, too, is Lady Macbeth. Moreover, there are minor characters such as Portia in *Julius Caesar.* Though she says little, she is a remarkable woman, whose bravery and anguish mark her out as potentially tragic. The question that hangs over her, however, is whether she is fully developed enough to be tragic. That, generally speaking, is the case with tragic women. Although there are some tragic heroines, they do not attract playwrights as do tragic heroes.

The second question can be answered in a similar way. There are tragedies centred round ordinary characters (they are often called domestic tragedies). But there are very few. A popular question about *Death of a Salesman* is whether or not Willy Loman is tragic. There is no reason why a salesman should not be tragic (remember that tragedy is a broad term), but Willy Loman is so stupidly blind that he fails to qualify as one. It should be possible to admire or stand in awe of a tragic hero, and, of course, 'ordinary' characters can be admirable. The fact remains, however, that domestic or everyday tragedy is a very rare thing.

## 14.4 THE FALL OF THE HERO

The main action of tragedy is the fall of the hero. This fall is both external and internal; externally the hero falls from power and respect and internally from peace of mind. King Lear starts the play as a king, and, though stubborn and wilful, he has personal authority and confidence. By the third act he is wandering, crazed and half-naked, across a heath in a terrible storm. There could hardly be such a striking fall: from riches to rags, from sanity to madness.

When you write about the fall of a tragic hero, you should explore the way his language changes. Consider the case of Othello. At first he speaks simply yet eloquently, the verse moving with the steady grandeur of great music. This is part of what he says to the Senate (the parliament of Venice) in the third act of the play:

> Most potent, grave and reverend signiors,
> My very noble and approved good masters:
> That I have ta'en away this old man's daughter,
> It is most true . . .

Othello is in control of his language. Look at the solemn, measured rhythm of the opening line, the dark cadences with which the lines close, and the grave honesty of the admission that he has 'ta'en away this old man's daughter', which culminates in the openness of 'It is most true'. The tragedy of Othello is enacted in the change from that speech to the rambling incoherence into which he later falls. Later on he speaks in disjointed prose about a handkerchief which he believes provides evidence for Desdemona's unfaithfulness:

> Handkerchief – confessions – handkerchief! To confess, and be hanged for his labour. First, to be hanged, and then to confess; I tremble at it. Nature herself would not invest herself in such shadowing passion without some instruction. It is not words which shake me thus. Pish! Noses, ears and lips. Is't possible? – Confess? – Handkerchief? – O devil!

Othello's control has gone. What he says is close to nonsense; he wildly jumps from one point to another, obsessively repeating 'handkerchief'. The fall of Othello is a fall in his language from noble coherence to ranting nonsense.

When you study a tragedy, you should ask yourself this question: why does the tragic hero fall? Many reasons have been offered, and, though none of them are completely satisfying, they are worth thinking about. The two most popular are: the hero has a fatal flaw, and the hero wilfully goes against the fixed moral laws of life.

The idea of the flaw is that the hero has a fault, which, under pressure, brings disaster. It is common to think of this flaw in terms of *excess*. Dr Faustus longs for learning *too* much, Hamlet is *too* thoughtful, and Othello *too* willing to believe rumour. For all their great qualities, a flaw makes them unstable.

However, the idea has two disadvantages: it seems too weak to account for the terrible consequences of tragedy, and it underestimates the evil which tragic characters *freely* bring about. The first disadvantage can be seen in *Macbeth.* The flaw of over-ambitiousness might explain why Macbeth wanted to become king, but can it explain why Macbeth plunges Scotland into a bloodbath? Here the second point comes in. What is tragic about Macbeth is not that he has a flaw but that a man with such a huge poetic imagination should *willingly* pursue evil. There is no point in killing Lady MacDuff and her children, and, what is more, Macbeth realises this. Nevertheless, he goes ahead with the murder. There is tragedy in that. If Macbeth were not free to act (even if he chose evil), there could be no tragedy at all.

The second reason for the fall of a hero – that of going against the fixed moral laws of life – does take account of freedom. The word that is often used is *hubris* – an arrogant and excessive pride and confidence in oneself. The *hubris* of a tragic hero is seen when he decides to go against the fundamental moral and religious laws of life. The hero either believes that he is right or that his task is more important than morality. As a result, he falls foul of the moral laws of the universe. In other words, the *hubris* of the hero is always shown to be *wrong.* This idea does do justice to the significance audiences find in tragedy. It also does justice to the mixed feelings an audience might have. For instance, Hamlet might seem justified in revenging his father's death, but when his revenge destroys Ophelia and Polonius, an audience might not be so sure. But in that lies the difficulty of the idea; audiences often find themselves approving of, or at least being interested in, action that they know is wrong. Tragedy, then, can't just work on a moral level.

Whenever you write about the fall of a tragic hero, you should remember that there is always an element of mystery. Fatal flaws and the moral laws of the universe are simply ways of trying to account for the terrible mystery of tragedy. But though they go some way in explaining it, they never explain it away. At the end of a tragedy both the characters and the audience (and probably the playwright) wonder why the terrifying events took place. Even when reasons are given for a fall, the strange mystery of it persists.

## 14.5 THE SENSE OF INEVITABILITY

The fall of a hero is often inevitable. The harrowing thing about *Romeo and Juliet* is that the young lovers seem powerless to avoid the catastrophe that overwhelms them. It is very painful for an audience to witness events which it sees as inevitable, particularly when the tragic hero can't see this. The inevitability of tragedy raises two closely related problems: the extent to which the characters are free or controlled, and whether the outcome of events could have been avoided at all.

The tension between freedom and control is certainly there in tragedy. In some plays there is tension between the fact that characters make free choices and the feeling that there are unseen forces controlling them. This is evident in the opening chorus of *Dr. Faustus*:

> Till swollen with cunning of self-conceit,
> His waxen wings did mount above his reach,
> And melting, heavens conspired his overthrow.

Marlowe compares Faustus with Icarus, who, in the Greek myth, flew too near the sun. His *hubris* – 'did mount above his reach' – comes from free will, but his fall – 'heavens conspired his overthrow' – suggests that he was controlled. *Macbeth* is a similar case; it is never clear whether Macbeth freely chooses or is controlled by the witches. The point about tension is that it can't be neatly sorted out one way or the other. The extent to which heroes are free or controlled, like the reasons for their fall, is a mystery.

The question of whether or not the outcome of events is inevitable is related to the idea that tragedy recognises moral, or religious, values. If there are no values, there can be no tragedy. But since tragedy recognises moral laws, it is clear why the fall of a hero is inevitable. A hero falls because he tries to break the unchanging, and unchangeable, moral order. This is why there can't be social tragedy; that is, tragedy based on the customs of the society. Customs change from age to age, so a hero who tries to break them and fails in one age would not inevitably fail in another. There is, then, the feeling in tragedy that events are always going to turn out disastrously, because characters have broken unchangeable moral laws. It will, for instance, always be wrong for someone to take upon himself the role of a revenger. If we ever came to believe that revenge *was* right, *Hamlet*, for example, would not be seen as tragic.

## 14.6 SUFFERING

In tragedies there is suffering as well as death. Suffering can be both physical and mental. In *King Lear* Gloucester suffers when his eyes are gouged out and when he is told, immediately afterwards, that the son whom he loved, Edmund, has betrayed him. Gloucester's suffering is like that of many tragic characters in that it is excessive. This is another terrible mystery: the tragic hero not only suffers, he suffers excessively. Lear, for instance, has been foolish and blind, but what he undergoes physically and mentally is far in excess of his crimes. He is, as he says, a 'man more sinned against than sinning'.

Some people point out that though the suffering of heroes is excessive, it does lead to greater self-knowledge. This is only partly true. Hamlet suffers intellectual, moral and emotional anguish, yet at the end of the play he is, if not happy, more composed and settled. But Lear gains no insight from his suffering because he is simply too old to learn. His suffering is appalling, and nothing can be said to lighten its terrible weight.

## 14.7 THE SENSE OF WASTE

Because tragedy shows the fall, excessive suffering and death of a great man, audiences are likely to experience a sense of waste. A great man has come to nothing. At the end of a play, therefore, there must be the feeling that a great human being has passed away. At the end of *Antony and Cleopatra* the cold and unfeeling Octavius is victorious, but his victory does not diminish the stature of the two lovers. Even the death of Macbeth leaves the audience with the feeling that greatness has passed away, because the new king, Malcolm, is not as impressive as the tyrant whom he replaces.

The sense of waste leads to a consideration of other feelings that tragedy arouses in the audience. Three are important: the sense of vastness, of fear and of pity.

There is something massive and universal about tragedy. Tragic action involves individuals, nations, and even the whole realm of nature. In *Antony and Cleopatra* two nations – Rome and Egypt – are locked in battle; in *King Lear* Britain is at war with France, and nature and the gods, it seems, are at war with mankind. The vastness of tragedy is moral and religious as well as physical. In tragedies audiences see the central issues of human life explored. In *Macbeth* there is good and evil, love and hate, and loyalty and rebellion. These are universal; hence the sense of vastness.

The fear that tragedy arouses is not that of being frightened or shocked, but the feeling of being in the presence of forces that are strange and terrible. *King Lear* shows what a fearful thing hatred is. Lear responds in hatred when Cordelia won't say she loves him, and when the other daughters refuse to do as he wants, he launches into horrible curses. Likewise, *Macbeth* shows how one man can plunge his country into a bloodbath, and *Antony and Cleopatra* shows that love can be destructive. These themes don't frighten as a horror film does but they are fearful in their power to disturb.

## 14.8 THE INVOLVEMENT OF THE AUDIENCE

One of the distinctive things about tragedy is that the audience is invited to understand what the hero is undergoing; it is not an external observer but feels what the hero is feeling. (This is why the soliloquy is so important in tragedy.) The response it makes is one of pity. It is pity because terrible things are happening, which the audience sees as inevitable and is consequently powerless to prevent. As it sits and witnesses the terrible decline of a character, its heart can go out to him or her, but it knows there is nothing that it, or any other character, can do. In *Othello* the pity and the sense of powerlessness are so great that members of the audience have been known to shout, in frustrated desperation, at the doomed and misguided hero. An audience can even come to pity a character whom it did not like at first. Such a case is Richard II. In the early part of the play he is vain, proud and foolish, but when he falls from power, the audience shares his grief and pities the lonely figure in the prison cell who tries to imagine that his prison is like the world over which he once ruled.

## 14.9 HOW THE AUDIENCE RESPONDS TO THE END OF TRAGEDIES

Although tragedy brings suffering and ends with death, it is the experience of audiences that it is moving but not depressing. It has puzzled many people that audiences don't leave the theatre in a gloomy frame of mind but with a feeling of uplift, and, strange as it may seem, even joy. Nobody has satisfactorily explained why this is so, but three important ideas have been advanced: the idea of catharsis, the idea of seriousness, and the idea of human dignity.

Catharsis is an idea that goes back to the Greek philosopher Aristotle. He said that tragedy aroused and then drove from an audience feelings of pity, so that, by the end, they felt relieved. Catharsis is the act of being relieved, or purged, of those feelings. As an explanation of tragedy it has a number of difficulties. It was thought out to explain *Greek* plays, so it is not necessarily applicable to later ones. In addition, it is based upon ancient ideas of medicine that few people accept nowadays. A further difficulty is that Aristotle did not elaborate on the idea, so it is not clear *exactly* what he meant. Nevertheless, it is quite useful not as an explanation but as a *description* of what happens to an audience. Audiences *do* feel uplifted after a tragedy and leave the theatre calm and serene. Milton put the idea this way in *Samson Agonistes*: 'And calm of mind, all passion spent.' That, for many theatre-goers, is what catharsis means.

Tragedy reminds the audience that life is serious. At the end of a play the audience might feel that they have been reminded of the depths of life, of the fact that things *matter*. It could be they have been reminded that life is vast and wonderful, or that human relationships are both wonderful and very difficult. For instance, an audience coming out of *Hamlet* might realise very powerfully that friendship matters, because it would have seen a play in which, for all its darkness, confusion and doubt, Hamlet is sustained by the loyalty and friendship of Horatio.

Finally, tragedy reminds an audience that people can be dignified and noble. It is not always easy to believe or remember this in everyday life. Wars and starvation suggest that human life is cheap, and in many industrialised societies people feel small and anonymous – like cogs in a machine. But in tragedy we see heroism, nobility, courage, patience and love. And we see these things in spite of flaws, wilful evil and appalling suffering. It is said of Othello that he is 'great of heart'. The same can be said of most tragic characters, and of human beings in general.

## 14.10 COMEDY: THE HAPPY ENDING

Examiners often remark that candidates write well on tragedy but badly on comedy. This is not surprising, because people have always found it more difficult talking about what is enjoyable and funny than what is serious and tragic. As a result, there are fewer ideas about comedy available. Nevertheless, you will have to find appropriate ways to write about comedies, because they are frequently set in examinations. To help you to do this five areas will be explored: the happy ending, comic characters, love, the relation of comedy to the audience and laughter. As you will see, some of these points correspond, though are different, to the points that were made about tragedy.

Tragedy ends in death; comedy ends happily. If the tragic vision of the world is bleak, the comic one is bright and celebratory. This is not to say that every event in comedy is happy. In many plays there is anxiety, anger and misunderstanding, but these dark elements give way to joy, love and understanding. It is always a mistake to write about comedies as if they were tragedies in disguise. They are not; comic vision recognises the stuff out of which tragedy grows but shows that there can be harmony instead of chaos, and life instead of death. Two very important elements of a happy ending are the idea of the lost being found and marriage.

One of the happiest things in comedy is the spectacle of characters moving from the distress of being lost to the joy of being found. In *Twelfth Night* the twins, Viola and Sebastian, both believe that the other has drowned. The central action at the end of the play is the moving scene in which they both recognise each other. In *The Comedy of Errors* a husband is reunited with his wife, and the sets of twins are brought together. In

*A Midsummer Night's Dream* finding is more a case of coming out of a delusion and discovering whom one really loves. In the scene in which the lovers, now freed from their delusions, wake up Helena says with joy and wonder: 'And I have found Demetrius like a jewel.' Even in *The Importance of being Earnest,* a very different play from those of Shakespeare, the plot concerns how Jack Worthing was lost by his governess. At the end of the play he finds out who he is and, to his delight, discovers that his real name is Ernest. A point you should notice about lost characters being found is that theme is often more important than action that prompts laughter. A comedy need not be funny but it must have a happy ending.

The happy ending of many comedies is marriage. Marriage is the happy conclusion of falling in love and the promise of birth and new life. It is a sign of love, harmony and hope. This is expressed by Hymen, the god of marriage, at the end of *As You Like It.* As he enters to celebrate the marriage of four couples he sings:

> Then is there mirth in heaven
> When earthly things made even
> Alone together.

'Made even' means reconciled, and 'Alone together' means brought together as one. That is what marriage does. It is important to remember that marriage is a social institution. Therefore, at the end of comedies there is a wonderful feeling of characters finding a place in human society. At the end of many plays the stage becomes crowded with characters to show this wonderful feeling of belonging. Shakespeare is realistic enough to show that not everyone joins in (Malvolio angrily rushes off, and Jaques goes back to the forest) but he shows that it is sad that not everyone can join in the happy, celebrating community.

## 14.11 **COMIC CHARACTERS**

Characters in comedies are much more ordinary than those in tragedies. Although there is a king and a queen in *Love's Labour's Lost* and a duke in *Twelfth Night,* the audience never feels that the fate of their country rests upon them. In comedy even kings and queens are human and pleasantly ordinary. Consequently, comedies are not dominated by towering, heroic figures. The names of plays confirm this: *Hamlet* and *Othello* are tragedies, whereas *The Taming of the Shrew* and *A Midsummer Night's Dream* are comedies. Tragic titles focus on individuals, comic ones on the nature of the action. The central characters of comedies come in pairs or groups. In *Much Ado about Nothing* there is Beatrice and Benedick, and in *As You Like It* Rosalind and Orlando. In a play such as *She Stoops to Conquer* there are a group of important characters: Hardcastle, Kate Hardcastle, Tony Lumpkin and Marlow. Two very important aspects of comic characters should be discussed at greater length: the centrality of women and the importance of stock characters.

Comedy, particularly Shakespearian comedy, is dominated by women. Men are tongue-tied or over-romantic, but the girls are witty, sensible and enterprising. Rosalind is a splendid example. When she is turned out of her uncle's court, she disguises herself as a man and with her cousin, another enterprising girl called Celia, she goes off into the Forest of Arden. When she finds the man she loves, she proposes to him that she will pretend to be Rosalind so he can woo her to gain confidence. At the end she organises the marriages. The idea of the enterprising girl is also present in Goldsmith. When Kate Hardcastle discovers that Marlow is too shy to marry her, she disguises herself as a serving maid. Even in *The Importance of being Earnest* the girls are more decisive than the men: both Gwendolen and Cicely decide they must marry a man who is called Ernest.

Marlow, we have seen, is a conventional character. There are many more in comedies. One reason for this is that stock figures are amusing. Ben Jonson was aware of this. In *The Alchemist* Subtle and Face take over an alchemist's premises and let it be known that they have discovered what all alchemists were searching for – how to turn ordinary metal into gold. This news brings many visitors, all of whom are stock characters. For instance, there is the worldly man, Sir Epicure Mammon, who wants to satisfy his appetite for wealth, women and food; and a puritan called Tribulation Wholesome, who, although he is as greedy as the other visitors, solemnly claims he wants the money for the members of his religious congregation. One of the reasons why they amuse is that they conform to conventions; the audience can say of them, 'How typical!'

The other reason why there are more stock characters in comedy than tragedy is that in comedy the action is very important. Many of the things that entertain in comedy do so because of what is done rather than who is doing it. The stuff of comedy is mistaken identity, deception, and disguise, and those things are amusing in themselves. For instance, the trick Tony Lumpkin plays on Hastings and Marlow in *She Stoops to Conquer* is funny, because there is something basically amusing about two men thinking they are in a hotel when they are really in a private house. Because that idea is amusing in itself, there is no special need for the characters of Marlow and Hastings to be very full because their being full wouldn't add to the humour.

Whenever you meet a stock character in a comedy, you should ask: why does the playwright introduce a stock character? Two answers have been offered: stock characters are funny, and stock characters can show that what is important is action. There is a third which particularly applies to Shakespeare: they serve as a contrast to the more fully developed and original characters. In *As You Like It* there are two very conventional characters – the love-sick Silvius and the girl he loves, the proud and disdainful Phoebe. In one scene Rosalind, a highly original character, overhears their conversation. She becomes so angry with Phoebe that she joins in. This has a comic result, for Phoebe falls in love with her (remember, she is dressed as a man), but the scene is important in another way. It shows how different Rosalind is from a stock character, and, consequently, the audience is led to see that her love is more real.

## 14.12 LOVE

If the central action of tragedy is the fall of the hero, the central action of comedy is another sort of fall – falling in love. Because love is very important, several aspects of it need to be explored: its suddenness, the ways in which characters speak about it, how it can be planned, and the kind of plots it produces.

In comedies falling in love is often sudden and surprising. In *As You Like It* Rosalind and Orlando fall in love, if not quite 'at first sight', after a very brief conversation. They meet at the wrestling match, and after Rosalind and Celia have failed to persuade him not to wrestle, Orlando overcomes the Duke's champion. Then he is overcome by her. When she gives him a chain as a token of his success, he stands in speechless admiration. Rosalind, as always, is never lost for a word, but even when she goes back to talk to him, he remains dumb. When she has gone he simply says: 'O poor Orlando, thou are overthrown!' He is – that is what love does. In *The Importance of being Earnest* love is at first hearing rather than first sight. Cecily says that the moment she heard about Ernest she fell in love with him!

Because love is sudden, it is spoken about in dramatic ways. Love is said to be a madness, a plague or a game. The thing that these three have in common is transformation. When characters are in love, they are transformed, and their picture of the world is transformed too.

When Malvolio is deceived into believing that Olivia loves him, he transforms himself. The letter that has deceived him has spoken of yellow stockings and cross-gartering. These he willingly wears when he comes to woo her. The scene is both very funny and painfully embarrassing. He is in love with her, but she is only thinking of Cesario. Her attendants say that Malvolio has gone mad, to which she says:

> I'm as mad as he,
> If sad and merry madness equal be.

In *A Midsummer Night's Dream* the Duke sums up the strange events that have happened to the lovers by saying:

> Lovers and madmen have such seething brains,
> Such shaping fantasies, that apprehend
> More than cool reason ever comprehends.

That speech touches on two things: the 'seething' brains of both lovers and madmen, and the fact that they both see the world in quite strange ways. Their minds – 'fantasies' – are 'shaping'; that is, they create in their minds the world they experience.

Love can be as sudden and devastating as the plague. When Olivia first falls in love she says:

> How now!
> Even so quickly may one catch the plague?

Two ideas are expressed in these lines. The idea of the suddenness of love and the comparison with disease. In the section on tragedy much stress was laid upon the mysteriousness of tragic action. The likeness between love and disease points to a similar mysteriousness in love. Love strikes suddenly and for no reason, as does the plague.

Love is compared to games, because games, or holidays, are joyful transformations of the ordinary working world. Throughout *As You Like It* there are frequent references to games, sports and holidays. At the beginning of the play Rosalind says to Celia: 'From henceforth I will, coz, and devise sports. Let me see, what think you of falling in love?' Later in the Forest of Arden (a place where life is transformed by love into a dream-like holiday) Rosalind playfully says to Orlando: 'Come, woo me, woo me; for now I am in a holiday humour and like enough to consent.' The image of games is deeply appropriate: love is playful, enjoyable and, above all, *not* like ordinary life.

You will remember that Jane Austen shows that love should be allowed to grow naturally, and that those who try to plan and plot are wrong. That idea is not found in Shakespeare's comedies; in his plays characters can be brought to love each other. The plot of *Much Ado about Nothing* turns on the attempts of Don Pedro and his friends to make Beatrice and Benedick fall in love. They succeed. Even in *As You Like It* plotting has a place. Although Rosalind and Orlando are in love, Rosalind needs to plot and plan in order to get the shy Orlando to declare his love. Comedy, then, shows that characters can be brought to love each other by trickery. The tricks that are used most are disguise and deception. Rosalind dresses up as a man and uses this disguise to get Orlando to court her, and Beatrice and Benedick are deceived into loving each other.

## 14.13 COMIC PLOTS AND THE AUDIENCE

One of the biggest differences between tragedy and comedy is in the construction of plots. Tragic plots can be quite simple – a central character falls from wealth and honour to degradation and humiliation. But comic plots are often very complex. Take, for example, *A Midsummer Night's Dream.* There are three sets of characters: the Athenian nobility, the Athenian workmen, and the fairies. The plot would be complex enough with those three groups, but within those groups there are further complications. The lovers are divided from the older generation and, even more violently, they are divided from each other. Indeed, the number of times the lovers change their loves is bewildering. The workmen (the mechanicals, as they are called) are a happy group, yet they are confused when Bottom is parted from them, and in the world of the fairies Titania and Oberon have quarrelled, so they lead separate lives. From the audience's point of view complexity is delightful. An audience enjoys seeing one character taking part in several plots and waits in eager anticipation to see how things will work out. The point you should remember is that it is love that makes a plot complex. At one point in *A Midsummer Night's Dream* Helena loves Demetrius, Demetrius loves Hermia, Hermia loves Lysander, and Lysander loves Helena. With a situation like that, the plot is bound to be intricate.

When you consider the complexity of comic plots, you are considering the relation of the play to the audience. Here, too, there is an interesting contrast to tragedy. In tragedy the audience is invited to feel what the tragic hero is feeling, whereas in comedy it remains much more detached. A comic audience overhears and overlooks rather than sympathises. This should be reflected in the way you write about comedy. It is quite proper to say 'we feel for Othello', but when writing about comedy, it is appropriate to indicate the distance between the action and the audience. You can do this by saying 'We observe and are delighted by the confusion . . .', or 'As onlookers we are amused by the misunderstandings . . .'

A very important element in the detachment of the audience is that it knows more about what is going on than the characters on the stage. Comic characters plot and deceive each other, so some hold an advantage over others, but as the audience knows *everybody*'s doings it can look down upon the action in the secure knowledge that, unlike the characters on stage, it is not deceived. An audience watching a comedy, in other words, enjoys a delightful feeling of superiority. Consequently, it can enjoy the spectacle of the deceiver who is also deceived. In *Twelfth Night* Sir Andrew Aguecheek is encouraged by Sir Toby Belch to challenge Viola (whom he thinks of as the boy Cesario) to a duel. There is a very funny scene in which Sir Toby and Fabian persuade both Sir Andrew and Viola that the other is a very fierce swordsman. They are so frightened by each other's reputations that they can hardly fight. Sir Toby clearly enjoys deceiving Sir Andrew and Viola, but the audience has the advantage over him because it knows what he does not – that Viola is really a girl.

## 14.14 LAUGHTER

The detachment of an audience makes laughter possible. Because many of the situations an audience laughs at are painful for the participants, a detachment from the feelings of characters is necessary. It has been stressed that comedy need not be funny, but the fact remains that it often is. Although it is very difficult to explain why something is amusing (a joke that has to be explained ceases to be funny), you should when you write about comedies, be prepared indicate how laughter arises. To help you to do this three ideas about what makes people laugh will be discussed: expectation, characters behaving like machines, and a sense of proportion.

Expectation can be funny both when it is fulfilled and denied. When Tony Lumpkin directs Marlow and Hastings to Hardcastle's house by telling them it is an inn, the audience expects the misunderstanding to be amusing and is not disappointed. However, when Christy Brown's father, whom everyone believed was dead, turns up, the audience laughs because the event contradicts what was expected. It is, therefore, a good idea to bear in mind what the playwright is leading you to expect. When it happens, there is the kind of humour associated with the phrase 'I could see it coming!'; and when it is denied, the comic reaction is 'I never expected *that* to happen!'

An audience also laughs when it sees characters being beaten or humiliated. The reason for this is that it sees characters' bodies simply as bodies. The more the human body approximates to a machine, that is, to something lacking personality, the funnier the actions become. It is possible to see bodies as machines because of the detachment of the audience. In *A Comedy of Errors* there is much confusion between the two twin sons and the two twin servants that results in the servants being beaten. In *Twelfth Night* Sir Toby and Sir Andrew enter, bleeding and sore, after a beating they have received from Sebastian. Because the audience is detached, it laughs at the sight of characters reduced to little more than puppets. When this kind of action is the major point of a play's humour, the result is farce rather than comedy. Farce can be a strangely disturbing experience. Characters are reduced to types, and bodies become machines, so that action is both frantic and absurd.

What usually saves comedy from being farce is a strong sense of proportion. Because we have a sense of proportion, we have an idea of how characters should and do behave. When that sense of proportion is not reflected in behaviour, we laugh. When Malvolio woos Olivia, he offends our sense of proportion. When he appears in his yellow stockings, Olivia thinks he is ill, so suggests he goes to bed. Malvolio takes this in quite another way: 'To bed! ay, sweet-heart, and I'll come to thee.' That is funny, because people don't say that kind of thing when they start to woo; Malvolio outrages our sense of proportion. From this you can see that what counts as funny often depends upon the manners of society.

## EXERCISES

1 Read the last scene of Shakespeare's *Julius Caesar* and then answer the questions below. Those who have killed Caesar, led by Brutus and Cassius, have been defeated by Mark Antony and Octavius. Cassius has committed suicide.

*Brutus:* Come poor remains of friends, rest upon this rock.
*Clitus:* Statilius showed the torch-light, but my lord,
He came not back; he is or ta'en or slain.
*Brutus:* Sit thee down, Clitus. Slaying is the word;
It is a deed in fashion. Hark thee, Clitus. *(Whispers)*
*Clitus:* What I, my lord? No, not for all the world.
*Brutus:* Peace then, no words.
*Clitus:* I'll rather kill myself.
*Brutus:* Hark thee, Dardanius.
*Dardanius:* Shall I do such a deed?
*Clitus:* O Dardanius!
*Dardanius:* O Clitus!
*Clitus:* What ill request did Brutus make to thee?
*Dardanius:* To kill him Clitus. Look, he mediates.
*Clitus:* Now is that noble vessel full of grief,
That it runs over even at his eyes.
*Brutus:* Come hither, good Volumnius, list a word.
*Volumnius:* What says my lord?
*Brutus:* Why this, Volumnius,
The ghost of Caesar hath appeared to me
Two several times by night; at Sardis once,
And this last night, here in Philippi fields.
I know my hour is come.
*Volumnius:* Not so, my lord.
*Brutus:* Nay, I am sure it is, Volumnius.
Thou seest the world, Volumnius, how it goes;
Our enemies have beat us to the pit. *(Low alarums)*

It is more worthy to leap in ourselves,
Than tarry till they push us. Good Volumnius,
Thou know'st that we two went to school together;
Even for that our love of old, I prithee
Hold thou my sword-hilts, whilst I run on it.

*Volumnius:* That's not an office for a friend, my lord.

*(Alarum still)*

*Clitus:* Fly, fly, my lord, there is no tarrying here.

*Brutus:* Farewell to you; and you; and you Volumnius.
Strato, thou hast been all this while asleep;
Farewell to thee too Strato. Countrymen,
My heart doth joy that yet in all my life
I found no man but he was true to me.
I shall have glory by this losing day,
More than Octavius and Mark Antony
By this vile conquest shall attain unto.
So fare you well at once, for Brutus' tongue
Hath almost ended his life's history.
Night hangs upon mine eyes; my bones would rest,
That have but laboured to attain this hour.

*(Alarum. Cry within, 'Fly, fly, fly!)*

*Clitus:* Fly, my lord, fly.

*Brutus:* Hence! I will follow.

*(Exeunt Clitus, Dardanius and Volumnius)*

I prithee Strato, stay thou by thy lord.
Thou art a fellow of a good respect;
Thy life hath had some smatch of honour in it.
Hold then my sword, and turn away thy face,
While I do run upon it. Wilt thou Strato?

*Strato:* Give me your hand first. Fare you well my lord.

*Brutus:* Farewell good Strato. *(Runs on his sword)* Caesar, now be still;
I killed not thee with half so good a will. *(Dies)*

*Alarum. Retreat. Enter Octavius, Antony, Messala, Lucilius, and the Army*

*Octavius:* What man is that?

*Messala:* My master's man. Strato, where is thy master?

*Strato:* Free from the bondage you are in Messala;
The conquerors can but make a fire of him.

For Brutus only overcame himself,
And no man else hath honour by his death.
*Lucilius:* So Brutus should be found. I thank thee Brutus,
That thou hast proved Lucilius' saying true.
*Octavius:* All that served Brutus, I will entertain them.
Fellow, wilt thou bestow thy time with me?
*Strato:* Ay, if Messala will prefer me to you.
*Octavius:* Do so, good Messala.
*Messala:* How died my master, Strato?
*Strato:* I held the sword, and he did run on it.
*Messala:* Octavius, then take him to follow thee,
That did the latest service to my master.
*Antony:* This was the noblest Roman of them all.
All the conspirators save only he
Did what they did in envy of great Caesar;
He only, in a general honest thought
And common good to all, made one of them.
His life was gentle, and the elements
So mixed in him that Nature might stand up
And say to all the world 'This was a man.'
*Octavius:* According to his virtue let us use him,
With all respect, and rites of burial.
Within my tent his bones tonight shall lie,
Most like a soldier, ordered honourably.
So call the field to rest, and let's away,
To part the glories of this happy day. *(Exeunt)*

(a) Look for all the mentions of suicide and death in the scene and think about the effect this has on the atmosphere of the scene.

(b) Even in death, Brutus stands out from the rest of the characters; how does Shakespeare make him such an outstanding figure? (You should look at how the others talk about him.)

(c) Try to describe the feelings of the characters and your own feelings at the death of Brutus.

(d) What is the effect of the two closing speeches from Mark Antony and Octavius?

2 Read the extract from the last scene of *As You Like It* and then answer the questions below. After much confusion and misunderstanding, four pairs of lovers come to be married: Rosalind and Orlando, Celia and Oliver, Phoebe and Silvius and Audrey and Touchstone. Hymen, the god of marriage enters to celebrate the marriages. Rosalind is the daughter of Duke Senior, and Celia his niece.

*Enter Hymen, Rosalind and Celia. Still music.*

*Hymen:* Then is there mirth in heaven
When earthly things made even
Atone together.
Good Duke, receive thy daughter;
Hymen from heaven brought her,
Yes, brought her hither,
That thou mightst join her hand with his
Whose heart within his bosom is.
*Rosalind: (To Duke)* To you I give myself, for I am yours. *(To Orlando)*
To you I give myself, for I am yours.
*Duke Senior:* If there be truth in sight, you are my daughter.
*Orlando:* If there be truth in sight you are my Rosalind.
*Phoebe:* If sight and shape be true,
Why then, my love adieu.
*Rosalind: (To Duke)* I'll have no father, if you be not he.
*(To Orlando)* I'll have no husband, if you be not he.
*(To Phoebe)* Nor ne'er wed woman, if you be not she.
*Hymen:* Peace, ho! I bar confusion:
'Tis I must make conclusion
Of these most strange events.
Here's eight that must take hands
To join in Hymen's bands,
If truth holds true contents.
*(To Orlando and Rosalind)*
You and you no cross shall part.
*(To Oliver and Celia)*
You and you are heart in heart.
*(To Phoebe)*
You to his love must accord,
Or have a woman to your lord.
*(To Touchstone and Audrey)*
You and you are sure together
As the winter to foul weather.
*(To all)*
Whiles a wedlock hymn we sing,
Feed yourselves with questioning,
That reason wonder may diminish
How thus we met, and these things finish.

*Song*
Wedding is great Juno's crown,
O blessed bond of board and bed!

'Tis Hymen peoples every town;
High wedlock then be honoured.
Honour, high honour, and renown
To Hymen, god of every town!

*Duke Senior:* O my dear niece, welcome thou art to me,
Even daughter, welcome, in no less degree!
*Phoebe (To Silvius):* I will not eat my word, now thou are mine;
Thy faith my fancy to thee doth combine.

(a) Look for all the words that are about harmony, love and friendship and think about what they contribute to the atmosphere of the scene.

(b) What do you imagine would be the effect on stage of the music and the rhymes spoken by Hymen?

(c) Think about the significance of Hymen's words:

Peace ho! I bar confusion:
'Tis I must make conclusion

(d) How would you stage this scene to bring out the importance of marriage?

CHAPTER 15

# THE THEATRE OF THE IMAGINATION

## 15.1 A PERFORMING ART

Drama is what is called a performing art. As a result, plays are the most immediate, the most intense and the most communal of all literary works. They are immediate because they are acted out in front of an audience, intense because what is said is concentrated into a few hours, and communal because they are enjoyed and judged by a group of people who have specially gathered to view them. Examiners frequently complain that candidates hardly ever convey the *dramatic* nature of what they are writing about. This is often because they have never seen plays performed. You should, therefore, try to see a performance of your set plays, or, failing that, see any plays, so that you will understand the kind of impact drama can have.

The fact remains, however, that most candidates for public examinations get to know plays from books rather than theatres. Instead of the immediate, intense and communal experience of the theatre, you will be faced with words printed on paper. What can you do to make these words live as drama? The answer is that you will have to learn to act out a play in the theatre of your imagination; that is, you will have to picture for yourself all the elements that go to make up a theatrical performance. The aim of this chapter is to suggest ways in which you can do this. Four areas of the theatre will be examined: atmosphere, staging, actors and performance.

## 15.2 ATMOSPHERE

When you see a play in the theatre, you are aware of its atmosphere. The play creates a particular mood or feeling. On the page a play often seems to lack atmosphere. What you must do in order to appreciate the play is look at three aspects which create atmosphere: the characters, the actions and, in the case of Shakespeare, the imagery.

You can sometimes tell what the atmosphere of a play is by looking at the characters. If there are a number of stock characters, the play is likely to be light-hearted. If, on the other hand, it concerns kings and soldiers, the atmosphere is likely to be grave and serious. Of course, characters are only a guide to what a play *might* be like. It is possible to have light-hearted plays about matters of state, and disturbing plays, such as Joe Orton's *Loot*, which contain stock characters. But as a guide it can be useful. For instance, if you look at the characters of *She Stoops to Conquer,* you will expect the atmosphere to be a happy, domestic one. The major characters are the Hardcastles, their children, a family friend, Sir Charles Marlow, and his son and friend. When you see the social status of the characters – comfortable, upper middle-class – you may anticipate that much of the humour will revolve around manners. In both cases you will be right. Goldsmith presents a happy, domestic play in which the misunderstandings which cause the laughter are social in character.

The actions of a play create atmosphere. Plays containing murders and battles are likely to be serious and even tragic, whilst eavesdropping, disguise and trickery produce an atmosphere of light-hearted merriment. There are, of course, exceptions. *Othello*, one of the most harrowing tragedies, depends upon dramatic action associated with comedy – deception and eavesdropping. *Othello*, however, *is* an exception. A play such as *The Importance of being Earnest* follows the general rule. There is a case of impersonation, the very funny requests of both Jack and Algernon that Canon Chasuble baptise them with the name of Ernest, and, at the end, a discovery which stems from Miss Prism recalling that, in a moment of absent-mindedness, she mistook the manuscript of the novel she had written for the baby she was looking after! Actions such as those are almost bound to produce a light-hearted atmosphere.

It is often remarked of Shakespeare that each of his plays has its own distinctive atmosphere. Each play is, as it were, a separate world. This is in large measure due to the way in which each play has its own set of images. In Part I on poetry it was pointed out that some poems are built around a single image. In Shakespeare, plays are built around a family of images, which are repeated as the action unfolds. Readers and theatre-goers often notice the recurrence of a word or image which gives a play a particular mood or colour. Consider *Macbeth,* which is full of recurring images: blood, clothes, darkness and night. Imagery of night occurs throughout. When Lady Macbeth hears that King Duncan is to stay with them, she calls upon 'thick night' to hide her proposed crime. She later speaks of Duncan's murder as 'this night's great business', and after the murder there are a number of references to the terrible storm: 'the night has been unruly', 'the obscure bird / Clamoured the live long night', and 'a rough night'. When Macbeth is eagerly looking forward to the murder of Banquo, he mentions night three times within ten lines: 'night's yawning peal', 'seeling night', and 'night's black agents'. The effect of these and other images is to create an atmosphere which is dark, threatening and 'thick' (a favourite word in the play) with evil.

Whenever you start thinking about how a play might be performed, you should start with the atmosphere. A good performance of a play will translate atmosphere into staging and acting, so in order to know what would be suitable, you should have a clear idea of what the atmosphere is like. You can only do this by studying the words of the play – the words that create characters, action, and the imagery which helps to create and make distinctive the play's mood.

## 15.3 STAGING: THE STAGE ITSELF

The next step is to think about the staging; that is, about all the physical conditions of a theatrical performance. There are four things you should consider: the stage itself (this is of particular interest in the case of Shakespeare), the scenery, the costumes and the lighting.

It is always a good idea to ask yourself this question: what kind of a stage would be most appropriate for this play? there are three types that are used in the modern theatre. The traditional stage is that of an acting space behind the proscenium arch, from which hangs the curtain. The audience, as it were, see the action of the play through the 'window' formed by the proscenium arch. This type of stage is appropriate to plays that have realistic settings and deal with the manners and social habits of everyday living. It would, for instance, be appropriate to perform *The Importance of being Earnest* on such a stage. A second type is the apron stage, which projects out into the body of the theatre, so that the audience sit on the three sides of the acting area. Some theatres that have apron stages have no proscenium arch, but others retain this feature. Apron stages bring the audience in and emphasise the *theatricality* of the theatre. When someone in the audience can look across the stage to another part of the audience, he or she will be very much aware of being in a theatre. As a result, plays that are deliberately theatrical work very well on apron stages. *A Man for all Seasons* is an example. The Common Man, who acts as a chorus as well as taking a number of parts, could talk to the audience and then join in the action of the play. The third type is a variation of the apron stage – theatre in the round. This is a stage which, rather like a circus ring, is surrounded by the audience except for the entrance and exit point. This type of stage works very well for small-scale works. Harold

Pinter's plays *The Homecoming* and *The Caretaker* can be effective in the round.

When you think about staging Shakespeare, it is useful to bear in mind the kind of stage for which he wrote. It was a very large apron stage with two doors for entrances and exits. In addition, between the two doors there was probably an inner stage which was screened off by a curtain, and, above the main acting area, a gallery or balcony. A number of scenes are understandable in the light of these conditions.

Because the stage projected a long way into a circular, tiered theatre, the soliloquy would be very effective. The actor would not be very far away from the audience, so could either address them directly or could allow them to overhear his or her innermost thoughts. The two doors would be useful for opposing armies. Towards the end of *Julius Caesar* Antony's army could enter at one door and Brutus's and Cassius's at the other. The inner stage could be used for eavesdropping, as in the scenes in which Beatrice and Benedick overhear the other characters talking about them, or discoveries, as at the end of *The Tempest,* when Miranda and Ferdinand are discovered playing chess. The balcony could be used as the ramparts of a castle. Richard II could appear on the balcony to Bolingbroke at Flint Castle.

Shakespeare's plays work well on most stages, though, of course, the effects are different with the type of stage used. It is certainly not the case that his plays only work on the kind of stage described above. Nevertheless, it is a good idea to imagine how Shakespeare's plays would have worked in the theatres of his day. When you study one of his plays, you can try reconstructing such a performance in your imagination, paying attention to the effects made possible by the size of the stage, the proximity of the audience, the two entrances, the inner stage and the balcony. When you do this, certain features of a play become evident. For instance, *Macbeth* is a lonely play in which, for much of the time, two isolated, mentally tortured characters occupy a vast stage. Messengers come and go, but the lonely and anguished Macbeth and Lady Macbeth remain in stark isolation.

## 15.4 STAGING: SCENERY

Stage scenery is usually the responsibility of the designer. If you like art, it is a useful exercise designing your own scenery for a play, but if not, you should still try to imagine what kind of sets would be appropriate. In some plays a specific set is required. For instance, it would be impossible producing *The Caretaker* without two beds and a pile of junk. Whilst other plays are not quite so specific, their words make it clear that a particular kind of setting is necessary. *She Stoops to Conquer,* for instance, needs a rambling domestic set, and *The Royal Hunt of the Sun* should have rich, exotic settings. Shakespeare can be produced with elaborate or plain sets, with sets that change each scene, or one that remains throughout the performance. The question you should always have in mind is that of appropriateness. For instance, in *The Winter's Tale* the scenes in Sicilia need to be very different from those in Bohemia, and in *Antony and Cleopatra* the Roman scenes must look different from the Egyptian ones. Whenever, then, you study a play, you should ask yourself: what kind of scenery would be appropriate to the atmosphere of the play?

## 15.5 STAGING: COSTUME

Costume, like scenery, should be appropriate to the play. It should express the particular character of an individual and contribute to the atmosphere of the play. It is, therefore, a useful exercise to ask yourself how you imagine the characters to be dressed. At the beginning of the play, Hamlet must look different from everyone else. He is still in mourning for his father (he talks of his 'customary suits of solemn black') whilst the rest are celebrating a royal wedding. You should try to picture the contrast and understand how it shows the difference between the brooding, inward-looking Prince and the practical, busy nature of the new king's court.

In the case of Shakespeare it is interesting to ask about the period of the play. With the exception of the histories, Shakespeare's plays lend themselves to being costumed in a number of historical periods. There have been eighteenth-century, Victorian, Edwardian, 1920s and 1960s productions of tragedies and comedies. When you are thinking about costume, you can ask yourself whether a particular historical period would be appropriate to a particular play. For instance, a 1930s setting of Julius Caesar would emphasise the threat of dictatorship and highlight Brutus's dilemma: should Caesar be killed in case he becomes a tyrant?

## 15.6 STAGING: LIGHTING

Although lighting is a recent introduction to the theatre, it is a very powerful way of creating atmosphere. You should always ask yourself how a scene should be lit. The tense, mysterious opening to *Hamlet* requires subdued lighting, while the wonderful sunrise scene in *A Midsummer Night's Dream,* when the lovers wake up and find that their confusing nightmare is over, would be very effective if the light gradually grew stronger and stronger, signifying the return of sanity and harmony. The point to remember about lighting – and also about scenery and costume – is that particular effects can interpret the play. *Twelfth Night,* for instance, can be played as a happy comedy and also as a rather melancholy play. Bright, clear light would help the former interpretation, and subdued light the latter.

## 15.7 ACTORS: AGE

The third major area to think about is that of the actors. When you stage a play in the theatre of your imagination, you will have some idea of what kind of actors would be suitable, and how you think they should perform their parts. Here the matters discussed in Chapter 12, 'The Language of Drama', are important. You are free to imagine the kind of movements an actor makes and the kind of groupings that would be suitable on the stage. In doing this you must remember that in many plays you are offered a *number* of opportunities. It is very rare that a play needs to be acted in one particular way. You should also remember that actors bring their own particular personality to bear upon a part. When, therefore, you think about actors, you should remember that the words of a play are a starting point for a number of different performances. With those qualifications in mind, you can think about three things: the age of an actor, the size of an actor and the voice of an actor.

To ask about the age an actor needs to be to play a part is to ask about how old a character is. This question only really arises in Shakespeare, because in most of the plays since his time the playwright makes the ages of characters clear. The point to remember in Shakespeare is that the age of a character has a bearing upon the interpretation of the play. Take, for example, the case of Malvolio. He is often presented as quite an old man, although there is no real support in the text for such an interpretation. If he is played as old, the scene in which he tries to stop the drunken riot caused by Sir Toby, Sir Andrew and Feste becomes a case of age rebuking youth. But how would the wooing of Olivia be played? If the actor is old, or just plays the part as an old man, the scene in which he approaches Olivia in his yellow stockings would be grotesque as well as funny. This scene would work very differently if the actor were young. The actor then could play Malvolio as someone deeply in love with Olivia but sadly inept in his courtship. Instead of the grotesqueness of age the audience would be presented with the pathos of love-sick youth. Both scenes could be moving but in quite different ways. The question of age can be usefully applied to other characters. Are the Macbeths old or young? How much older is Claudius than Hamlet? Is Don Pedro much older than Benedick and

Claudio? Should Antony be played as a mature man or as someone very much in decline?

## 15.8 **ACTORS: SIZE**

It is worthwhile asking what contribution an actor's size makes to a performance. Lady Bracknell is a domineering figure in *The Importance of being Earnest* but if she were played by someone who was small there would be the added comedy of the smallest person on stage ordering everybody else about. Likewise, O'Casey's *Juno and the Paycock* would have a comic opening if the Captain were a big lumbering man and Juno were short. The size of the actors would reflect the farcical elements in the play – a wife violently angry with her husband – but might cause problems when, towards the end, the action becomes more tragic. It is worth asking about the size of actors playing Shakespeare. It would, for instance, be very poignant if Othello were played by a big man and Iago by a small man, because the spectacle of a big, heroic figure of evident nobility brought to a state of inhuman jealousy by a slight, spare man would show how vulnerable Othello was.

## 15.9 **ACTORS: VOICE**

Voice should be appropriate to character. The man who plays Sir Thomas More in *A Man for all Seasons* should speak in a quiet, thoughtful manner, so an actor with a voice that is either deep or soft would be most suitable. In comedies it is very important for voices to match parts. It would, for instance, be difficult to imagine Lady Bracknell with a high-pitched voice or Sir Andrew Aguecheek with a hearty, deep one. In other parts, particularly tragedies, the quality of voice matters less. However, it is important to ask yourself how you imagine Hamlet or Macbeth to sound. A Hamlet with a slow, heavy voice might bring out the brooding elements but would be less suited to the playful aspects of the character. Likewise, an actor with a rich, romantic voice could do justice to the poetic side of Macbeth but might be less suited to portraying the character's ruthless side.

## 15.10 **PERFORMANCE: THE PRESENCE OF ACTORS**

When you have thought about the kind of actors that would be suitable, you can go on to consider the last area – how the play is performed. There are a number of points you should consider: the effect of an actor's presence, the use of the pause, the contribution of music and dance, the effect of spectacle, ghosts and fights.

When you see a play, you realise that a character can be very effective even if he or she says little or nothing. The mere fact of a character's presence can be dramatically telling. When you read a play, you will have to remind yourself that though a character is not saying anything his or her very presence might be effective. Pinter's *The Caretaker* begins with an intriguing scene. A man stands all alone in a room, he looks about him, turns and exits. Although he says nothing, the audience will find itself asking a number of questions. Who is he? What is he doing? Where is he going? Will he be seen again? When you read a play with a scene such as that in it, you will have to imagine the strange and intriguing presence of a silent character. In the scene from *The Winter's Tale* discussed above in Chapter 12, 'The Language of Drama', the boy Mamillius remains on stage after the violent entry of his father, Leontes. While his parents argue, he stands silent. This could be played so as to be very moving, because before Leontes's entry he was very talkative. His silent presence, no doubt the result of sheer bewilderment, could be touching and effective.

## 15.11 **PERFORMANCE: THE PAUSE**

In a theatre the audience is very much aware of pauses. When an actor stops speaking, the audience feels that the pause indicates that either something important has or will happen. In modern plays pauses are part of the text. Pinter and Becket clearly give a great deal of thought to where they are placed. When, therefore, you can act out a play in the theatre of your imagination, you have to imagine the expectation and the tension caused by pauses. Pinter's *The Homecoming* starts with Max asking Lennie whether or not he has finished with the scissors:

> *Max:* What have you done with the scissors? *(Pause)* I said I'm looking for the scissors. What have you done with them? *(Pause)* Did you hear me? I want to cut something out of the paper.
>
> *Lenny:* I'm reading the paper.
>
> *Max:* Not that paper. I haven't even read that paper. I'm talking about last Sunday's paper. I was just having a look at it in the kitchen. *(Pause)* Do you hear what I'm saying? I'm talking to you! Where's the scissors?

The pauses bring home the annoyance of Max, who wants attention, and the frustration of Lenny, who wants to get on with his newspaper. They also give the audience time to see that these are the emotions that are present, and time, too, to see that the situation is tense and also slightly comical. In other words, the pauses direct the audience's attention to what Pinter thinks is significant in the relation between Max and Lenny.

In the case of Shakespeare, there are no pauses in the text. Therefore, when you study a play you have to ask: would pauses be suitable in this scene, and, if so, where? When in *Macbeth* the body of Duncan is discovered, there is confusion and panic. It emerges that the grooms (attendants) appear to have been responsible for the murder, and Macbeth admits that he has killed them:

*Lennox:* . . . they stared, and were distracted;
No man's life was to be trusted with them.
*Macbeth:* O! yet I do repent me of my fury,
That I did kill them.
*Macduff:* Wherefore did you so?
*Macbeth:* Who can be wise, amazed, temperate and furious,
Loyal and neutral, in a moment . . .

It is a very tense moment: will the real murderer –Macbeth – be discovered, or will everyone believe that the grooms were responsible? If there were a pause after Macbeth's 'That I did kill them', Macduff's question would sound very threatening. If, too, there were a pause before Macbeth answered Macduff's question, it would seem as if he were searching for an explanation to hide his guilt. You should not only imagine where pauses come in order to realise the dramatic tension of the scene. A pause can also interpret a scene in a particular way. If, for instance, there were *no* pause before Macbeth's reply, it would indicate that Macbeth had already anticipated the question and had thought out a reply. Macbeth would then be interpreted as a ruthless schemer rather than a man learning painfully how to be evil.

## 15.12 PERFORMANCE: THE CONTRIBUTION OF MUSIC AND DANCE

The effects of music and dance are very difficult to imagine. On stage music can have a transforming effect upon a scene, and dance adds a physical excitement that is very difficult to convey in words. Hard as it is to imagine their impact, you can approach the contribution of music and dance by reminding yourself of certain things. You can recall what was said in Chapter 11, 'The Conventions of Drama', that a successful song should echo and contribute to the mood of the scene, and that dances were understood by the audience as an expression of harmony and concord. You can also ask yourself what kind of tone would be suitable. When you come across a song (and remember, it is not only Shakespeare who includes them), you should look very closely at the words in order to judge their tone and then decide what kind of tune would match them. You can be quite free in thinking about suitable kinds of tune; there have been successful productions of Shakespeare that used the rhythms of pop music. In the case of dance you can always write about the impact it makes. Drama is not just a matter or words; the vigorous physical movements of dance can be a very impressive contribution to a play. If you have to write about a scene that includes dance, you should remember that drama is a performing art, and so point to the way in which the play comes over through words, action and dance. You can do this by asking what kind of dance would be suitable: rapid and lively, slow and languid, smooth and graceful? The dance in *Romeo and Juliet,* for instance, will be different from the ones in *The Winter's Tale*; in the former the dance is a courtly affair, in the latter it is part of rustic celebrations.

## 15.13 **PERFORMANCE: SPECTACLE**

When you want to talk about the total impact of words, action and dance, a useful word to use is 'spectacle'. Some scenes in plays demand the colour of settings and costume, the stylised gestures of actors, the accompaniment of music, and the excitement of dance. Such a scene is the wedding masque in *The Tempest.* The allegorical figures speak in elaborate, lyrical verse. It would be appropriate to imagine them richly costumed, moving with delicate, stylised steps, and being accompanied by mysterious music. Other plays also present opportunities for spectacle. In Shakespeare the Egyptian scenes of *Antony and Cleopatra* require to be performed in a lush and spectacular fashion, and in the modern theatre a play such as *The Royal Hunt of the Sun* requires a colourful and dramatic production. When you read a play, you should look out for moments of potential spectacle and try to imagine the impact they make.

## 15.14 **PERFORMANCE: GHOSTS AND FIGHTS**

Ghosts are often a problem, particularly in Shakespeare. All you are given in the text of a play is 'Enter a ghost'; it is up to you to do the rest. You could think how a ghost could be presented. Eerie music, weird lights and a hollow, sepulchral voice present a popular solution, but some audiences get so used to that kind of presentation that ghosts cease to arouse feelings of strangeness and mystery. Alternatively, the ghost could be played by someone who was very tall or very thin. The actor could move in a very stylised way, and speak slowly, dreamily or in a monotone. You could also ask yourself what the impact would be if there were no ghost physically present. In some plays the absence of an actor playing a ghost would have a considerable effect. Macbeth is the only one who sees Banquo's ghost. If the audience can also see him, it looks upon Macbeth as a man who is either especially sensitive or especially guilty. But if there is no ghost for the audience to see, it views Macbeth as the guests at the banquet do – as a strange and rather terrible man who is troubled by hallucinations.

The main difficulty you will have with stage fights is to imagine the impact they have upon the audience. Stage fights, in order to be effective, must appear to be savage and violent. You will have to imagine that. You can think of the noises – the clash of swords, the gasps for breath, the sounds of bodies crashing on to the stage – and picture the fear in the faces, the desperate movements and the sight of blood. Recalling fights you have seen on television may help you, but they are often tame in comparison with the sight of real people wielding real weapons. Fights bring home the immediacy of drama. The best thing you can do, as with all matters relating to the acting out of a play in the theatre of your imagination, is to try to realise the impact, which is basic to all theatre, of seeing real people performing in front of you.

## EXERCISES

**1** The following passage is the close of the first act of Peter Shaffer's *The Royal Hunt of the Sun.* Atahuallpa is the Inca king who is thought by himself and his people to be divine; Valverde is the priest of the invading Spanish army, and Pizarro is their leader. Read the passage carefully and then answer the questions below.

> *(The music crashes over the stage as the Indian procession enters in an astonishing explosion of colour. The King's attendants – many of them playing musical instruments: reed pipes, cymbals, and giant marraccas – are as gay as parrots. They wear costumes of orange and yellow, and fantastic head-dresses of gold and feathers, with eyes embossed on them in staring black enamel. By contrast, Atahuallpa Inca presents a picture of utter simplicity. He is dressed from head to foot in white: across his eyes is a mask of jade mosaic, and round his head a circlet of plain gold. Silence falls. The King glares about him.)*

*Atahuallpa (haughtily):* Where is the god?
*Valverde (through Felipillo):* I am a Priest of God.
*Atahuallpa:* I do not want the priest. I want the god. Where is he? He sent me greeting.
*Valverde:* That was our General. Our God cannot be seen.

*Atahuallpa: I* may see him.

*Valverde:* No. He was killed by men and went into the sky.

*Atahuallpa:* A god cannot be killed. See my father! You cannot kill him. He lives for ever and looks over his children every day.

*Valverde:* I am the answer to all mysteries. Hark, pagan, and I will expound.

*Old Martin:* And so he did, from the Creation to Our Lord's ascension. *(He goes off)*

*Valverde (walking among the Indians to the right):* And when he went he left the Pope as Regent for him.

*De Nizza (walking among the Indians to the left):* And when he went he left the Pope as Regent for him.

*Valverde:* He has commanded our King to bring all men to belief in the true God.

*De Nizza:* He has commanded our King to bring all men to belief in the true God.

*Valverde and De Nizza (together):* In Christ's name therefore I charge you: yield yourself his willing vassal.

*Atahuallpa:* I am the vassal of no man! I am the greatest prince on earth. Your King is great. He has sent you far across the water. So he is my brother. But your Pope is mad. He gives away countries that are not his. His faith also is mad.

*Valverde:* Beware!

*Atahuallpa:* Ware you! You kill my people; you make them slaves. By what power?

*Valverde:* By this. *(He offers a Bible)* The Word of God.

*(Atahuallpa holds it to his ear. He listens intently. He shakes it.)*

*Atahuallpa:* No word. *(He smells the book, and then licks it. Finally he throws it down impatiently.)* God is angry with your insults.

*Valverde:* Blasphemy!

*Atahuallpa:* God is angry!

*Valverde (calling):* Francisco Pizarro, do you stay your hand when Christ is insulted? Let this pagan feel the power of your arm. I absolve you all! San Jago!

*(Pizarro appears above with drawn sword, and in a great voice sings out his battle-cry.)*

*Pizarro:* SAN JAGO Y CIERRA ESPANA!

*(Instantly from all sides the soldiers rush in, echoing the great cry.)*

*Soldiers:* SAN JAGO!

*(There is a tense pause. The Indians look at this ring of armed men in terror. A violent drumming begins, and there ensues:*

*THE MIME OF THE GREAT MASSACRE*

*To a savage music, wave upon wave of Indians are slaughtered and rise again to protect their lord who stands bewildered in their midst. It is all in vain. Relentlessly the Spanish soldiers hew their way through the ranks of feathered attendants towards their quarry. They surround him. Salinas snatches the crown off his head and tosses it up to Pizarro, who catches it and to a great shout crowns himself. All the Indians cry out in horror. The drum hammers on relentlessly while Atahuallpa is led off at sword-point by the whole band of Spaniards. At the same time, dragged from the middle of the sun by howling Indians, a vast bloodstained cloth bellies out over the stage. All rush off; their screams fill the theatre. The lights fade out slowly on the rippling cloth of blood.)*

(a) Would you include any other pauses in the dialogue, and where and why would you place them?

(b) How do you imagine the Incas and the Spaniards are dressed?

(c) The music is said to be 'savage'. Try to imagine what kind of music would be suitable and what effect it would have.

(d) Read very carefully the stage directions for THE MIME OF THE GREAT MASSACRE. Try to imagine how you would stage it. You could think about such matters as the grouping of the actors, the lighting, the actions of the killers (stylised or realistic?) and the kind of stage that would be suitable.

2 Read the following extract from act 4 scene 4 of *The Winter's Tale* and answer the questions below. Perdita is dressed in a special way for the feast, and so, you may imagine, are the rest of the characters. The atmosphere is one of celebration.

*(Enter Shepherd, with Polixenes and Camillo disguised; Clown, Mopsa, Dorcas, and others.)*

*Shepherd:* Fie, daughter! when my old wife lived, upon
This day she was both pantler, butler, cook;
Both dame and servant; welcomed all, served all,
Would sing her song and dance her turn; now here,
At upper end o' th' table, now i' th' middle;
On his shoulder, and his; her face o' fire
With labour, and the thing she took to quench it
She would to each one sip. You are retired,

As if you were a feasted one and not
The hostess of the meeting: pray you, bid
These unknown friends to's welcome; for it is
A way to make us better friends, more known.
Come, quench your blushes and present yourself
That which you are, mistress o' th' feast: come on,
And bid us welcome to your sheep-shearing,
As your good flock shall prosper.

*Perdita: (To Polixenes)* Sir, welcome:
It is my father's will I should take on me
The hostess-ship o' th' day: – *(To Camillo)* You're welcome, sir.
For you there's rosemary and rue; these keep
Seeming and savour all the winter long:
Grace and remembrance be to you both,
And welcome to our shearing!

*Polixenes:* Shepherdess, –
A fair one are you, – well you fit our ages
With flowers of winter.

*Perdita:* Sir, the year growing ancient,
Not yet on summer's death, nor on the birth
Of trembling winter, the fairest flower o' th' season
Are our carnations, and streaked gillyvors,
Which some call nature's bastards: of that kind
Our rustic garden's barren, and I care not
To get slips of them.

*Polixenes:* Wherefore, gentle maiden,
Do you neglect them?

*Perdita:* For I have heard it said
There is an art which in their piedness shares
With great creating nature.

*Polixenes:* Say there be;
Yet nature is made better by no mean
But nature makes that mean: so, over that art,
Which you say adds to nature, is an art
That nature makes. You see, sweet maid, we marry
A gentler scion to the wildest stock,
And make conceive a bark of baser kind
By bud of nobler race: this is an art
Which does mend nature, change it rather, but
The art itself is nature.

*Perdita:* So it is.

*Polixenes:* Then make your garden rich in gillyvors,
And do not call them bastards.

*Perdita:* I'll not put
The dibble in earth to set one slip of them;
No more than, were I painted, I would wish
This youth should say, 'twere well, and only therefore
Desire to breed by me. Here's flowers for you;
Hot lavender, mints, savory, marjoram;
The marigold, that goes to bed with' sun,
And with him rises weeping: these are flowers
Of middle summer, and I think they are given
To men of middle age. Y'are very welcome.

(a) How would you design costumes for the play? Would you clothe Polixenes and Camillo, who have come to spy on the gathering, in a different way from the shepherd and his son, the clown?

(b) How would you imagine the shepherd delivers his speech? What actions and gestures would he use, and how should the actors be grouped on the stage?

(c) What is the impact of Perdita giving flowers to the characters? How do you imagine it should be staged?

(d) There is tension between Polixenes and Perdita: how would you like it to be acted out on stage?

# PART IV
# AS YOU STUDY

# CHAPTER 16



# READING, NOTES, PREPARATION

## 16.1 READING

If you are taking an examination in English Literature, you should aim to know the books you are studying thoroughly, more thoroughly, in fact, than either your teacher or your examiner. They are not taking the examination!

But what does it mean to know a book thoroughly? It can't just be a matter of knowing the names of all the characters and remembering all the lines. What you should aim at is *understanding*. In fact, the title of this chapter could be extended to 'Reading *and re-reading – with understanding*'. If you don't understand what you are reading, you are not really reading.

The question, then, is: how can I read a book with understanding? Before advice on that question can be given, three preliminary points must be made.

First, you should read the *whole* book. There is no place in proper reading for skipping passages. Since a book, be it a novel, play or poems, is something that an author intended to write, you can only grasp that intention by reading all of it.

Second, you should try to read in a place that is quiet. Nowadays, many people find this difficult because they are so used to having background music; some even say that without it they feel distracted. Nevertheless, if you are to do justice to a book you *need* silence. This is particularly important in the case of poetry, or drama written in verse. Background music, particularly if it has a strong rhythm, is bound to clash with the rhythms of the lines you are reading. The result will be that you do not fully take in what is before you.

Third, you should read frequently. If you read a novel over a very long period of time, you will miss the shape of the plot and the development of characters. With poetry, frequent reading is necessary because poetry is an unusual form of literature. In order to appreciate the way, for instance, rhythm enacts meaning or the ambiguity of words is exploited, you need to read frequently in order to accustom yourself to the way poets use words.

## 16.2 READING WITH UNDERSTANDING

Now for the question: how can I read a book with understanding? The best advice that can be given is to bear in mind a number of questions as you read. If you find you are losing the thread of the book, or your concentration is slackening, you can bring the book sharply into focus again by putting a question to yourself. Of course, some questions are more appropriate to one book than another, and the list that follows is not exhaustive. You can always look back through the separate chapters on poetry, novels and drama to find further questions to ask. The point to remember, however, is that the questions you put to yourself are intended to help you read with understanding. Therefore, the basic one that can apply to any book is this: do I understand what I am reading? The questions that follow are all aspects of that one.

Of any poem, novel or play you can ask: am I following what is happening? This can apply to the argument of a poem, the developing relation between characters in a novel, and the growth of a plot in a play. A simple way of answering the question is looking back through the preceding lines or pages and trying to understand how arguments or events have developed. It is usually worthwhile doing this. If you miss a connection in the argument or story, you may find yourself increasingly puzzled as you read further.

In the case of novels, plays and, in some cases, narrative poems, you can ask: why are the characters behaving in this way? This question turns on the motives of characters. In most literature the author is interested not only in what characters do but in *why* they do it. If you feel you are not in touch with the characters of a book, you can always stop and think about their reason for behaving as they do. If you cannot find a satisfactory reason, it may be that the author is not bothered about motivation but merely wants to establish a new situation in the plot.

When you are reading a book for the first time, it is easy to misinterpret its mood. Therefore, you should ask: am I in touch with the mood? Mood is usually two-fold. The first is atmosphere. You can think hard about how the settings build up the atmosphere of a book in a way that is appropriate to its meaning. The second is tone. This comes down to asking about the attitude of the author, and considering such matters as how he or she views the characters and passes judgement upon them.

When you question the motives of characters and inquire about the mood of a book, you are thinking about the way the author is writing the book. This, of course, is central to understanding what a book is about. Another question directly concerning authorship is this one: can I see how the plot is being constructed? It is a good idea to ask yourself this question, because many students, to put it simply, fail to see the wood for the trees. They understand individual incidents but can't see the book as a whole. Therefore, as you read, you can ask yourself whether you can see the problem from which the plot grows and whether it is built on parallels and contrasts – in other words, whether you can see the plot and not just a sequence of events.

The above questions are more applicable to novels and plays than to poetry. In the case of a number of poems by one author or an anthology based on a common period or theme, you can ask: how similar is this poem to the others? This is very important. One of the hardest things at 'O' and 'A' Level is seeing connections between a number of short poems. If, as you read, you can bear in mind the other poems, you can begin to see them as a group rather than as separate pieces.

There is one question that applies to any work of literature: how am I being invited to respond? It is a particularly good idea to ask this question if you find that your concentration is slackening. Reading a book is a collaboration between you and the author. The author is inviting you to feel, to think, and to judge as you read. If you are not paying proper attention, you will take the book in as a set of facts but no more. It is, then, a good idea to stop and ask yourself what you are feeling about the characters. As you do so, you must remember that your feelings will be appropriate if they arise out of a response to what the author is trying to do.

There is a final point that must be made about reading with understanding. It is this: if you read a book attentively, you will be studying it. Sometimes, it is thought that reading and study are two entirely different activities. They are not. Studying is reading done with an awareness of what it is you are looking at and of what is going on in your mind.

## 16.3 MAKING NOTES

Although reading and study are not separate activities, there is one thing you should do when you are studying that you are unlikely to do if you are just reading for pleasure – make notes. There are two ways of making notes, and if you are wise you will do both.

If you own the book you are studying (and if you don't, it is a good idea to buy one) you can make brief notes in the margin. Because margins are not very broad, you will not be able to write very much. All you will be able to do is underline important parts or make the briefest of comments on what is happening. Nevertheless, this is very valuable. If you mark your book in this way, you have a guide to the important parts and some notes that will help you interpret what is happening.

But notes in the margins of books are not enough. You are foolish if you try to rely solely upon them. What you need as well is a notebook in which you can write at greater length about the ideas that occur to you. Sometimes notes in the margin of a book are so brief that you forget what you meant by them. If you have a notebook in which you can write down your ideas at length, you will not fall into this trap. But what should you put into your notebook? Here are a few ideas.

Some students find it helpful to write down a brief summary of the plots of novels or plays. This can take a number of forms. You can summarise the bare bones of the plot in one or two paragraphs. The advantage of this is that it helps you see what problems the plot is based on and what issues it raises. Another approach is to give a brief summary of what happens in each chapter or scene. This has the advantage of ensuring that you don't get the order of events confused. A further exercise, which is more appropriate to drama than novels, is to draw up a chart of characters and scenes, noting who appears in which. This can be helpful in seeing who the major characters are and estimating the extent to which they dominate the stage. When making notes on poetry, you can briefly record the issue with which each poem deals.

Summaries of plots, however, are not detailed, and to know a book well you must think about it in detail. You should, therefore, make detailed notes about chapters, scenes, lines, and words. You can do this in a number of ways. You should try to recognise anything that puzzles you and frame it as a question. Sometimes the question yields more writing; you could, for instance, briefly explore two ways of answering it. But some questions are simply useful on their own and can be left to prompt more thought when you read through your notes. Many of the notes you will want to make will be on the significance of something. That is to say, you will want to express *why* an event is important. This could be because it shows a character developing, because it focuses the main theme of the book, or parallels another part of the work. When you note down that an event is significant, you will be interpreting the book's *meaning.* (More will be said about this in the Chapters 17 and 19.)

Your notes will also be about your reactions. It is a good idea to record how you feel about a word, a line or what a character does, particularly when you are reading the book for the first time. The impressions you receive from a first reading are especially valuable, because you don't know what to expect. Among your impressions you will want to say something about the quality of the book. You should note whether you think a scene is handled well, and also remark upon it if you think it is done badly. If you can see a reason for this, you should, of course, give it.

Notes can easily get out of hand. Some students make too many. This is unwise; you should remember that examinations test your thinking about works and not your notes on those works! Another difficulty is that notes can become jumbled. You can avoid this by remembering to take four precautions. You should make it clear what the notes on the page are about by writing clear headings. You should work out a convenient form of abbreviations and stick to it: for instance, you can call Shakespeare Sh. The third thing you should do is leave a line between each remark. You will find it is much easier revising if each point appears separately on the page. The last thing you should do is find a method of distinguishing between particular and general points. Particular points are about the immediate words or lines of a stanza, chapter or scene; general points are about what the author is doing in the book as a whole. As you read and make notes about particular points, you will find that ideas start to occur to you about the whole book. You can keep a separate section for these notes, or you can put them in with the others but distinguish them by putting them in brackets or writing them with a different coloured pen. Either way you will have a fund of ideas for thinking about the work as a whole.

## 16.4 **RE-READING**

Many people who don't take examinations re-read their favourite books. They do so because they find the books rich and rewarding. It is to be hoped that the books on 'O' and 'A' Level syllabuses are like that, because when you study for an examination, you will have to re-read your set works. Indeed, some teachers say that reading only really begins with re-reading, that is to say, you can only really think about a book when you are familiar with its plot and characters. That view may be an extreme one, but it does point to the fact that in order to get to know a book well, re-reading, or, in the case of plays, re-viewing is essential. And when you re-read a book, you will be surprised to see what you have missed or forgotten. To re-read a book is to see new aspects of a character, to respond more deeply to the atmosphere, to understand its themes more deeply, and to appreciate more keenly how it is written. Sometimes a line that you ignored will jump at you from the page, and on other occasions you will find that what you didn't like because it seemed far-fetched is now quite credible. Furthermore, you will find that as your experience of life grows, your response to literature will grow too.

Since, then, re-reading is essential to study, what can be said about reading a book with an examination in mind? You will find that you have to do three kinds of work: preparation, class-work and follow-up notes. If you are taking an examination on your own, preparation and class-work will not apply to you, but follow-up notes will.

## 16.5 PREPARATION

If you know that a poem, chapter or scene is to be discussed in class, you will have to read or re-read it to prepare yourself. You should remember that the more familiar you are with the work under discussion, the more you will be able to contribute and to gain from the class. Preparation, if it is done properly, can be a lengthy business. First, you must read the sections that are going to be discussed. It is always helpful if you can read them more than once, particularly with poetry.

But reading is not all you should do. The discussion of literature usually centres on an examination of the meaning of a book, on appreciation of how the author establishes that meaning, and the thinking through of the pleasures, questions and judgements that occur to you in the act of reading. In order to prepare yourself for this you should make notes that you can use in class. These need not be extensive. The best thing to do is read the sections to be discussed and notice what you notice. In other words, try to be aware of the impressions and thoughts that are forming in your mind. It is these that you should commit to paper. You will usually find they are of three kinds: notes on the meanings of a passage, questions arising from the passage, and difficulties you have had in understanding. You should try to write these down in as clear a form as you can and then bring them to lesson for discussion.

## 16.6 CLASS-WORK

In class you should do three things: listen, make notes and talk. You should listen not only to what your teacher says but also to the contributions of your fellow students. Teachers don't have a monopoly of wisdom, and quite often the questions and puzzlements of other students can suggest new and interesting lines of thought. When you hear something of interest, you should, of course, make a note of it. As with ordinary notes, you can do this by jotting a remark down in the margin of your book and putting a slightly more developed version of that idea in your notebook. In order to avoid confusion, you should try to take notes in class in the way in which you have been advised to take them in your own time. And remember: in many classes you will be left to make notes yourself, so don't wait to be told – get on with it!

Talking can be as important as writing because it is a way in which you can master the ideas of a book. When you make a point that has arisen from your preparation, ask a question about what someone has said, or disagree with a remark, you are finding words to express your understanding of the book. As soon as you speak, you will realise that there is a great difference between having a hunch in your mind and having the appropriate words to express it. Talking in class will help you bridge the gap between the two, because the more you speak, the more you will learn to master the necessary words.

## 16.7 **FOLLOW-UP WORK**

But the place where you must master words is on paper. This is where follow-up work comes in. When the lesson is over, *your* work begins. It is up to you to understand and master what has been said in class. The best way to do this is by more reading and writing. You should re-read the passages under discussion and you should try to write about the ideas that emerged in the lesson. What you will be left with in the way of notes will be jottings in your book and slightly longer remarks on paper. You should look through these in the light of the passages discussed and see if any of them can be taken further. You may find that there are one or two important ideas in your notes. You should try to master these. Given that there is a great difference between understanding an idea when it is explained to you and finding the right words to express that idea yourself, you should attempt to write as clearly as you can about the ideas that have emerged. Sometimes all you will need to do is explain the idea, while on other occasions you will find that the idea leads you to explore other issues. If you can do one or two pieces of follow-up writing of between half a page and a page in length, then you will be working satisfactorily.

The more re-reading and writing you can do, the easier you will find revision. In fact, the most useful revision is not the intense work done in the weeks leading up to the examination but the steady, week by week business of reading, re-reading and writing. If at the end of every week you can look through what you have studied, what you have learned from your reading and re-reading will become part of the way in which you think about books. It is obvious that you will want to work harder when you are faced with examinations, but you will find that revision much easier if re-reading is a regular feature of your work.

# CHAPTER 17

# INTERPRETATION

## 17.1 THE IMPORTANCE OF INTERPRETATION

The idea of interpretation often frightens students. They either think it is a matter of discovering meanings that have been deliberately hidden by the author or of dreaming up fantastic ideas about what the book really means. Now whilst it is true that some meanings in books are not immediately obvious to readers and that books that seem to be about, say, love, may, with study, be seen to be more concerned with other things such as growing old or selfishness, it is misleading to think of interpretation in those ways. Interpretation is the business of finding out what the meaning, or meanings, of the book is. Another way of putting that is to say that interpretation is finding out the significance of a work, of saying what it is about, what it adds up to.

For instance, when you say that *Hard Times* is about how the human spirit can be distorted by false education, you are interpreting Dickens's book. Likewise, when you say that *The Winter's Tale* is about, among other things, reconciliation, you are also giving an interpretation. You should notice that in both those cases interpretation is not a matter of telling the story but pointing to what is important, and that is another way of saying what is the meaning or the significance of the work.

The question, then, that you should ask about any literary work is: what is its meaning or significance? When you answer that question, you will be interpreting the work. That question, however, does not tell you *how* to go about looking for meaning. Sometimes, of course, you will read a work and some things will strike you as important. If that happens, you can start thinking about their significance and so start the business of interpretation. But sometimes you will need more help. In these cases it is a good idea to try a number of approaches. You can approach the work through the characters (this is sometimes called the psychological approach), or you can turn to society and ask what the author is showing you about that. A third approach is through ideas. You can ask what issues are central to the work. Two further approaches are those through literary form and history. The approach through literary form concentrates on how the work is constructed, and the approach through history asks whether the period in which the book was written can help us to see the work's importance. Let us look at these five approaches to interpretation, and try them out on one work – Jane Austen's *Emma.*

## 17.2 INTERPRETATION THROUGH CHARACTERS

The approach through characters is very popular. It finds the meaning of works in what they show about characters' thoughts and feelings, the views they have of themselves, the way they change and grow, and the way they establish, maintain or break relationships. If you interpret a work in this way, you will have to consider the effect characters have on you, the feelings they arouse in you, and the judgements you make about them. You will know it is worthwhile taking a psychological approach to a novel if the author takes an interest in the motives and reactions of characters. Therefore, if you find, as you do in George Eliot, long passages exploring characters' minds, you will know that this approach will be fruitful.

There are many passages in *Emma* in which Jane Austen either says what Emma is thinking or recounts events from Emma's point of view. Emma has definite views of herself (she says she will never marry), and equally definite views of others (she does not think, for instance, that Robert Martin is socially good enough to marry Harriet Smith). Jane Austen, however, makes it quite clear that Emma does not know herself, and consequently misjudges other characters. For much of the time she tries to find a suitable marriage partner for Harriet Smith. She has no difficulty in persuading herself that Harriet would be happy with Mr Elton and even the romantic Frank Churchill, and no difficulty either in persuading herself that each of them take an interest in Harriet. But it is not till Harriet thinks that Mr Knightley is in love with her that Emma wakes up to the reality of the world about her and the reality of herself. She realises she has been blind (the word is very important) in encouraging Harriet to hope for marriage from the Eltons and Churchills of the world, and, even more important, she wakes up to her own true feelings: 'It darted through her, with the speed of an arrow, that Mr. Knightley must marry no one but herself!'

That metaphor (a very rare thing in the book) enacts her awakening, an awakening which is both painful and yet wonderful. It is also the moment when an approach through character makes sense: *Emma* is about growth towards understanding, about the painful (and funny) path Emma treads from blindness to real sight and, in her own case, *insight.* Once the approach through character has made sense with Emma, it can make sense of other characters. Mr Knightley, too, is someone who has not really known himself. Throughout the novel he has played the role of father and guide to Emma (her real father, Mr Woodhouse, never advises or guides her) but, at the end, he recognises that he loves her. In his case, too, the novel is about how he grows towards a clear vision of life and himself.

## 17.3 INTERPRETATION THROUGH SOCIETY

The social approach to literature emphasises not so much the personality or inner feelings of characters as the relation they have with each other. A social interpretation of literature sees these relations in terms of the traditions and customs of society. There is, therefore, much stress in a social interpretation on the classes to which characters belong. For instance, it is important to see who is rich and who poor, who is rising in society and who is falling, and who earn their living from a trade, a profession or from family land. A social approach also looks on the institutions of society. One of the most important of these is marriage. It is important to ask who marries whom, whether they come from the same class, and the extent to which it is a marriage of love or a means of social improvement.

A social approach to *Emma* is profitable in a number of ways. Although all the characters are middle class, some are professional like the lawyer John Knightley, some in trade (there is an important scene in a shop), and Mr Knightley runs the family estate. The question of marriage is very important. At the beginning of the novel (it starts and ends with a marriage) Mr Weston, a man who by trade in London has made enough money to buy a small estate, marries Miss Taylor, a governess. Socially it it not an equal marriage. The marriage between Mr Elton, the vicar, and Augusta Hawkins is not equal either. He has a social position but her family, though wealthy, are not quite as respectable. For Augusta Hawkins, then, marriage is socially advantageous. Frank Churchill is wealthy but he marries the poor but educated Jane Fairfax. Socially, then, they are not equals. It is interesting that the only marriage that is an equal one is the most important – Emma's to Mr Knightley. She is the daughter of a highly respected family and he owns the big estate. In addition, though this is a point about character, they are intellectual equals.

What do such marriages tell us? Jane Austen recognises that marriage – the basic institution of society – can, even within one class, be entered into for different reasons and can, therefore, be very different from one case to another. It is interesting, however, that the most important marriage is an equal one. This probably indicates that whilst Jane Austen recognises the variety of marriages that do occur, her ideal is one in which the partners are socially and intellectually equal. A social interpretation, therefore, reveals that her view of marriage is that it should maintain the stability of society by being, as near as possible, between characters of the same social positions.

## 17.4 INTERPRETATION THROUGH IDEAS

The approach through ideas is not very different from the ones through characters or society. It sees works of literature as being about attitudes and concepts. It is a philosophical approach. Literature is seen to be about the ideas of, for example, honesty, ambition, freedom of choice or guilt. You can tell whether the approach through ideas will be fruitful if the book contains passages in which ideas are either discussed or scenes which are the expression of ideas occur. For instance, in *1984* there are long discussions of political ideas, and the scenes in which Winston rewrites history are examples of the idea that the ruling party can even change the past. The aim of the approach through ideas is to be able to say that the book deals with such-and-such ideas. These ideas can, of course, be psychological or social.

*Emma* can be said to be about self-deception and true self-knowledge, and about marriage. For much of the time Emma is deceived. Her deception is wilful. She *wants* to believe that Mr Elton loves Harriet, so everything that happens is interpreted in that light. As we have seen, she eventually wakes up. She realises that she has been misleading herself and Harriet, and consequently feels foolish and guilty. (The morality of manipulating other people is also one of the ideas of the book.) This awakening leads her to self-knowledge. *Emma,* thus, is about the psychological ideas of deception and self-knowledge. It is also about the social one of marriage. Jane Austen is interested in the idea of marriage. She observes why people marry and also leads the reader to ask whether some marriages are more suitable and satisfying than others. In short, *Emma* is about ideas that are both psychological and social.

## 17.5 INTERPRETATION THROUGH LITERARY FORMS

The approach through form opens up a different set of problems. It asks how plots are constructed; what place the narrator has in relation to events; whether or not the author is deliberately trying to write a particular kind of book, say, an allegory, comedy or tragedy; or, in the case of poetry, how the stanza form, rhythm or sounds contribute to the meaning of a work. A formal approach stresses the importance of parallels, balances and contrasts. These can be events, images, individual words or lines. Of course, formal interpretations are never complete because they can't tell you what is *significant* about a work. They can, however, help you in making other interpretations because, for example, a psychological understanding of characters must be given formal expression in a book.

We have already touched on two formal aspects of *Emma*. Parts of *Emma* are written in the third person, yet it is quite clear that it is Emma's thoughts and not Jane Austen's that are being given. To put the point formally, you could say that the narrative is effectively first person although grammatically it is in the third. Thus Emma on the future Mrs Elton: 'She was good enough for Mr. Elton, no doubt; accomplished enough for Highbury – handsome enough – to look plain, probably, by Harriet's side.' That is in the third person yet it is not direct speech. It is narrative expressing Emma's viewpoint. Note the grudging use of 'enough'. The reason why Jane Austen writes in this form is because the novel is about how Emma imagines and interprets the world. Third person narrative that gives a first person view is the formal expression of that. Emma *thinks* she is seeing the world clearly but, in fact, she is interpreting it as she would like it to be.

The second formal feature already touched upon is the way the novel starts and ends with a marriage. The marriages, as it were, serve as a frame for the novel, giving it a neat and satisfying shape. But the formal device of framing the book in this way helps to draw attention to marriage. In itself it can do no more, but a reader can be alerted by this to think about the marriages of the book. He or she will then see that marriage is important and will be able to appreciate the start and finish of the book as the formal expression of the importance of marriage in the novel.

## 17.6 INTERPRETATION THROUGH HISTORY

The starting point of historical interpretation is that a work will reflect the thoughts, feelings and customs of the age in which it was written. It follows from that that knowledge about the period will help a reader understand books. A knowledge of manners, for instance, will help a reader judge the relations between characters. It is also useful to know what the society valued. This includes such things as the books they read, the games they played, the ideas they discussed, the things they took for granted, and the clothes they wore. In some cases it is useful to know what they thought. It is difficult to read Shakespeare without a knowledge of how important the monarch was in Elizabethan England and also of how religion played a very important part in people's lives. You can see from this that historical interpretations can be close to ones concerned with society and ideas. You can't interpret the society of a book unless you have some idea of what society was like in the period in which it was written, and the ideas in a book are bound to reflect those that were held at the time. It is not, however, *just* a case of books reflecting their time. What matters is what an author *makes* of the thoughts, feelings and customs of his or her age.

In order to understand *Emma* you should know about the importance of large estates in early nineteenth-century England, the position of governesses, the difficulties of travel and the position of the church. Let us, however, look at how a knowledge of the period helps in two areas – manners and reading. Manners are important in the novel, and it is also important to note what Jane Austen makes of them. The fact that Emma commends Mr Elton for his manners indicates that they were highly regarded at the time. This is what she says about them:

> In one respect, perhaps, Mr. Elton's manners are superior to Mr. Knightley's or Mr. Weston's. They have more gentleness. They might be more safely held up as a pattern. There is an openness, a quickness, almost a bluntness in Mr. Weston, which everybody likes in *him* because there is so much good humour with it – but that would not do to be copied.

The fact that Emma draws attention to manners in this way shows the importance they have, but the passage also indicates Jane Austen's attitude. Emma assumes that manners are a matter of copying a model; Mr Elton's, she says, could be held up 'as a pattern', whereas Mr Weston's 'would not do to be copied'. When, however, we learn that Mr Elton is only putting on a show to impress Emma and when we see that, after his marriage, he is calculatingly rude to Harriet, we see that Jane Austen is using a current interest in manners to indicate her belief that the best manners are those, like Mr Weston's, that are a genuine expression of his character and not copied like Mr Elton's.

She also uses the matter of reading to indicate her judgements. Emma likes popular novels, as does Harriet Smith. In the late eighteenth and early nineteenth century there were many books written for ladies. They were romantic, shallow and cheap. If a reader knows this, the following passage will be of particular significance. Emma has asked Harriet whether Mr Martin, a young farmer who has taken an interest in Harriet, reads. This is part of Harriet's answer:

> And I know he has read *The Vicar of Wakefield*. He never read the *Romance of the Forest*, nor the *Children of the Abbey*. He had never

heard of such books before I mentioned them, but he is determined to get them now as soon as ever he can.

Unknown to Harriet, those words are a judgement on her and Emma. The *Romance of the Forest* and *Children of the Abbey* are cheap and sentimental, whereas *The Vicar of Wakefield* is a masterpiece. Robert Martin's reading is unfashionable but shows real taste. The reader who knows about fashions in reading will be able to appreciate that point.

There is a final point that should be made about historical interpretation. It is helpful to study an edition that has some explanatory notes. Such editions usually explain the historical background and sometimes go on to indicate how the author handles the ideas of his or her time. If you don't own an edition with notes, it is a good idea to buy one. There are many available in the shops, and some of them are quite cheap.

## 17.7 INTERPRETATION AND THE READER

It would be a mistake to give the impression that interpretation is just a matter of approaching every poem, novel or play five ways. Some works of literature, for example, only require to be looked at from one or two viewpoints. Furthermore, interpretation is always personal. This means that one reader is not going to stress the same points as another. You will find that the way you interpret a book reflects your general interests and beliefs. If, for instance, you are interested in politics, you will tend to take a social approach, and if your interests are historical, you will find pleasure in studying how the work is related to the period in which it was written. You should, however, remember that interpretation is not just a matter of saying what you enjoy about a work. One of the points about *Emma* is that it is dangerous to read your own wants and prejudices into a situation. That is something you should avoid doing with books.

There are three things you should remember, which should prevent you from looking at books from a merely personal viewpoint. These are the words, the views of others and the idea of intention.

Because it is all too easy to imagine that a book says something, you should look at its words very closely to see what it is they are really saying. Quite often we form general ideas about books which, whilst they are not exactly false, are still too sweeping. The remedy for general ideas is to study the words closely to see if they qualify, or even deny, the impression you have received. An example is the way Jane Austen presents Emma's treatment of Harriet Smith. It is very easy to see Emma as a selfish manipulator of Harriet's feelings. This is not entirely untrue but it does need qualifying. In one chapter Emma persuades Harriet to reject Robert

Martin's proposal of marriage. Emma's behaviour is not commendable, but Jane Austen does show that Harriet is a rather shallow person. She is not happy about rejecting Robert Martin, but when Emma speaks of Mr Elton she brightens up. Jane Austen, therefore, shows that although Emma was wrong to manipulate her, Harriet is a weak and foolish girl whose feelings for Robert Martin are not very strong.

The second thing you should do is make yourself aware of other people's interpretations, by listening to what other people say and reading books of criticism. If you are in class, you should listen to and, of course, take notes on, what your teacher and fellow students say. You should listen particularly hard to views with which you *don't* agree.

Literary criticism is the phrase given to the business of interpreting and judging literature. School, college and public libraries, as well as bookshops, usually have a large selection of critical works. You should read them to find new ideas, new questions to ask and new lines of interpretation, though it is important to remember that literary criticism is most helpful when you know the books you are studying well and when you already have views about them. You will then be able to appreciate the fact that it is possible to interpret books in a number of ways and will be in a position to judge the value of the ideas given to you by literary criticism.

Finally, it is not easy to think about interpretation without discussing the intentions of the author. If a work has a particular meaning, it is difficult to escape the idea that that meaning is there because the author intended it. Literary works are specially designed by authors, so to interpret a work is to follow the creative mind of the author. This means that when you write about the meaning of a work, you should remember to mention the author. You can write about how the author presents the psychology of the characters, or explores ideas in the writing of a book.

## EXERCISES

**1** Try interpreting your set books from the psychological, social and ideas points of view. Which do you find the most helpful?

**2** Examine the forms of all the books you are studying. Do their forms help you to interpret them?

**3** Try to find out as much as you can about the historical period in which your books are written, and try to see how the authors have used the ideas and customs of their time.

**4** Select one or two passages from your set books and examine the words closely. To what extent do the words modify the general interpretations of these works you have made?

# CHAPTER 18

# EFFECTIVENESS

## 18.1 JUDGING EFFECTIVENESS

Many examination questions ask you to judge how effective a work of literature is, though they might not always use the word 'effective'. Some questions ask you to comment on the 'achievement' of an author, or invite you to write about the 'success' of a particular work. However, they are getting at the same thing – how well an author has written.

Judging the effectiveness of a poem, novel or play is not easy. In most cases you need to take your time. It would be foolish to judge a work simply on your first impressions, but equally you should never forget what you thought about a book when you first read it. You should recognise what your early judgements were but allow yourself to make new ones. It is always wise to be tentative, and always unwise to rush into a judgement that you regard as final. The best way to approach the problem of effectiveness is to ask questions about the work. What follows are a number of questions about poetry, novels and plays, and some general ones that can apply to any work.

## 18.2 QUESTIONS ABOUT THE EFFECTIVENESS OF POETRY

When you are thinking about the effectiveness of a poem, you ask about how interesting the words are, their appropriateness to the subject, the function of the imagery, rhythm and form, and whether the words enact the meaning. Let us examine these questions in more detail.

This can be asked of any poem: are the words interesting? When asking this question, you should remember that words can be used in very many ways. If you look back to Chapter 2, 'Words and Meanings', you will see the different effects that are created by metaphor, similes, images, symbols, and so on. Yet the effectiveness of words does not depend upon their being a figure of speech. Words can interest a reader by summoning associations or being direct and simple. Take, for example, the end of the first stanza of W. B. Yeats's 'The Wild Swans at Coole':

> Upon the brimming water among the stones
> Are nine-and-fifty swans.

Those words are effective although they are direct and simple. 'Brimming' is a strangely impressive word which suggests fullness and the marvellous shimmering quality of water in lakes. 'Water' and 'stones' are simple words, yet their very simplicity impresses because they point to the plain, unadorned yet wonderful reality of natural things. There is a stately, measured exactness about the phrase 'nine-and-fifty'. 'Fifty-nine' would sound horribly trite, but 'nine-and-fifty', because the phrase is built up steadily, sounds serene and poised. Of course, it is unlikely that those words will impress you upon first reading (though they might). In most cases you have to read a poem a number of times in order to recognise which are the interesting words.

A more specific question to ask is: are the words appropriate to the subject? Readers have long felt that an effective poem is one in which the words match the subject matter. A poem that deals with important subjects such as religion, morality or important events should, it is felt, use elevated words, whereas one that deals with ordinary things should use everyday ones. Two modern examples will make this clear.

In the fourth section of *Little Gidding* Eliot writes about the descent of the Holy Spirit. In order to bring out the momentous character of the event, he uses elevated words:

> The dove descending breaks the air
> With flame of incandescent terror
> Of which the tongues declare
> The one discharge from sin and error.

You will see that the 'tongues' don't merely speak, they 'declare'; and what they 'declare' is not a let-off or even a pardon but a 'discharge'. Those elevated and powerful words indicate that the subject matter is weighty. By contrast, look at these lines from John Betjeman's 'In Westminster Abbey'. Betjeman beautifully captures the tones of a well-meaning, honest but rather shallow lady who has gone into the Abbey to say her somewhat self-centred prayers:

> Now I feel a little better
> What a treat to hear thy Word.

The ordinary, everyday phrases – 'a little better' and 'what a treat' – are delightfully appropriate to the speaker. The words Betjeman has chosen are effective because they match his subject – a pleasant, middle-class lady who fails to appreciate that prayer is not quite the same as nice chat over afternoon tea.

A similar kind of question can be asked about the imagery: is the imagery appropriate to the subject? One of the pleasures of imagery is that of finding it expressing in its own concrete yet imaginative way the theme of the poem. Tennyson does this in 'Mariana'. It is a bleak poem in which the speaker, a woman, hopelessly waits for her estranged lover to return to her. The imagery of the poem beautifully enacts the desolation, boredom and frustration she feels. This is the first stanza:

> With blackest moss the flower-plots
>   Were thickly crusted, one and all:
> The rusted nails fell from the knots
>   That held the pear to the garden wall.
> The broken sheds looked sad and strange:
>   Unlifted was the clinking latch;
> Weeded and worn the ancient thatch
>   Upon the lonely moated grange.
> She only said, 'My life is dreary,
>   He cometh not,' she said;
> She said, 'I am aweary, aweary,
>   I would that I were dead!'

The imagery is of things overgrown or broken down: the 'flower-plots' are 'thickly crusted' with 'blackest moss', and the 'ancient thatch' is 'weeded'; 'rusted nails' fall from knots, sheds are 'broken' and look 'sad and strange' and the 'unlifted latch' clinks. Such imagery prepares us for her lamenting refrain. We can see from the imagery that her life is 'dreary' and understand, so near to death is everything, that she, too, wishes she 'were dead'. The imagery of the poem is no mere afterthought or decoration; it both creates and expresses the resigned hopelessness of the abandoned Mariana in her 'lonely moated grange'.

Since the rhythm of a poem should be appropriate, you can ask: is the rhythm appropriate to the meaning? An effective rhythm is not one that is regular (good rhythms are very rarely exactly regular) but one in which the stresses, and the weight of the stresses, fall on the crucial words. Indeed, in the best poems the rhythm of the words and the meaning of the words appear as *one* and not two things. For instance, when you read the opening lines of Donne's 'The Good-Morrow', are you not simply aware of the awakened astonishment of the poet:

I wonder, by my troth, what thou and I
Did, till we loved?

Yet those lines read as an expression of awakened astonishment because the rhythm so perfectly expresses the meaning. The rhythm is roughly iambic, but 'wonder' is stressed heavily, and the pace of 'thou and I' (note that the important words are stressed) is a steady crescendo leading to the achievement of 'Did'. That 'Did' breaks the rhythm, yet its urgency and ardour, so close to everyday speech, is felt by the reader to be emotionally right. The reader has the experience of listening to one thing, not an easily separable meaning and rhythm.

The question that can be asked about form is similar to the ones already given: is the stanza form appropriate to the subject of the poem? The test of a successful stanza form is close to the one used of rhythm: if you get the feeling that the idea could not have been said so effectively had it been in another form, then you can judge the stanza successful. Another way of putting the point is to say that the length of line and the rhyme scheme have an inevitable sense of rightness. For example, are not heroic couplets deeply appropriate to the strict, disciplined and deft turn of Pope's mind. Look at this couplet from his *Essay on Man*:

Know then thyself, presume not God to scan;
The proper study of mankind is Man.

The first line is an instruction (in grammatical terms it is an imperative), and the second completes it by firmly supplying a reason. What makes the couplet deft is the rhyme scan / man, but this deftness is not just that of pleasing harmony of sound that delights the ear. The rhyme sums up the meaning of the couplet – 'man' should study, that is 'scan', himself. In short, the instruction is: scan man.

The final question sums up all the ones above: does the poem enact its meaning? Enactment is a matter of all the aspects of words – associations, rhythms, sounds – combining to express the meaning. And meaning, of course, should be understood widely to include emotions as well as ideas. Enactment can be understood to apply to a poem as a whole and to individual parts. Blake's 'The Tyger', for instance, enacts throughout its six verses the attractive energy and fearful terror of the creature. Those impressions are enacted by the whole of the poem. An example of an individual line enacting its meaning can be found in Philip Larkin's 'The Whitsun Weddings'. In one delicately beautiful line – 'Thence the river's level drifting breadth began' – Larkin enacts the sense of peace and spaciousness felt by a railway traveller who sees the landscape broaden out over and beyond a wide, gently flowing river.

## 18.3 QUESTIONS ABOUT THE EFFECTIVENESS OF NOVELS

When you are thinking about the effectiveness of novels, it is good to start where examination questions do – with characters. There are three that can be asked about them. The first is: can the characters in a novel be understood? The word 'understood' must cover all the ways in which a reader can appreciate what it is a character is feeling and why he or she is feeling it. If a character has feelings that are utterly contradictory, then no understanding is possible. However, it is important to remember that a reader can understand a character whom he or she does not like. Take, for example, Mrs Elton from *Emma.* She is quite awful – showy, interfering, bossy and affected. Yet it is clear to the reader *why* she is like that – she wants to be accepted by the society into which she has married. This is what she says to Emma about her first meeting with Mr Knightley, whom she has met at the Westons:

> 'Knightley!' continued Mrs. Elton; – 'Knightley himself! – Was not it lucky? – for, not being within when he called the other day, I had never seen him before; and of course, as so particular a friend of Mr. E's, I had a great curiosity. "My Friend Knightley" had so often been mentioned, that I was really impatient to see him; and I must do my caro sposa the justice to say that he need not be ashamed of his friend. Knightley is quite the gentleman. I like him very much. Decidedly, I think, a very gentleman-like man.'

Mrs Elton offends Emma and the reader, yet, awful as she is, Jane Austen makes it possible for us to understand her. She wants to feel at home so she boldly talks of 'Knightley', when everybody else (including Jane Austen – and the reader!) refers to him as '*Mr.* Knightley'. She also tries to impress by talking in a fashionable way. Her husband she affectedly calls 'Mr. E.' and my 'caro sposa'. Awful as she is, we understand her. It is because we see that she is putting on a show that we find her an effective character.

The second question to ask about character is: does the author use access to a character's mind to good effect? The answers to this question will be different, depending upon whether the novel is written in the first or third person. In the case of first person narratives the mind of the narrator must either be interesting in itself or must undergo a series of interesting experiences. Jane Eyre is interesting in herself. There is a very remarkable tension in her between passion and duty. She is a girl who desires love and yet also someone who strictly adheres to her moral code. For instance, she passionately loves Mr Rochester but feels she must not live with him while his first wife is still alive. Pip in *Great Expectations* undergoes very interesting experiences – fear, dread, guilt, ambition, love, disappointment, sickness, remorse and self-realisation. In the case of third person narratives access into the mind of a character must show why that character acts as he or she does. Winston Smith in *1984* is effective, because Orwell vividly shows why he seeks to rebel against society. We see his disgust at living conditions, feel the dread of the ever-present eyes of authority, understand how all the good things in life have been corrupted, and glimpse with him the possibility of a better world – a world without lies, fear and oppression.

The third question to ask about character is: has the author been fair to his or her characters? It is quite clear that authors create characters whom they invite readers to like or dislike. When, however, an author's feelings get out of hand and a character is praised or condemned too much, a novel is made less effective. Successful novels, by contrast, contain characters who are unattractive yet presented fairly. Such a character is Mr Casaubon in *Middlemarch*. He is not a man for whom the reader is likely to feel affection, and it is equally clear that George Eliot judges him a failure who has a damaging effect upon Dorothea, his young wife. Yet George Eliot is never unfair to him. She presents him as a sad, disappointed man who is all too painfully aware that he is a failure. Moreover, she knows that her readers find him cold. At one point she directs her readers' attention away from Dorothea towards him. One chapter begins in this way:

> One morning, some weeks after her arrival at Lowick, Dorothea – but why always Dorothea? Was her point of view the only possible one with regard to this marriage? I protest against all our interest, all our effort at understanding being given to the young skins that look blooming in spite of trouble; for those too will get faded, and will know the older and more eating griefs which we are helping to neglect. In spite of the blinking eyes and white moles objectionable to Celia, and the want of muscular curve which was morally painful to Sir James, Mr. Casaubon had an intense consciousness within him, and was spiritually a-hungered like the rest of us.

That is George Eliot being fair. She protests against always seeing life from the point of view of the young. Mr Casaubon, she insists, and insists strongly, had 'an intense consciousness within him, and was spiritually a-hungered'. We are turned away from Dorothea and asked to consider what it must be like to be Mr Casaubon.

You can ask a question about the plot of a novel. A good one is: is the problem from which the plot grows an interesting or important one? Of course, what is thought to be important will differ from reader to reader, but it is generally held that problems such as a failed marriage, the struggle to overcome an unhappy childhood or the fight to resist evil are ones that engage people deeply. Yet it is not good enough simply to base a novel round an important problem. The novelist must really present the complexity of the situation if the plot is to be effective. Again, it is George Eliot that succeeds in doing this. *Middlemarch* presents, among other things, the failed marriage of Casaubon and Dorothea. But George Eliot never simplifies their relationship. She shows that whilst they grow further apart they remain sensitive to each other's needs. At one point Dorothea agonisingly asks: 'What have I done – what am I – that he should treat me so?' Yet, at the end of the very same chapter there is this touching moment:

> When her husband stood opposite to her, she saw that his face was more haggard. He started slightly on seeing her, and she looked up at him beseechingly, without speaking.
>
> 'Dorothea!' he said, with a gentle surprise in his tone. 'Were you waiting for me?'
>
> 'Yes, I did not like to disturb you.'
>
> 'Come, my dear, come. You are young, and need not to extend your life by watching.'

Neither understands the other, so in that sense their marriage is a failure, yet they are understanding and sensitive in this scene. She sees that he is 'haggard', and he speaks in a tone of 'gentle surprise'. By refusing to simplify the marriage, George Eliot makes the novel effective and increases its poignancy.

It is important to ask about the effectiveness of the setting. The most direct question is: does the setting reinforce the theme of the novel? You must remember that setting can be the society depicted, or the landscape and townscape. In *1984* the theme of the book – the destruction of humanity by an oppressive society – is expressed in the settings. What we learn of the people in general and what we see of rotting London houses show how life is narrow and brutalised. Likewise in *Tess of the D'Urbervilles* the scenes in Talbothays are effective because the society and landscape reflect Tess's joy in finding love. The society at the farm is a happy communal one in which the owner eats with his workers. The landscape is rich and overflowing with life. Both these settings show that Tess is at home in a rich and wonderful world.

The last question you can ask about novels is concerned with their themes or issues: does the novelist have something interesting and important to say about human life? Novels that either say nothing or are confused in what they say are ineffective, so the first thing you must be sure about is that a view of life does emerge in a book. But you don't have to agree with the view in order to find the book effective. Effectiveness depends upon the force and complexity with which a view is presented. Take, for example, William Golding's *The Spire.* The book is very forceful; it concentrates intensely on the dean's attempts to build a spire on his cathedral. It is also complex; the spire stands for so many things – prayer, ambition, sexuality, art and pride. Yet it is a book that divides readers. Some agree with the negative judgement passed on human ambition, whilst others do not. Both groups, however, can agree upon the effectiveness with which the important themes are communicated.

## 18.4 QUESTIONS ABOUT THE EFFECTIVENESS OF DRAMA

All the questions you can ask about the effectiveness of drama turn upon whether or not a play is *dramatic.* A basic one is about language: do the words of the play invite action? In order to answer that question you will have to think hard about whether the words invite gestures, movements and groupings. Plays that in no way invite action can't be called dramatic. The point about plays that do is that the actions invited by words are various. Look at this passage from *Macbeth* in which Macbeth is persuading the murderers to kill Banquo by showing that Banquo is the enemy of all of them:

> So is he mine; and in such bloody distance,
> That every minute of his being thrusts
> Against my nearest of life: and though I could
> With bare-faced power sweep him from my sight,
> And bid my will avouch it, yet I must not . . .

The words 'thrusts / Against' and 'sweep him from my sight' cry out for accompanying gestures, but there could be a number of appropriate ones. Does 'thrusts / Against' invite the actor to point to his heart or his head, and does the word 'sweep' indicate that the dramatic gesture (it must be that) should be with one or both arms? The words, then, provide different opportunities for dramatic expression.

A similar question can be asked about the theme of a play: is the theme acted out in the words of the play? A play will be effective if its central issues are both spoken about and acted out. In *King Lear,* for instance, there is a great deal of talk about seeing and blindness. When Lear foolishly decides to disown his youngest daughter, he is told to 'see better'. In the sub-plot Gloucester can't see that Edgar is a good son and that Edmund is plotting against him. But there are also actions. In one of the most terrible scenes in the whole of Shakespeare Gloucester has his eyes put out. His moral blindness (blindness to people, that is) has become physical blindness. The terrible irony of the play, however, is that once he is physically blind, he begins to 'see' clearly what has happened to him. At a crucial moment he 'sees' that he was 'blind': 'I stumbled when I saw.' What makes the words effective is the fact that the audience can see they come from a blind man. The theme of seeing and blindness is in the action as well as in the words.

As drama is a literary form that very obviously depends upon conventions, you can ask: are the conventions used in an interesting way? Plays can't be understood unless the audience recognises dramatic conventions, but unless those conventions are extended, the play will not be enjoyable. What Shakespeare often does is allow a character to grow beyond the conventions of the role he or she is playing. He often does this with villains. Take, for instance, Oliver in *As You Like It.* The first scene presents him as unnaturally cruel to his brother, Orlando, and viciously scheming. However, when he is left alone at the end of the scene, his soliloquy is not what convention would lead us to expect:

> Now will I stir this gamester: I hope I shall see an end of him; for my soul, yet I know not why, hates nothing more than he. Yet he's gentle; never schooled and yet learned; full of noble device; of all sorts enchantingly beloved; and, indeed, so much in the heart of the world, and especially of my own people, who best know him, that I am altogether misprized . . .

The only thing there that convention would lead us to expect is the hope that he will 'see an end of' Orlando. But what follows is an enlargement of character beyond the convention of the villain. He virtually praises Orlando, and stands in wonder at his qualities. Moreover, he admits (painfully?) that he has no idea why he hates him, and there could be sadness in the thought that everyone loves Orlando and looks down on him. What Shakespeare is doing is making a character grow out of a convention. This helps to make the play effective.

There are two questions that can be asked about characters. The first is: are the characters distinctive? Of course, if a dramatist has decided that some characters need only be stock ones, it is foolish to say that they should have been fuller. However, unless the play is a farce, characters of some individuality are needed. You should also see if there is a balance in a play between those who are fairly fully drawn and those who are not. In Bolt's *A Man for all Seasons,* for instance, the Common Man plays a number of stock roles. This is appropriate, because detailed characterisation could not add anything of importance. But the play is a serious one, so characters who are distinctive are required. Sir Thomas More, of course, is created in some detail, as is Cromwell, Rich and Margaret. The balance between the stock and the distinctive characters is good, because the play moves from lightness to seriousness, depending upon who is on stage. This gives the play variety and makes it effective.

The second question about character is this: does the play create a vigorous and immediate sense of life? This question depends not so much upon the personality of one or two characters but the *impression* the actions of characters make upon the audience. The action of the play need not be striking. Becket's *Waiting for Godot* is a play in which actions are few but the dialogue is varied and lively, so an immediate sense of life is created. In this passage the two tramps, Estragon and Vladimir, are wondering what Godot will offer them:

*Estragon:* What exactly did we ask him for?
*Vladimir:* Were you not there?
*Estragon:* I can't have been listening.
*Vladimir:* Oh . . . nothing very definite.
*Estragon:* A kind of prayer.
*Vladimir:* Precisely.
*Estragon:* A vague supplication.
*Vladimir:* Exactly.
*Estragon:* And what did he reply?
*Vladimir:* That he'd see.

That is lively, quick-fire dialogue in which there are remarkable changes of mood. Vladimir is cautious in reply to Estragon's first question and then sadly vague ('Oh . . . nothing very definite') in his answer. However, when Estragon makes some suggestions he is much more assured – 'Precisely', 'Exactly'. It would be right to say that the characters create a vigorous and immediate sense of life.

The final question that can be asked about drama concerns the plot: is the plot well handled? In order to answer that, you will have to see whether all the elements of a plot are held harmoniously together and whether they naturally grow to produce a credible conclusion. The question is more likely to be asked about comedies than tragedies, for comedies demand complex, well-made plots. Take, for instance, the plot of *Twelfth Night.* Shakespeare has several elements that he has to hold together. One of the ways in which he does this is by drawing the audience's attention to the similarities and differences between those elements. At the beginning of the play we hear of Olivia who, because of the death of her brother, has withdrawn from the world. In the second scene, however, we are shown Viola, who believes her brother is drowned. Instead of withdrawing from the world she adopts a disguise and seeks employment at court. That is not the only case of similarity and difference in the plot. Orsino, who loves Olivia, adopts a very romantic attitude in loving. Olivia, however, when she falls in love is very practical. She asks questions such as: 'How shall I feast him?' That is very sensible and down to earth. She is thinking about what she will give Cesario (Viola in disguise) to eat.

The plot ends when Orsino goes to visit Olivia and, although it is not seen, Sir Toby pursues his idea of challenging Cesario to a duel. This brings the twins on to the stage together, and enables Shakespeare to close the play effectively. He can allow all the characters to see what has confused them and also stage the beautiful and touching reconciliation between Viola and her brother, Sebastian.

## 18.5 TWO GENERAL QUESTIONS ABOUT EFFECTIVENESS

There are two questions that you can ask of any literary work, whether it be a poem, novel or play. The first is: has the author fulfilled his or her intentions? If you decide that the author had a particular intention in mind when the work was written, a way of judging its effectiveness is by asking whether that intention has, in fact, been fulfilled. You can often decide what the intention of the author was by looking at the events of the plot as a whole. The plot shows you how the author intends a character to be interpreted and judged. You then have to look at the work closely to see if what was intended has been achieved. You must prepare yourself for disagreements with your fellow students. What, for instance, was Jane Austen's intention with regard to Fanny Price in *Mansfield Park*? Some readers would say she is meant to be a quiet and reserved heroine, whom readers will both like and judge as being good. Many readers find her to be that, but others agree that though that was Jane Austen's intention, the character actually created does not fulfil it, because she is cold and self-righteous. Lawrence's *Sons and Lovers* presents another problem. What were Lawrence's intentions? Should a reader approve of Paul Morel and think that Miriam was a bad influence on him? That might be what Lawrence intended, but many readers both like her and feel she is treated unfairly by Paul *and Lawrence.* In some cases, however, the intentions of an author are clearly and marvellously fulfilled. Bulstrode in *Middlemarch* is intended to be an unattractive character for whom the reader has increasing sympathy. He is that, and we do.

The second question concerns form: does the work hang together as a whole? One of the pleasures of reading literature is of finding works in which every part contributes to the general effect. This is very clearly the case with short poems, but is also true of longer works. However bulky and rambling some of Shakespeare's plays appear to be on first acquaintance, you may find that close study shows you that each element blends in with the others to make a satisfying whole. Sometimes even a single line can take you into the heart of a play. When the mad Ophelia enters, she asks: 'Where is the beauteous majesty of Denmark?' That poignant question takes you to the heart of *Hamlet*. The 'beauteous majesty of Denmark'–

the late king – is dead, and his son, Prince Hamlet, has been (possibly) driven out of his wits and (certainly) driven out of the country. When the question is asked, there is no beauty nor majesty left. And that is one of the themes of the play – the whole society is corrupted and rotten.

## EXERCISES

**1** Recall your first impressions of a book. How helpful do you now find them in judging whether or not a book is effective.
**2** Try to say why you think a poem, novel or play is effective.
**3** Look at the poems, novels or plays you are studying in the light of each of the above questions examined. Do they make you change your mind about the effectiveness of your set works?
**4** Try to say what you think the intentions of the authors were in writing the books you are studying. Do you think the authors have fulfilled these intentions?
**5** Try to say how the books you are studying hang together as a whole. If you think they don't, try to say why not and whether you think they are less effective because of that.

# CHAPTER 19

# QUESTIONS

## 19.1 THE FORM OF QUESTIONS

If you are studying for an 'O' or 'A' level, you will write essays, both as part of your course of study and in the examination room. The chief complaint that teachers and examiners have about essays is that they do not answer the questions. The reason for this is that most students don't think hard enough about the wording of the questions and so they don't show in their essays that they really understand what is being asked of them. The aim of this section is to look at the *kinds* of question that are asked at 'O' and 'A' level, and how you can prepare for them.

No matter whether you are being asked to write about poetry, novels or plays you will find questions in four forms: the direct question, the quotation, the parts question and the passage question.

The direct question is the one that asks you straightforwardly about the work. It is usually in the form of how, why, or, particularly at 'O' level, what or where. For instance, you might be asked: 'How does Dickens show the reader that Pip is a snob?' or 'Why does O'Brien want to make Winston betray Julia?'

The quotation question puts an idea forward for discussion by borrowing or inventing a remark about the work. The quotation is often followed by 'Discuss', 'Do you agree', or an invitation to think about the work in the light of the remark. For instance, you might find questions such as these:

> 'Wilfred Owen has only one subject – war – and that makes his poetry of limited interest to the reader.' Discuss.

> 'William Golding has a gloomy view of people.' Do you agree that Golding's view of people in *The Lord of the Flies* is a gloomy one?

You should remember that you are not forced to agree or disagree with the quotation. You can agree with some parts and not with others, or say that the remark is true of some aspects of the work but not all of it.

The parts question is the one in which you are asked how an author, or book, deals with one or two of a list of items. For instance, questions have been set on the following lines:

> Discuss Shakespeare's treatment in *The Winter's Tale* of *two* of the following: song and dance, the court, women, children and young people, disguise, the passing of time.
>
> Write briefly about the importance of three of the following characters in *A Man for all Seasons:* Rich, Roper, Chapys, More's wife, Norfolk, the King.

The passage question comes in a number of forms. What they all have in common is the fact that a passage is printed on the examination paper and you are asked to write about it. It might be a poem from an anthology, part of a chapter from a novel, or lines from a play. You could be asked specific questions about the passage or given a general invitation to write about it. In some 'O' and 'A' level examinations you are given what is called an 'unseen' passage: that is, something from a work you have not studied. Again, the questions could be specific or general. Specific questions sometimes take the following form: 'Examine the effectiveness of the metaphor in the third line'. General questions are often put this way: 'Write about the following passage from a modern novel bringing out whatever you find of interest in it.'

When we turn to the *content* of questions, we find more variety, but diverse as they are, certain types can still be seen.

## 19.2 QUESTIONS ON POETRY

Questions about poetry are usually about style, theme, or the problems they present, or they are passage questions.

Questions about poetic style are set at both 'O' and 'A' level, though they are more numerous at the latter level. What they all share is the idea that poets write in their own way, and that, therefore, each poet's work is distinguished by an individual manner. Questions about style ask you to write about that individual manner by identifying what features make it distinctive. Hence, the following questions could be set:

> What features of Milton's poetic style are present in the first two books of *Paradise Lost*?
>
> Readers have admired the individual voice of Dylan Thomas. With close reference to at least three poems show what are the basic characteristics of that voice.

Consider the poetic qualities of Hopkins as they are present in 'The Wreck of the Deutschland'.

Sometimes questions specify the aspects of style about which you are to write. They might ask you about the narrative skills of a poet, about a poet's dramatic manner, about his or her imagery, use of a stanza form or variety of sound and rhythm. An extension of this type of question is the one that asks you to say what features of a poet's style make him or her metaphysical, or romantic. A further variation is the question that asks what aspects of a poet's style has made him or her popular. Quite often, at both 'O' and 'A' level, questions about style include something on the effectiveness of the writing.

In general, questions about style can be prepared for. You should prepare notes on the distinctive features of a poet's manner – choice of language, imagery, stanza form, rhythm, sounds and tone. It is insufficient just to make a list of these. For each one you will need two or three examples about which you can write in detail. You can also work out your arguments for why you find the poet's work effective or not. Questions about popularity or the extent to which they are representative of a particular group of poets should also be prepared for in detail.

Questions about the themes of a poet are set at both 'O' and 'A' level. It is not easy to generalise about them because they are as varied as the diverse subjects of different poets. You could be asked how a poet treats love, the passing of time, failure, the future, nature, the city, work or leisure. Sometimes, questions include a line or two, and you are asked to say how central they are to the poet's work as a whole. Another way of putting the question is to invite a comment on the emotional or intellectual outlook of the poet. Sometimes you are asked to assess the poet's ideas by considering the extent to which they are still relevant or whether they are limited by being, for instance, too concerned with personal problems.

Clearly, you should prepare for questions such as these by identifying the basic themes and attitudes of the poet. You should, of course, gather specific examples. You can also anticipate some questions by considering whether the poet shows certain limitations, and whether the ideas present in the work have a lasting value. A good starting point for identifying a poet's basic concerns is the question: what is this poet interested in?

Problem questions are usually only set at 'A' level. Their starting point is the realisation that there is something odd, difficult or controversial about a poet's work. It seems odd, for instance, that Donne should write passionate love *and* religious poetry, or that Chaucer's Wife of Bath should be given a surprisingly honest and even explicit *Prologue* but go on to tell a conventionally romantic *Tale.* Wordsworth might be thought of as difficult because most of his subject matter is very ordinary and yet he responds very warmly to it. Poetical works become controversial when critics disagree about them strongly. Some might say that *Paradise Lost* is thrilling, others that it is cold, austere and hard to read. A special form of this type of problem is the harsh words one writer uses of another. Yeats, for instance, dismissed Owen, and Eliot found fault with Milton.

You can prepare for these questions by reading poetry in a questioning manner. You can constantly ask yourself whether there is anything odd or difficult about the work, and reference to works of criticism will bring you face to face with controversies. What you need to show is that you understand *why* the poetry is problematic. To do this you have to be able to write about it in detail and be able to show how different views of it have emerged. It is also of great value if you can show the strength and limitations of these views, either by showing that the poetry does not work in the way critics claim it does or by showing that a critic has only seen half the truth.

Passage questions are usually much more detailed at 'O' than at 'A' level. 'O' level questions often print one or two poems and then ask a number of questions. The most common question is the one that asks you to comment on the meaning of effectiveness of particular words, lines, sounds or rhythm. Other questions are about your impressions of a line or the extent to which a poem is typical of an author. Most of these questions tell you to write in detail. At 'A' level you are usually invited (particularly in the case of unseen poems) to compare and contrast the subject matter, verse form, language and imagery of two poems.

At both 'O' and 'A' level you must write about the words before you. What you should always try to do is show how they enact their meanings. Examiners give no rewards to students who simply say that the poet uses metaphors or writes alliteratively. You must show how the meaning and emotional impact is present in the metaphors and the alliterated words. This means you must never be content with just using critical terms – you must try to use a broader language dealing with thought and feeling. Another mistake to avoid is that of leaving the poem or poems 'in bits'. Whilst you should avoid simple paraphrasing, you must show how the poem is constructed, how it develops, how the tone changes and what its conclusion achieves. A very common mistake is that of assuming you know what the tone of the poem will be simply by looking at the subject matter. Not all poems about death are gloomy, nor are all poems about spring happy. You should read the poem a number of times, trying to sense its particular emotional character. Above all, you should write in detail, trying to show how individual words and phrases work within the poem.

## 19.3 QUESTIONS ON NOVELS

Questions about novels are very varied indeed. The most common ones are about character, theme, style and the attitude of the author.

Most questions at 'O' level and over half at 'A' level are about character. The 'O' level ones can be very simple. You may be asked to write about how a character changes, how he or she reacts to events or other characters, about a particular aspect of a character, or about your reactions to him or her. You could also be asked to write about how some characters differ from others, and you could be asked to say which of the two you prefer and why. 'A' level questions are more complex. Many ask you to see how characters contrast or complement each other. They sometimes go on to ask you to consider the importance of a character in the design of the whole novel. Questions are also concerned about motives. There are also questions about how novelists handle characterisation. Some might ask you whether all the characters are presented in the same way, whether some are closer to caricature than others, and whether, within one novel, there is a sufficient range to make the work varied and interesting.

It is easy to prepare for the simple questions. You can make detailed notes on the various aspects of each character, particularly noting their reactions to major events, to each other, and the important changes that take place in them. In the case of the more complex ones, you should make similar notes but bear two other points in mind: their place in the design of the novel, and the way they are presented by the author. In dealing with the first point you will need to tie in the characters with the novel's themes, and with the second you will need to think about the relation between narrator and character, and about whether the characters reveal the author's views about people in general. No matter whether you are preparing for 'O' or 'A' level you should look for the telling incident or piece of dialogue. If you can write about those, your work will be detailed and convincing.

Questions about themes are set at 'O' and 'A' level. They are often concerned with their development. Questions such as the following might occur:

Trace the development of the relationship between Jane and Mr Rochester in *Jane Eyre.*

Examine carefully the ideas about education in *Hard Times.*

Consider how George Eliot handles marriage in *Middlemarch.*

Another popular approach is to pose a question in terms of a tension between two ideas, or to invite the student to consider the interrelation between two themes. Some questions ask you to comment on the significance of the title, and others, particularly at 'A' level, require you to argue about the *importance* of a particular theme. Another form of the question is to take two themes and ask whether one is handled more effectively than the other.

When you prepare notes on themes, you should pay particular attention to how they emerge and change. In doing this you will need to note events in which a change becomes evident. If you can detect a change in the attitude of the author, you must note that. Notes should also be made on the interrelation of themes and the significance of the title. As you do this, you will have to ask which themes are the most important. You will usually find that the important ones are those which are the concern of the central character or are seen in the lives of more than one of the characters.

Questions about style are usually only set at 'A' level. Most of them are about the techniques of novel writing. For instance, you may be asked about the viewpoint of the author, about how the author relates events, about the pace of the plot's development, about the changing views the reader is offered and the contribution of the background. In other words, the questions ask you to think about *how* the novel is written.

The best way to prepare for these questions is to study the book as a work of art that has been specially created by the author. If you always bear in mind that that is what it is, you will start to notice how the novelist is working. If you want more specific help in compiling notes, you can think about particular topics such as the narrative viewpoint, access to characters' minds, the nature of the plot, the pace of events and the role of background. If you can locate specific events in which the style of the author's writing is particularly evident, then you should use them in detail in your answers.

Questions about character, theme and style are also questions about the attitudes of an author, in that the only way in which the attitudes of the author can be known is through these elements. The difference is one of focus; in questions about the attitudes of an author, character, theme and style are examined for what they reveal about the author's outlook on life. Therefore, there are questions about why an author attacks certain ideas, or why he or she shows sympathy for certain characters. It is sometimes proposed in the form of a quotation that an author approves of one character, or set of ideas, but disapproves of others. Sometimes a quotation from the author about his or her intentions is offered for discussion, and sometimes there is a question about the author's views on life as a whole. For instance, students are frequently asked whether or not Hardy is a pessimist.

Your thinking about these matters should emerge in and through your consideration of character, theme and style. As you think about these areas, you should ask yourself: does this writing tell me anything about the attitudes of the novelist? The development of the plot is often crucial. What happens to characters and how they react to their circumstances usually shows you what an author thinks. Sometimes, of course, the attitudes of an author are made plain in the tone or the way they openly declare what they think. Nobody could miss the anger of Dickens in *Hard Times,* or miss his statements about education in the same novel. When the attitude of an author is less plain, you should try to show the problem of coming to a firm conclusion.

## 19.4 QUESTIONS ON DRAMA

Questions about drama are similar to those about the novel in that there are ones about character and theme. But there are also questions about the dramatic effectiveness of plays, genre questions and, particularly in the case of Shakespeare, passage questions.

Character questions are set at 'O' and 'A' level. Some of them are no different from questions about novels; they ask about the changes in a character, contrasts between characters, relationships, the beliefs of characters or particular aspects such as their treachery, deception or ambition. Some go further and ask you to assess your feelings about them. You may be asked to say how amusing or sad you feel a character to be or estimate the degree to which the playwright invites you to feel sympathetic. 'A' level character questions are not very different from 'O' level ones. The most common distinguishing mark is the invitation to think about a character's contribution to the play as a whole.

The best advice that can be given about these questions is to look closely at the wording. Some ask for no more than character sketches, whilst others ask you to think about characters dramatically. For instance, a question that asked 'Trace the breakdown of Willy Loman in *Death of a Salesman*' would require no thinking about the play as a piece of drama at all. All you need do to prepare for such a question is make sure you know the major changes that occur in the characters of the play you are studying. If, however, the question asks 'Trace carefully Arthur Miller's treatment of Willy Loman in *Death of a Salesman*', you must pay attention to how the playwright presents and develops characters. When making notes, it is always wise to prepare for the second type of question rather than the first, because material for the second will cover answers of the first kind.

Theme questions at 'O' and 'A' level also tend to be simple. The questions usually fix on an important element in the play and frame a question round it. Questions that may come up are:

How important is the theme of revenge in *Hamlet*?

Examine the theme of deception and self-deception in *Twelfth Night*.

Trace the development of the idea of 'Nature' in *King Lear*.

'O' level questions rarely ask anything more of you than the ability to identify and follow through a particular theme. At 'A' level, questions often go further; you may be asked to decide which of two themes is the more important, to write about your response to them, or defend or attack a suggestion about the main theme of the play.

You should prepare for the simpler questions by looking for particular incidents in which the theme of the play is evident. If you can point in detail to three or four moments, you will avoid writing vaguely – something that examiners do not like. When you prepare for 'A' level questions, you should constantly look for reasons *why* a theme is important and *how* it emerges in the play. This preparation will make you think about the play as a whole. You will have to think about how the plot expresses the themes of the play, about the contribution of recurring words or images, about the dialogue and the characters. In other words, you should try to show that a theme emerges in and through the whole play.

Questions about dramatic effectiveness ask you to think about plays as drama. Sometimes questions simply ask what is dramatically effective about a play. When they are more specific they might ask about the dialogue (very popular in the case of Pinter and Becket), about the relation between words and action, and about the kind of audience that would find the play enjoyable. Most of these questions will only be set at 'A' level. At 'O' level you may find questions about dramatic importance of the setting and atmosphere.

The best preparation you can make for these questions is to think about the play you are studying in the light of three of the points made in the chapters on drama. The first is the nature of dramatic language – its ability to invite gesture and movement. The second is the nature of a dramatic plot – its need to act out the themes rather than merely report them. The third is the need to act out the play as you read it in the theatre of your imagination. It is a good idea to keep a separate set of notes on the play's dramatic effectiveness, or you may be unable to think about the play other than in terms of character or theme.

Genre questions are closely related to those about dramatic effectiveness. Genre means a kind or type of literature. In drama it is often applied to comedy and tragedy. Quite often at both 'O' and 'A' level you will be asked to think about the nature of comedy or tragedy in relation to the play you are studying. A popular question is one that gives a definition and asks you to say how helpful it is in understanding your play. Another popular question is the one that suggests that a particular play is, for instance, too sinister to be a comedy or contains too much laughter to be really tragic. Sometimes the question invites you to consider whether a play stands between two types; it might be said to be closer to farce than comedy, or, in the case of Shakespeare, more of a problem play than a comedy.

These questions ask you to assess how helpful critical terms are. To answer them well, you need to see that critical terms are useful but that they sometimes force you to bring expectations to a play that the play will not fulfil. You need to show that terms like comedy and tragedy are quite flexible, and that you can be flexible in using them. Therefore, you should go into an examination room with a general idea of what tragedy and comedy is like but also aware of the points in the plays you have studied that don't fit in with these general ideas. You can then write about how, say, the play extends ideas of comedy, departs from them entirely, or fails to capture the necessary comic spirit.

Passage questions (also known as gobbet questions) are set at both 'O' and 'A' level. They are similar to questions about poetry in that at 'O' level they are much more specific than at 'A' level. The usual practice is to print between thirty and sixty lines. At 'O' level you can expect questions on such matters as the state of mind of a character, the effectiveness of an image, and the dramatic effectiveness of the scene. At 'A' level there are sometimes specific questions inviting you to write about who speaks, to whom and in what circumstances, dramatic significance, and the way in which the ideas are expressed. There are also more general questions that invite you to write about the passage as a whole. These questions may also invite you to comment on its themes, the development of character, the significance of it being in verse or prose, its imagery, and the place of the passage in the development of the plot.

For advice about how to write in detail on drama you should turn back to Part III on drama. You should look at the words and respond to them as pieces of dramatic writing. It is also a good idea to bear two other points in mind. The first is to look and respond to the changing mood of a passage. So often good dramatic writing is perpetually changing in its emotional intensity. The mood of a scene can intensity, relax, grow to a minor climax and then gradually release its tension to become peaceful. As you write about such changes, try to show that you respond to them. Examiners often complain that students write without relish, interest or sensitivity to a play's mood. The second thing you should remember is the play as a whole. You should write mostly about the passage before you, and you should not waste time in telling the story. If you do see a parallel with another part of the play, an important change in a character, a central image or an important word that is used elsewhere, you must comment on it. Examiners are also impressed if you can show them that you can see the play as a whole by writing about the place of the extract in the plot.

## 19.5 ARGUMENT AND EVIDENCE

There is one last piece of general advice you should follow. When answering a question, you should maintain a balance between argument and evidence. Examiners are impressed by candidates who can see the issues behind a question and can present a clear view of them. They welcome essays that state the problems contained in the question, develop these problems in appropriate ways, and conclude by showing which arguments are sound and which unsound. But to do this, you need evidence. You must refer (in detail, if possible) to specific passages. And usually it is not good enough just to quote. If you quote a passage in support of an argument, you must show, even if only briefly, what there is in the passage that supports your argument. You can do this by singling out a word or phrase, pointing to the central ideas in the quotation, or showing how the words of the quotation enact its meaning.

## EXERCISES

**1** Look through all the questions you have been asked to write on your set books and see if you can understand exactly what they are asking you to do.
**2** Prepare revision notes for all your set books in the light of the kinds of question you may find in the examination.
**3** Work out some questions of your own for each of your set books. It is a good idea to work out one for each of the types set out above.
**4** Practise writing in detail about the important passages in each of your set books.
**5** Plan out answers for questions, making sure you strike a balance between the argument as a whole and the evidence required to back it up.

# CHAPTER 20

# EXAMINATIONS

## 20.1 REVISION

It is foolish to leave revision to the few weeks before an examination. Throughout your course of study you should find time to look through your work. The best thing to do is to look through what you have done every week. You should read through the material, do any writing that you think is necessary, and try to relate the new material to what you already know of the book.

Once you have finished your first study of a book you should re-read it. (More advice on this is given in Chapter 16.) You can do this in one of two ways. You can either read the book through without taking notes or you can make further notes as you read. It is wise not to exclude the possibility of making more notes, as new ideas may occur to you as you read. You can also turn to criticism to give you more ideas.

Throughout your course you will be making notes. As the examination approaches, you should make some that are specifically concerned with it. The best thing to do is make separate notes on the important aspects of the book – its themes, style, characters, plot and effectiveness. It is also wise to look through the kinds of question that are usually asked and prepare notes on these. A convenient way of compiling revision notes is to buy a cheap exercise book and devote two or three pages to each of the topics. But you should not forget that it is the book upon which you are going to be examined and not your notes! Therefore, make sure that in your revision notes you keep a record of the page numbers of important passages.

There are a number of ways in which you can revise. One is simply reading your set books. This is particularly important with poetry. Because many poems are short, you can easily read a number of them each day and so make yourself more familiar with them. It is also a good idea to look at the set work in the light of your notes. If you have both open on the table before you, the one can illuminate the other. Ideas in your notes may remind you of the importance of something in the text, and the work itself may help you to see how some of the ideas in your notes relate to each other. A third way of revising is that of reading through your revision notes with possible examination questions in mind. This will help you to be more flexible in the use of your notes, and so you may avoid the danger of only seeing the book you are studying in terms of your notes.

It is a good idea to do some writing as part of your revision. You can plan answers and write in detail about important passages. You should also practise writing quickly. Examinations at 'O' level often allow you thirty-five minutes a question, and 'A' level rarely gives you more than fifty minutes. If you are not required to do timed essays in class, you should certainly do some in your own time. Find yourself an examination question and answer it in the time allowed. As soon as you start practising, you will find that you have not much time, so you should write a number of essays to get used to it.

Learning quotations is necessary. If you have revised your work once a week, you will find that many quotations have stuck. Still, you should learn some more. Care should be given to selecting the passages you wish to commit to memory. Pick those that you can use in a number of ways; that is, those passages that are useful when talking about more than one aspect of a book. Two rules of learning should be observed. The first is that as soon as you can do without the book from which you are learning the better. You can read the passages for learning three or four times but then try to recall what you have learned. You will find that the sooner you do without the book, the quicker you will learn. The second rule is regular repetition. You must never assume that once you have learned a quotation you will remember it for ever. You should practise reciting those passages you have learned once or twice a day. Some people like to write the passages for learning out and pin them on their bedroom walls. This is a good idea, as long as you use them to prompt yourself when you forget. In general it is pointless to learn very long quotations. It is much better to know fifteen short (two or three line) quotations than three or four very long ones. It is also worth remembering that in examinations you can use phrases even when you have forgotten the whole line or sentence. For instance, you may remember that Macbeth speaks of pity as being like 'a naked newborn babe'. You can use the quotation as part of a sentence and then comment on, say, the sense of vulnerability created by the word 'naked'.

## 20.2 EXAMINATION TECHNIQUE

Examination technique helps you to make the best of what you know in an examination. Although the subject here is English Literature, the following advice is applicable to nearly all examinations.

Although revision is hard work, you should make sure you are not tired when you take the examination. If you have revised thoroughly, there is no need to stay up late the night before an examination. Even if the examination is in the afternoon, late night revision is both unnecessary and undesirable. The plain fact is that you should be fresh and alert before the examination.

Teachers are never tired of telling their students to answer *all* the questions. The advice is so obvious as to seem almost unnecessary, but every year hundreds of candidates ruin their chances either by failing to answer all the questions or by only answering some of them in part. This is where the value of doing timed essays as part of your revision comes in. If you are used to writing essays of the required length, you are much less likely to mistime your efforts. If you do find you are spending too much time on an essay (this can easily happen with the first one you do), you must stop and start another.

Above all, you must decide at the very beginning of the examination which questions you are going to answer. When you are allowed to look at the paper, read through *all* the questions and decide there and then which ones you are going to do. This method has two advantages. First, it quickly gets rid of all your anxiety about the paper. Naturally, you will be worried about what is in the paper and you will probably be troubled about which ones you should do. If you can get over all that anxiety by deciding which questions you are going to answer, you can then use all your mental energy on the questions themselves. The second advantage is that you will find that your unconscious mind is already thinking about the questions you are to do. You may find an important idea about a question you are yet to do pops into your mind as you are answering another. You should briefly jot the idea down in case you forget it, and immediately return to the essay you are doing.

## 20.3 IN THE EXAMINATION ROOM

Some of the aspects of writing in the examination room have already been covered in Chapter 19, but some advice still remains to be given.

You should make sure you are answering the question. To do this, you should read it through three or four times to determine what it is asking. It will be helpful in answering that question to look out for two things. You can see what kind of a question it is. Study of the previous chapter will prepare you for that. You can also look for the key words – the words that tell you exactly what the examiner requires of you. Popular key words are: effective, successful, aims, purpose, dramatic and contrast. If a question asks you to write about the effectiveness of a character, you will have to make sure you don't give a character sketch. Unless you take note of the presence of the word 'effective', you may just write about what a character is like and so fail.

Sometimes a question can easily be broken down into parts. If you decide to do such a question, you usually have the shape of the essay sorted out for you. For instance, look at this question on *Macbeth*:

> Consider the role of the witches, and comment on their contribution to the play and the appeal they have for audiences.

Any answer to this question should be in three parts. There should be a lengthy part on the role of the witches, for which you will have to think about their place in the plot and the problem of what effect they have on Macbeth. There should then be a section on their contribution. You could write about how they create atmosphere and how they are similar to, or different from, other characters who appear to influence Macbeth. Finally, there should be a section on why they appeal. You could write about the opportunities they offer to a producer, and the effect that is created by the fact that they open the play.

When you are writing quickly, it is not always easy to be clear. The best thing you can do is remember that you are communicating with the examiner, and that you should therefore produce what he or she wants. Examiners look for four things in an essay. The first is an understanding of the issues of the question. The best way of showing this is by writing a brief opening paragraph in which you explain the problems behind the essay and say what you are going to argue about them. The next thing an examiner is looking for is a coherent argument. You should make sure that you move from point to point in a logical way. The third requirement is evidence that is discussed in detail. You must show that you know which parts of the book are necessary for answering the question and you must be able to show how and why they are necessary. The last thing is a conclusion. You must draw together all that you have said and show what it adds up to. Practice at writing essays like this is, of course, necessary.

You must remember to write in a way which is appropriate to the wording of the question. If you are asked to discuss critical terms, you must show that you can handle them. An essay on imagery, for instance, requires you to use terms such as figurative, simile and metaphor. An even more important point is to make sure you are answering in the right person. If you are asked about Shakespeare's treatment of a character, you should write in the third person. If, however, you are asked what *you* think about a book, you must answer in the first person. Examiners often complain that students don't write in a personal way. To say 'I felt this' or 'I think that' certainly helps.

## 20.4 SOME WARNINGS

You should never reproduce in an examination an essay you have written during the course of study, unless, that is, the wording of both questions is exactly the same. You will, of course, use material from essays you have done, but whatever you use, be it argument or evidence, you must frame it according to the demands of the question. For instance, both the following questions are about Jocelin, the central character in Golding's *The Spire*:

Do you find Jocelin a likeable character?

Do you think that Golding is inviting the reader to approve of Jocelin?

Answers to both questions would include common material, but if you had done the first during a course of study and reproduced it in answer to the second in an examination, you would fail. The first asks you for your response to the character of Jocelin; the second asks you to think about whether the author invites the reader to judge Jocelin favourably or unfavourably.

Some students find answering questions on poetry difficult. Because of this they often get stuck with just one or two poems. That is not good enough. In poetry answers you are expected to show that you can talk about a number of poems in the light of the question. When you are answering a poetry question, you should ensure that you can mention six or seven poems in some detail and refer more generally to others. It is also desirable to refer to two or three poems *together* when you are dealing with an aspect of the poet's work rather than looking in detail at one poem and then leaving it to look in equal detail at another. Examiners are rightly impressed by students who can move with ease from one poem to another when they are making a point about the poet's style or interests.

A third point you should heed is that answers should frequently mention the name of the author, particularly with novels and drama, where weak students often ignore the author altogether. You should mention the author because, as was stressed in Chapter 6, works of art are not just 'ordinary life' but objects specially made by authors. To use the name of the author indicates to the examiner that you understand that point. You can prepare for this by practising writing about how, for instance, Orwell presents, develops, or view what happens in his books.

A further point very much related to the last one is that you should avoid speaking of the characters as if they were real people. Again, this point has been made before. Characters in novels or plays only exist in the words on the page and should, therefore, only be spoken about in terms of them. A way of avoiding treating a character as if he or she were real is to speak of him or her in relation to the author or the reader.

When you are thinking through an examination question, you should not be afraid to disagree with it. Students are often worried about taking their own line because they wonder whether the examiner will like what they have written. The point to remember is that you must answer the question. If you are asked to say why you think a play has proved popular on the stage, you can't deny that it has been popular. If, however, you are asked whether you think a play is dramatically effective, you must tell the examiner what you think. There is an alternative to either agreeing or disagreeing. In quotation questions you are given a view of the work. Quite often the view is true in parts but not wholly true, in which case you can say that you agree to a certain extent. Even if you take an unusual line of argument, you will be rewarded as long as you can produce a good case, backed up by evidence. Examiners are concerned that you should argue clearly, not that you should agree with them.

The final point is that you should leave yourself time to look through your answers. This applies in most examinations. When you are writing quickly, you tend to miss out words, mis-spell common words and make simple grammatical errors. If you leave yourself sufficient time to read through your paper, you can correct these. Because you think you know what you have written, you may not see the mistakes you have made, so you must read with great care, looking at every word.

# GLOSSARY

**Abstract and concrete.** A word is abstract when it refers to a quality such as goodness or evil, and concrete when it refers to something that can be detected by the five senses. Literature needs both kinds of words. Ideas are abstract but they are made real by concrete examples. The opening of R.S. Thomas's 'Poetry for Supper' has an abstract word followed by concrete ones:

> Listen, now, verse should be as natural
> As the small tuber that feeds on muck . . .

The concrete words 'tuber' and 'muck' give body to the abstract 'natural', thus making it more effective. (See also **Image and imagery**.)

**Act and scene.** The major structural divisions of a play are called acts, and their sub-divisions scenes. An act or scene changes to indicate either the passage of time, a new action or a change of place. Shakespeare's plays have five acts, whereas most modern plays have two or three.

**Allegory.** A story which seeks to demonstrate philosophical or religious beliefs. Each element in the story stands for an aspect of the belief that the story is seeking to explain. There could, for instance, be allegorical figures representing Truth, Goodness or Virtue. In Bunyan's *Pilgrim's Progress,* the central figure, Christian, is the Christian soul who sets out from the city of destruction (man's fallen state) as a pilgrim travelling towards the Heavenly City (the eternal home of the redeemed).

Some works are very near to being allegory. The novels of William Golding have many allegorical elements. In the *Lord of the Flies* Simon is a Christ-like figure who is killed because the boys do not want to listen to the good news that he brings.

**Alliteration.** The repetition of the same consonant sound. Alliteration is usually both pleasing and memorable; pleasing because readers enjoy the pattern of sounds, and memorable because repeated sounds impress themselves upon the mind. There is no point in just mentioning that alliteration occurs, unless you can go on to discuss its effect. To help you describe the effect of alliteration you can ask whether or not it produces a distinctive tone, and whether or not it is regularly spaced. The former effect is the more important, because alliteration, whether or not it is regularly spaced, is always capable of contributing to the tone of a poem. For instance, the alliteration on the 'f' sound is regular in one line from Owen's 'Exposure' – 'With sidelong flowing flakes that flock, pause, and renew' – and irregular in another – 'Pale flakes with fingering stealth come feeling for our faces' – yet both create a furtive tone. The flakes may seem delicate but they are sinister in the way they bring a deathly cold to the exposed soldiers. (See also **Assonance** and **Consonance.**)

**Allusion.** A reference to another book, event, person or place. The allusion is usually implied or hinted, so the reader is given the pleasure of seeing it and understanding the effect it creates. Sometimes the effect is to make what is being said more significant, more ambiguous or more amusing. In Pope's *The Rape of the Lock,* Belinda is shown to have bright and sparkling eyes:

Bright as the sun, her eyes the gazer strike,
And, like the sun, they shine on all alike.

It is a radiant picture but one qualified by the allusion to St Matthew's Gospel, where Jesus says that God sends the sun to shine on everybody. The presence of that allusion suggests that those fascinated by Belinda, and maybe Belinda herself, have a distorted sense of values in that they confuse the human with the divine.

**Ambiguity.** The capacity of a word or words to mean two or more different things. In poetry this capacity is valued, because the meanings of poems are thereby enriched. When discussing ambiguity, you should show that the same words could have different meanings. For instance, in Blake's 'London' there are the lines:

How the Chimney-sweepers cry
Every blackening Church appalls . . .

'Blackening' is ambiguous. Does it meant the soot from chimneys has blackened the Church, or is the Church actively blackening society? You will also probably need to discuss the tone of the poem, because a poet often makes it clear that a poem is deliberately ambiguous.

**Assonance.** The repetition of vowel sounds in adjoining words. The effect of assonance is similar to that of alliteration; that is to say, it helps to create tone. It is also worthwhile noting whether or not it is regularly spaced. Assonance is rarer than alliteration yet it can be very effective. In these four lines from Donne's 'Song', the repetition of the 'i' vowel creates a tone of lamentation and regret:

When thou sigh'st, thou sigh'st not wind,
  But sigh'st my soul away,
When thou weep'st, unkindly kind,
  My life's blood doth decay.

(See also **Alliteration** and **Consonance**.)

**Audience.** Those who view a play, and, by extension, those for whom any work is written. When you are reading a play, you will have to put yourself in the position of being the audience. The best way to do this is to be aware of all the resources of the theatre – actors, staging, scenery, costume, lighting and music – and imagine how these could be used in the production of a play. Then you will be imaginatively close to the experiences of the audience.

**Ballad.** A poem, usually of simple construction, that tells a story. Many English and Scottish ballads are quatrains, in which the first and third lines are longer than the second and fourth. Many of them are traditional and deal with love, war, travel and adventure. They are enjoyable because they are direct, fast moving and contain brief but telling details. For instance, the repeated line 'And no birds sing' from Keat's 'La Belle Dame sans Merci' is sufficient to convey the poem's terrible bleakness.

**Black comedy.** Comedy that invites laughter at serious or painful aspects of life such as disease, pain, failure and death. Joe Orton's comedies can be described as black, and some moments in Shakespeare's problem plays – *Measure for Measure, All's Well that Ends Well* and *Troilus and Cressida* – come near to it.

**Blank verse.** Poetry that is written in lines of unrhymed iambic pentameter. It is very common in English and can be used for telling a story or thinking about ideas and feelings. It is worthwhile noticing how regular and insistent its rhythms are.

Shakespeare uses blank verse in his plays. There is usually no point in drawing attention to this, unless there are very interesting variations in the rhythm of a line. Such variations are usually the expression of deep emotion. For instance, Hamlet's order to his mother, 'Look here upon this picture, and on this', could be scanned in the usual way, but that would not reflect its emotional quality. To do that justice, the line should be scanned:

/ / ∪ / / / ∪ / ∪ /
Lóok hére upón this pícture, and ón this . . .

It is also important to notice when Shakespeare uses verse which is *not* blank verse. For instance, the witches in *Macbeth* and the fairies in *A Midsummer Night's Dream* speak in trochees rather than iambs. Trochees sound different, thus making the witches and fairies seem strange, non-human creatures. (See also **Metre**.)

**Cadence.** The rise and fall in pitch the voice makes when at the end of a line, a sentence or caesura. The emotional impact of poetry is often created by cadences. There is no technical language to describe their effect, though they are often said to be 'rising', 'falling' or 'steady'. When you write about cadences, you should try to characterise the emotional effect they create. For instance, the close of the passage about skating from Book One of Wordsworth's *The Prelude* is effective because the steady cadence enacts the peace of untroubled sleep:

and I stood and watched
Till all was tranquil as a dreamless sleep.

**Caesura.** The break in a line of poetry. The convention for marking a caesura is ‖. Caesuras are important because they mark changes in tone, in argument and emotion. They can also produce comic effects, particularly when what follows the caesura is very different from what preceded it.

When writing about a caesura, you should never just point to its existence but try to describe the impact that it has. For instance, the caesura in the last line of Yeats's 'An Irish Airman Foresees His Death' is effective because there is no break in the previous line (there are very few in the poem) and because it enacts the clear-sighted thoughtfulness of one who has come to a momentous decision:

> A waste of breath the years behind
> In balance with this life, ‖ this death.

**Caricature.** The deliberate distortion or exaggeration of a character's features or manners in order to ridicule or amuse. The reaction of reader or audience is often affectionate amusement. Sometimes the term is used against an author when it is suggested that his or her characters are near to caricature. But this criticism can only be used if the author aimed at creating a real character and failed.

**Comedy and tragedy.** A comedy is a play in which the confusions of characters, often prompted by love and furthered by deception or misunderstanding, eventually work out so that the play closes happily. The action of comedy is usually amusing, and the plot intricate. Tragedy is a play in which a character (often called the hero) falls from power, influence or happiness towards disaster and death. Often a hero is wilful and seems to bring destruction upon himself. This wilfulness is called *hubris.* The action arouses feelings of awe in the audience, who often leave the theatre with a renewed sense of the seriousness and significance of human life. The word catharsis is often used to describe the audience's feelings. It means the purging from the mind of the feelings of pity and fear the play has aroused.

You should be careful not to impose these, or any other definitions of comedy, upon Shakespeare's plays. All definitions should be used as general guides and not as rules. Though comedy and tragedy usually apply to plays, the terms can be used of both poems and novels.

**Complex.** A line, sentence, image, scene or whole work which consists of several closely connected ideas or feelings. You can use the term when you are trying to stress that the meaning, emotion or construction of a work is rich and varied. It is important to understand that the term implies that though a work has many elements, it is still unified. Therefore, it is often used as a term of praise. You should not, however, assume that only complex literature is good. There is also a pleasure and a value in simplicity.

**Conceit.** A highly elaborate image that seems on first acquaintance far-fetched but yet which, with thought, is seen to be appropriate. It is strange but true. You should try to convey the sense of shock, the challenge to thought, and the pleasure of discovering that the image is apt. The most famous example is from Donne's 'Valediction forbidding morning', where he speaks of a husband and wife's souls as being a pair of compasses:

> If they be two, they are two so
> As stiff twin compasses are two,
> Thy soul the fixed foot, makes no show
> To move, but doth, if the other do.

The shock is that the insubstantial soul should be compared to 'stiff twin compasses'; the challenge to thought comes when the third and fourth lines are read, and the pleasure is of seeing that the image is delightfully logical – she is stable but will move as he moves, because they are really one.

**Consonance.** The repetition of the same consonant sounds in two or more words in which the vowel sounds are different. The effect is of interest when the words are related in meaning as well as in sound. In W.H. Auden's '"O where are you going?" said reader to rider' there is a line: 'Behind you swiftly the figure comes softly.' The consonance of 'swiftly' and 'softly' is interesting because both words are concerned with the stealthy and slightly sinister approach of the strange 'figure'. (See also **Alliteration, Assonance** and **Half-rhyme.**)

**Consonants and vowels.** A consonant is a sound produced by stopping the breath, and a vowel by allowing the air to pass through the mouth without stoppage. Vowels are a,e,i,o,u and, in some cases, y; all other letters are consonants. The terms are useful when writing about the effects of sound in poetry. It is often important to note whether a vowel is long or short. For instance, the long vowels of Herbert's 'Sweet day, so cool, so calm, so bright' create a meditative and tranquil effect, whereas the short 'i's in the following lines from T.S. Eliot's 'The Love-Song of J. Alfred Prufrock' are nervous and slightly irritable:

> Oh, do not ask, 'What is it?'
> Let us go and make our visit.

**Convention.** An agreement between author and reader or audience that a device, form or procedure stands for the reality of what is being conveyed. A convention is never 'true to life', but reader and audience accept that it represents that feature or aspect of life. For instance, a stage is accepted by the audience as being a battlefield, a palace or a drawing room. Conventions are present in all types of literature, and as long as the reader understands that that is what they are, no difficulty is caused.

Sometimes the word 'conventional' is used to indicate disapproval. This is a different use. It means that an author is in no way original but simply uses other people's ideas. You must be careful not to confuse the two uses of the word.

**Counterpoint.** A word borrowed from music to indicate how some syllables in an otherwise regular line produce variations on the set rhythm. You should only use the term if you want to discuss the emotional or intellectual effect of the variation. The opening of Larkin's 'Church Going' is basically iambic until the last three emphatic words of the second line, which have the effect of enclosing the poet in the church, the poet's thoughts in his head, and the reader in the poem:

> Once I am sure there's nothing going on
> I step inside, letting the door thud shut.

The counterpointing of the rhythm fixes poet and reader in one place and prepares them both for the serious and sensitive meditations that are to come. (See also **Metre** and **Scansion.**)

**Denotations and connotations.** The denotations of a word are its standard range of meanings, the connotations its additional meanings that emerge through association, suggestion, and emotional undertones. Writers, particularly poets, often exploit a word's connotations, so you should look to see if their words work in this way. For instance, the denotations of the word 'flat' are a smooth, unbroken surface; its connotations are lifeless, dull and uninteresting.

**Diction.** The selection of words used in a work. The term is only useful if you can characterise the diction. For instance, an author may use words drawn from everyday life (John Betjeman often does this in his poetry), from religion, from politics or from another academic subject, such as a science. When you write about diction you should try to show the effect of selecting a particular range of words.

**Enactment.** This word stands for the way in which all aspects of words – their sounds, rhythms, and the shapes they make in lines and stanzas – contribute to the meaning of what is being said. You should use the word to avoid the idea that poetry is just made up of form and content. Enactment insists that words are not divisible into what they say and how they say it, and that *how* something is said shapes *what* is said, and vice versa. In Byron's 'So, we'll go no more a-roving', the repetition of the 'o' sound, the heavy stresses on 'go' and 'roving', the casual 'so' at the beginning of the line, and its repetition at the start of the second line enact the langour of one who is wearied by much experience:

So, we'll go no more a-roving
So late into the night,
Though the heart be still as loving,
And the moon be still as bright.

**End-stopped and run-on lines.** An end-stopped line is one in which the grammatical unit, be it clause or sentence, is coterminous with the line. Thus, there is the satisfaction of finding the line and the sense ending together. A run-on line (sometimes called an enjambed line) is where the grammar, and thus the sense, is left unfinished at the end of the line. Run-on lines create pleasurable feelings of expectation, as the reader has to look further for the full sense of what is being said.

**Epic simile.** The comparison of one thing in terms of another in which the idea introduced to make the comparison (the vehicle) is developed in a lengthy passage to form a vivid picture. Epic similes are effective when there is an appropriateness in the comparison. For instance, in Book I of Milton's *Paradise Lost* the fallen angels rising from the burning lake of Hell are compared to the plague of locusts brought down upon Egypt by Amram's son – Moses:

As when the potent rod
Of Amram's son in Egypt's evil day
Waved round the coast, up called a pitchy cloud
Of locusts, warping on the eastern wind,
That o'er the realm of impious Pharaoh hung
Like night, and darkened all the land of Nile:

So numberless were those bad angels seen
Hovering on wing under the cope of hell . . .

The appropriateness is not just a visual one; Milton shows that both the locusts and fallen angels were a plague – the former upon Egypt, the latter upon the whole of mankind.

**Epigram.** Either a brief, usually witty, statement or a short poem which makes a simple but often dramatic or humorous point. You will probably use the first meaning more than the second. Often it is useful to call a deft line or remark epigrammatic. By that you are saying it is punchy and memorable. T.S. Eliot's 'Whispers of Immortality' has a grimly epigrammatic thrust:

Webster was much possessed by death
And saw the skull beneath the skin;
And breastless creatures underground
Leaned backward with a lipless grin.

**Expectation.** The effect of being led to think that something is going to happen. Short stories, novels and plays all build up expectations in readers and audiences. Expectations are built upon what is known about events and characters, and also on what the characters themselves expect to happen. Whenever you write about expectation, you should stress that it is the author, or playwright, who is responsible for creating it. (See also **Surprise** and **Relief**.)

**Farce.** A branch of comedy in which the characters are reduced to stock figures, and the action is often frantic and even violent. Thus, in farce characters can be beaten or humiliated and the audience reacts with laughter, because it has not been invited to see the characters as having any sort of distinctive personality. Elements of farce creep into some plays. For instance, the middle scenes of *Dr. Faustus* can be said to be farce, and the innumerable beatings of servants in Shakespeare's *The Comedy of Errors* introduce farce into a carefully constructed comic plot. (See also **Tragedy and Comedy**.)

**Flat and round characters.** Terms introduced by E.M. Forster to indicate characters in novels who have little personal identity (flat), and those who are given much more individuality (round). You should use the terms with care, because characters in novels are rarely simply flat or round. (See also **Stock character**.)

**Genre.** A word borrowed from the French which means a literary type or kind. Comedy, tragedy and satire are genres, but nowadays it is also common to speak of poetry and the novel as genres, too.

**Half-rhyme.** The effect that is created when the consonants of two words in a rhyming position have the same sounds but the vowels do not. In effect, it is consonance functioning in the place of rhyme. The effect of half-rhyme (or para-rhyme, as it is sometimes called) is to make the ear expect a rhyme which is denied. The result is that the words often sound strangely out of tune with each other. In Owen's 'Futility' the feeling that death has distorted the natural progress of life is enacted in the half-rhymes. He is speaking of the sun:

Think how it wakes the seeds, –
Woke, once, the clays of a cold star.
Are limbs, so dear-achieved, are sides,
Full-nerved – still warm – too hard to stir?

Whenever you write about half-rhyme, you should try to bring out how it leads you to expect a rhyme which you do not get. (See also **Consonance** and **Rhyme**.)

**Heroic couplets.** These are lines of iambic pentameters that rhyme in pairs. They are assertive and self-affirming and are consequently appropriate for argument. For instance, Pope in *An Essay on Criticism* neatly conveys the ideal of economy in verse in a heroic couplet which is itself economical:

Words are like leaves; and where they most abound,
Much fruit of sense beneath is rarely found.

They are, however, also used in narrative poems. Many people do not find them easy to read, because they seem repetitious. They should be read slowly, and it is often interesting to note whether the sentences of the poem are coterminous with the couplets. When they are not, and run-on lines occur, readers usually enjoy the variation. (See also **Metre**.)

**Image and imagery.** Any figurative or descriptive language that appeals to one of the five senses is called an image. Images could also be metaphors, similes, symbols and personification, as well as examples of non-figurative description. Images are impressive because they make ideas concrete. They also create atmosphere and can be used to establsh a pattern within a poem. It is sometimes helpful to show how an image works in some detail. For instance, in *Macbeth* Macduff tries to put into words the horror of finding that Duncan, King of Scotland, has been murdered. He uses a very complex imagery to do this:

Confusion now hath made his masterpiece!
Most sacrilegious Murther hath broke ope
The Lord's anointed Temple, and stole thence
The life o' th' building!

The death of Duncan is first seen in the image of 'Confusion', as an artist or craftsman, making his 'masterpiece'. Then 'Murther' (murder) is seen as a thief breaking into a religious building. (See also **Abstract and concrete**, **Metaphor and simile**, **Personification** and **Symbol**.)

**Irony.** The effect produced when a reader sees that there is a gap between the words that are being said and the real significance of those words. There are different kinds of gaps. The gap between words and truth occurs when something the reader knows to be mistaken is said. A second type of gap, or discrepancy, is between the words and meaning. This occurs when the reader sees that the real significance of what is being said is very different from what the speaker supposes. The gap can lie between intention and result. A speaker can intend something but the reader will see that the result will not be what is expected. This is also called dramatic irony. There is also the irony of one character interpreting the world one way, whilst the reader is led to see that this is false. In all cases of irony, someone is put at a disadvantage because others, usually the author and reader, can see more clearly than he or she can.

When you write about irony, you should make clear who is placed in a position of advantage and who is at a disadvantage. You should also remember that irony can produce different emotional effects. It can be bitter, comic, serious, tragic, sad, and so on. In your writing you should try to bring over how irony can make the reader or audience change attitudes to a character. For instance, you may be horrified by the callous inhumanity of Lady Macbeth, who believes that, after the murder of Duncan, 'A little water clears us of this deed'. When, however, she walks in her sleep and is seen to be perpetually washing her hands, you may see the terrible irony that 'a little water' can't clear her of guilt. When you see the irony, your horror may turn to pity.

**Lyric.** A poem, usually of no more than forty or fifty lines, and often much shorter, which expresses the thoughts and feelings of the poet or of an imagined speaker. The tones of such poems are varied, but they are often personal, reflective, and frequently deal with love or other powerful emotions. Sometimes writing that is smooth, fluent and intimate is described as lyrical. Most people's idea of poetry is lyrical. It is useful to remind yourself that poetry can be narrative, didactic and satiric as well. (See also **Song.**)

**Masque.** A highly elaborate entertainment in verse and song with lavish costumes and sets that was popular in the sixteenth and seventeenth centuries. The characters are often gods or allegorical figures. Shakespeare's *The Tempest* contains a masque to celebrate the betrothal of Ferdinand and Miranda. Milton's *Comus* is also a masque. If you have to write about masques, you will have to imagine the visual impact that they make on stage. (See also **Allegory**.)

**Mental landscape.** The effect created when a landscape is portrayed in terms of the feelings of the author, or character who moves through it. The outer world thus reflects the inner world of thoughts and feelings. The effect is particularly popular in late eighteenth- and nineteenth-century literature. Mental landscapes are often strange and impressive, conveying a sense of mystery and vastness. They can also express very powerfully the feelings of poet or character. George Crabbe's 'Peter Grimes' achieves both; the rejected Peter moves through a strange and rather eerie landscape:

> At the same times the same dull views to see,
> The bounding marsh-bank and the blighted tree;

(See also **Pathetic fallacy** and **Personification**.)

**Metaphor and simile.** The comparison of one thing in terms of another; in metaphor there is an implicit identity, whereas in simile the comparison is introduced by the words 'Like' or 'as'. Metaphors are thus more compressed and economical than similes, though similes are closer to ordinary speech, and there is a distinct pleasure in following through the comparison from the object being presented to that in terms of which it is presented. If you wish to distinguish one from the other, the terms 'tenor' (the object presented) and 'vehicle' (that in terms of which it is presented) can be useful. Thus, in the metaphor for a church from Larkin's 'Church Going' – 'this special shell' – church is the tenor and shell the vehicle, or in Larkin's simile from 'Ambulances' – 'Closed like confessionals' – the tenor is ambulances and the vehicle 'confessionals'.

**Metre.** The regular rhythms of poetic lines, created by a sequence of stressed or unstressed syllables. A recurring unit of stressed and unstressed syllables is called a foot. Special names are given to these recurring feet, and also to the number of feet in a line. Common English metres are the following:

*iambic:* unstressed syllables followed by a stressed syllable;
*anapaestic:* two unstressed syllables followed by a stressed syllable;
*trochaic:* a stressed syllable followed by an unstressed syllable;
*dactylic:* a stressed syllable followed by two unstressed syllables.

The names for the number of feet in a line are as follows:

monometer – one foot
dimeter – two feet
trimeter – three feet
tetrameter – four feet
pentameter – five feet
hexameter – six feet
heptameter – seven feet
octameter – eight feet

There is usually little point in merely labelling a metre. If you wish to discuss metre, you should try to characterise the effect it has by showing how it helps to enact the meaning of the poem. (See also **Blank verse, counterpoint, Heroic couplets, Scansion** and **Stanza**.)

**Monosyllabic and polysyllabic.** Words of one syllable such as 'did', 'good', 'said' and 'would' are monosyllabic. In poetry and verse drama they are effective in making the lines feel emphatic, forceful and strong. Consider the force of the opening of Donne's 'Hymn to God the Father':

> Wilt thou forgive my sin where I began
> Which was my sin though it were done before.

The monosyllables enact the dark, serious strength of the poet's plea.

Words of more than one syllable are polysyllabic. When a number of polysyllabic words are used in a line the effect is likely to be flowing, lyrical and sometimes even majestic. Notice how the polysyllabic words in Hopkins's 'The Windhover' help to enact the flowing and majestic movements of the falcon in flight:

> I caught this morning morning's minion, king-dom
> of daylight's dauphin, dapple-dawn-drawn Falcon . . .

**Narrator.** The narrator is one who tells a story. The narrator can, but need not, be the novelist. Narrators can tell their stories, or narratives, in the first or the third person. If the story is told in the first person, there is only access to the mind of the narrator. If, however, the story is narrated in the third person, it is possible to see into all the minds of the characters. When an author knows everything that goes on in characters' minds, he or she is called an omniscient (all-knowing) narrator.

**Onomatopoeia.** The effect that is created when the sounds of words mime or resemble the sounds of the object being described. Individual words such as 'crash' or 'buzz' are onomatopoeic, but the term is more generally used of an effect created by a number of words. Onomatopoeia is usually worth discussing when it creates atmosphere. In Keats's 'Ode to a Nightingale' one stanza closes with this line: 'The murmurous haunt of flies on summer eves.' The onomatopoeic 'murmurous' combines with the long vowels and the alliteration on 'm' and 's' to produce an atmosphere of languid ease.

**Overtones and undertones.** The associations of a word or words. Overtones are the clear and obvious associations, while undertones are those meanings which are hinted and implied. However, the two words are often used interchangeably to refer to words' wider meanings and emotional colouring. It is often very useful to point out the overtones and undertones of a word. You can do this by pointing to the number of ways in which a word is used in ordinary speech.

**Pathetic fallacy.** The way in which a writer gives human feelings to an object that could not possibly have them. The effect it creates is very close to personification. Its origin is probably in the very common practice people have of transferring their own feelings about something to the thing itself. Therefore, pathetic fallacy is often an indication of what the writer or character is feeling. In Tennyson's 'Ulysses' the sea 'Moans round with many voices'. The word 'moans' indicates the state of mind of the protagonist. (See also **Mental landscape** and **Personification.**)

**Pathos.** The arousing of tenderness, pity or sorrow in a reader or an audience by the presentation of a sad or moving scene. The pity of reader or audience is often due to the helplessness of the characters. Thus, the distraught Ophelia's speech about the sad decline of Hamlet at the end of act 3 scene 1 is full of pathos. When writing about pathos, you should strike a balance between showing how the emotions are aroused and recording what you feel about the scene.

**Persona.** A specially created voice or self in a poem, novel or short story. In most cases a persona speaks in the first person singular, though in some cases, particularly poems, this need not be so. Personas give works unity by showing the reader that everything in the work is the expression of a particular viewpoint. Because of this, it is wise to discuss personas in terms of tone and attitude. You should remember that a persona is not to be identified with the writer, and that a writer can adopt as many as he or she chooses.

**Personification.** The effect created when a non-human object or quality is written about as if it were a human being. Keats personifies the Grecian urn when he calls it a 'still unravished bride of quietness', and Gray personifies wealth and beauty when he writes of 'all that beauty, all that wealth e'er gave'. You should always try to characterise the effect of personification. Often, it makes the object seem close to both author and reader, and, in some cases, it can make the object or quality personified seem more lively and engaging. (See also **Mental landscape** and **Pathetic fallacy.**)

**Plot.** The sequence of events in a narrative poem, novel or play that are held together by the motives of characters, or other causes. Plots usually grow out of a problem, so it is useful to see what that is. It is also important to see how the plot is constructed. Some are built around contrasts and parallels, some around mysteries, and others grow out of a particular character's aims or the structure of society. In drama, plots should act out the themes of the play. (See also **Sub-plot**.)

**Problem plays.** A group of plays written by Shakespeare which, though they have a comic form, deal with dark and serious aspects of life. They are sometimes called the 'dark comedies'. *Measure for Measure,* for instance, has the comic form of confusion working towards a happy ending, and many comic conventions such as disguise and deception. Yet it deals with a man sentenced to death, and the attempts of a corrupt official to seduce a nun. Other problem plays are *All's Well that Ends Well* and *Troilus and Cressida.* Sometimes *Hamlet* is said to be closer to a problem play than a tragedy.

**Protagonist.** Originally the hero in a Greek play, but now it is also used to mean the speaker in a narrative poem or dramatic monologue. The protagonist is usually a specially created voice. The poet can thus explore a realm of experience different from his or her own. When writing about the protagonist of a poem, you should make sure that you don't confuse him or her with the author of the poem.

**Relief.** The effect experienced by readers and audiences when the tension created by expectation is released. Sometimes a reader or audience responds to relief by laughter, but on other occasions, as in tragedy, a feeling of seriousness is left when the anticipated event has occurred. (See also **Expectation** and **Surprise**.)

**Rhyme.** The identity in two or more words of the final vowel and any consonants that follow it. When the rhyming words are monosyllabic, the rhyme is said to be masculine, as in 'bold' and 'old', and when they are polysyllabic, they are said to be feminine, as in 'ending' and 'bending'. (You will also note that in the feminine rhymes the last syllable is unstressed.)

Whenever you write about rhyme, you should bring out the effect it creates. Rhyme creates harmony and also the pleasing effect of completing or resolving an idea. When words rhyme, they tend to be more noticeable and hence more important in the poem. When the words rhymed are important, the whole meaning of the poem can be focused. Rhymes, particularly feminine ones, can also be funny. (See also **Half-rhyme**.)

**Satire.** The art of exposing folly or wickedness by mocking it. Sometimes a whole work is called a satire, but more often it is thought of as a quality or function of an author's writing. For instance, Dickens satirises the civil service in *Little Dorrit* by creating the Circumlocution office – a massive department whose aim is to prevent anybody from doing anything. You should remember that satire is a moral art. That is to say, it does not merely poke fun at something but ridicules it in the name of important values.

**Scansion.** The examination of metrical patterns in verse by noting the sequences of accented and unaccented syllables. If you wish to draw attention to a pattern, you should mark accented syllables with a / and unaccented ones with a ∪. There is usually no point simply in labelling a line (see **Metre**) unless you can discuss any variations, or show that it effectively enacts the meaning of the line. (See also **Blank verse, Counterpoint, Heroic couplets** and **Stanza**.)

**Soliloquy.** A speech delivered when a character is either alone or isolated on the stage. A soliloquy can be public, in which case the character directly addresses the audience, or private, in which case the audience overhears the character talking to himself or herself. In Shakespeare, soliloquies are usually only given to important characters. For instance, Hamlet has a number of private soliloquies, and Iago a number of public ones. Characters very rarely tell lies in soliloquies, so you should pay particular attention to them.

**Song.** Either a lyrical poem which might be set to music or verses intended to be sung in a play. In the first case, you could ask yourself whether the rhythm and sounds of the poem are appropriately light or flowing. In the second, you should ask how it contributes to the mood or meaning of the play. When you are imagining what a play would be like on stage, you can ask yourself what kind of tune would be suitable. (See also **Lyric**.)

**Sonnet.** A poem of fourteen lines. A number of forms have been created, but the two most popular are the one constructed in an octave (eight lines) and a sestet (six lines), and the one in three quatrains (four lines each) and a couplet (two lines). When you write about a sonnet, you should look for the tightness of the argument and the depth of the emotional range. It is worth noticing how they end: is the end artificial, or does it naturally arise out of the rest of the poem and satisfactorily conclude it?

**Stanza.** A group of lines in a poem that form its basic, structural unit. The shape of a stanza is formed by the number of lines and often by the rhyme scheme. If you choose to write about the stanza form of a poem, you should seek to show how it moulds the meaning of the poem. You can also ask whether the stanza is appropriate to the mood and meaning of the poem.

Famous stanza forms are *terza rima* (three lines, usually rhyming ABA,BCD), *quatrain* (four lines), *rime royal* (seven lines, rhyming ABABBCC), *ottava rima* (eight lines, rhyming ABABABCC), and the *Spenserian stanza* (nine lines, rhyming ABABBCBCC). The last line of the Spenserian stanza is an *alexandrine* – a line of six (a hexameter) rather than five stresses; this line closes the stanza in a leisurely, even languid manner. (See also **Rhyme**.)

**Stock character.** A character in a play or novel who is no more than a representative type. Such characters have no individuality and usually possess only one or two characteristics. They are often comic. (See also **Flat and round characters**.)

**Subjective and objective.** A thought is subjective when it is concerned with the personal reaction of somebody, and objective when it ignores what the individual feels about something but concentrates on the object itself.

Writing about literature should always be a blend of both. You should write about the words of a poem, novel or play, and about your subjective reactions to these.

**Sub-plot.** A minor plot which often echoes the concerns of the major plot. You can use the term of both novels and plays. The relation between major and minor plots deserves attention.

**Surprise.** The effect created when expectation is not fulfilled. It can, therefore, only be discussed in relation to expectation. Novelists often spring surprises upon readers by unusual coincidences or the reappearance of a character. Shakespeare rarely works by surprise. The rejection of Falstaff and the last scene of *The Winter's Tale* are rare exceptions. (See also **Expectation** and **Relief**.)

**Suspension of belief.** A term introduced by Coleridge in relation to the conventions of the theatre. When a member of an audience accepts stage conventions, including things like ghosts or witches, he or she willingly suspends belief or disbelief. That is to say, conventions are accepted as real in the theatre, and the issue of whether or not they can be believed in outside the theatre is not raised.

**Symbol.** An object that stands for, points to and shares in a significant reality over and beyond it. Blake's 'The Tyger' stands for and points to creative energy but it is also an instance of that creative energy. Some symbols are traditional, while other symbols are specially created by authors. You can learn about traditional symbols, but need to be alert to the resonances of words and their context to recognise ones that are newly made by a poet or novelist. For instance, when you read Shelley's 'Ode to the West Wind', it is important to know that the wind is a symbol for inspiration. When, however, you read Ted Hughes's 'Hawk Roosting', you should try to see that the way the hawk is presented makes it a symbol of the terrible destructiveness that Hughes believes is at the heart of nature.

**Syntax.** The construction of sentences; that is, the order of words and their relation with each other. As the construction of a sentence controls the meaning and emotional impact of what is being said, it is always wise, particularly when thinking about poetry or verse drama, to study syntax. It is important to see whether the sentences are long or short, whether they have many or few clauses, and whether, as is usual in English, the subject comes before the object, or the other way round.

**Theme.** The subject, concerns, issues and preoccupations of a poem, novel or play. The word is usually spoken of as meaning the significance of events rather than the events themselves.

**Tone.** The emotional and intellectual attitude, manner, or poise of a piece of writing. A useful way of assessing the tone of a work is by asking how the author is speaking to you – the reader. In ordinary conversation you would pick up the tone from the way the words were delivered; when you are dealing with words on the page, you should allow their diction, rhythm and sounds to do this for you. Because tone is emotional, you must always try to characterise it. Thus, you may say the tone of a work is intimate, sly, innocent, hectoring, aggressive or fierce. You should remember that all literary works have a tone, and though it is sometimes difficult to detect, you can always try to discuss it.

**Unities.** At one time it was believed that a good play should comprise one action, should take place in a day, and should happen in one place. These three requirements were called the unities. Most English drama ignores them, although Shakespeare's last play, *The Tempest*, comes quite close to observing them.

**Villanelle.** A verse form (originally from France) of five three-line stanzas and a final quatrain, in which the first and third line of the first stanza appear alternately in the following stanzas and form a couplet in the final one. A popular modern example is Dylan Thomas's 'Do not go gentle into that good night'. When writing about villanelles, you should bring over the pleasure of finding that the recurring line has an appropriate place in the succeeding stanzas. Sometimes its new place brings out fresh meanings in the line. For instance, the line from Dylan Thomas is an order in the first stanza and a statement of fact in the second. In grammatical terms it changes from the imperative to the indicative mood.

# SUGGESTIONS FOR FURTHER READING

GENERAL BOOKS

The following books deal with a number of literary topics; some are in the form of glossaries, some general introductions, and others show how literary thinking can illuminate non-literary matters.

M.H. Abrams: *A Glossary of Literary Terms* (Holt, Rinehart and Winston)
David Daiches: *Critical Approaches to Literature* (Longman)
Tom Gibbons: *Literature and Awareness* (Arnold)
Philip Hobsbaum: *Essentials of Literary Criticism* (Thames and Hudson)
Robin Mayhead: *Understanding Literature* (Cambridge University Press)
John Peck and Martin Coyle: *Literary Terms and Criticism: A Student's Guide* (Macmillan)
Ian Robinson: *The Survival of English* (Brynmill)

POETRY

Most of the following books are introductions to practical criticism; that is, to the reading of individual poems. Suggestions about editions of individual poets can be found in the section headed LITERARY WORKS below. A number of the books listed above also deal with the reading, appreciation and interpretation of poetry.

Charles Barber: *Poetry in English: An Introduction* (Macmillan)
Paul Fussell: *Poetic Metre and Poetic Form* (Random House)
D.W. Harding: *Experience into Words* (Chatto and Windus; Penguin)
Ruth Miller and Robert A. Greenberg: *Poetry: An Introduction* (Macmillan)
James Reeves: *Understanding Poetry* (Pan)
Allen Rodway: *The Craft of Criticism* (Cambridge University Press)

NOVELS

Of the following books, some are general introductions and others, in addition to general material, discuss individual novels.

Walter Allen: *The English Novel* (Phoenix; Penguin)
E.M. Forster: *Aspects of the Novel* (Arnold; Penguin)
Ian Milligan: *The Novel in English: An Introduction* (Macmillan)
John Peck: *How to Study a Novel* (Macmillan)

DRAMA

The following list includes general books on drama and some works on Shakespeare and his theatre.

Eric Bentley: *The Life of the Drama* (Methuen)
John Russell Brown: *Shakespeare's Dramatic Style* (Heinemann)
S.W. Dawson: *Drama and the Dramatic* (Methuen)
J.L. Styan: *Shakespeare's Stagecraft* (Cambridge University Press)
G.J. Watson: *Drama: An Introduction* (Macmillan)
Raymond Williams: *Drama in Performance* (Muller; Penguin)

LITERARY WORKS

Works set at 'O' and 'A' level are usually available in a number of editions; the series listed below all have notes and critical comments.

Macmillan Shakespeare
Macmillan Students' Hardy
Macmillan Students' Novels
The Penguin English Library
Penguin English Poets
The New Penguin Shakespeare
The Signet Classic Shakespeare

CRITICISM

The following series are either short books dealing with literary works or concepts, or collections of essays by a number of writers.

Casebooks (Macmillan)
The Critical Idiom Series (Methuen)
Macmillan History of Literature
Macmillan Master Guides
Macmillan Modern Dramatists
Penguin Critical Anthologies
Studies in English Literature (Arnold)
Text and Context (Sussex University Press)
Text and Performance (Macmillan)
Twentieth-Century Interpretations (Prentice-Hall)

# GENERAL INDEX

K



L



M



N



O



P



Q

# INDEX OF AUTHORS AND WORKS

## T